SOUNDS IRISH, ACTS GLOBAL

Music Industry Studies

Series Editor: Sarah Raine, University of Leeds

Founding Series Editor: Dave Laing†, Honorary Research Fellow at the University of Liverpool and Senior Research Associate at the University of East Anglia.

In recent years, there has been a rapid growth of interest in the music industry, from policy-makers, educationalists, the media and others. This new series aims to satisfy the demand for in-depth knowledge and analysis of all facets of the industry, from recording to live music and the publishing sector. It will include both historical and contemporary approaches and draw on contributions from economics, geography, sociology, legal studies, cultural studies and other disciplines.

Published:

Beyond 2.0: The Future of Music
Steve Collins and Sherman Young

She's at the Controls: Sound Engineering, Production and Gender Ventriloquism in the 21st Century
Helen Reddington

Forthcoming:

Elements of Music Management
Sally Gross

The Handbook on Music Business and Creative Industries in Education
Edited by Daniel Walzer

Venue Stories: Narratives, Memories, and Histories from Britain's Independent Music Spaces
Edited by Fraser Mann, Robert Edgar and Helen Pleasance

SOUNDS IRISH, ACTS GLOBAL

EXPLAINING THE SUCCESS OF IRELAND'S POPULAR MUSIC INDUSTRY

MICHAEL MARY MURPHY AND JIM ROGERS

SHEFFIELD UK   BRISTOL CT

Published by Equinox Publishing Ltd.

UK: Office 415, The Workstation, 15 Paternoster Row, Sheffield, South Yorkshire, S1 2BX
USA: ISD, 70 Enterprise Drive, Bristol, CT 06010

www.equinoxpub.com

First published 2023

© Michael Mary Murphy and Jim Rogers 2023

All rights reserved. No part of this publication may be reproduced or transmitted in any form or by any means, electronic or mechanical, including photocopying, recording or any information storage or retrieval system, without prior permission in writing from the publishers.

British Library Cataloguing-in-Publication Data
A catalogue record for this book is available from the British Library.

ISBN-13   978 1 78179 779 2   (hardback)
          978 1 78179 780 8   (paperback)
          978 1 78179 781 5   (ePDF)
          978 1 80050 382 3   (ePub)

Library of Congress Cataloging-in-Publication Data
Names: Murphy, Michael (Michael Mary), author. | Rogers, Jim, 1969- author.
Title: Sounds Irish, acts global : explaining the success of Ireland's
  popular music industry / Michael Mary Murphy and Jim Rogers.
Description: Bristol, CT : Equinox Publishing Ltd, 2023. | Series: Music
  industry studies | Includes bibliographical references and index. |
  Summary: "Sounds Irish, Acts Global critically examines both the history
  of Ireland's popular music industry as well as the current music scene
  in the country. This book is of interest to business students as well as
  popular music scholars in addition to non-academic readers"-- Provided
  by publisher.
Identifiers: LCCN 2023001184 (print) | LCCN 2023001185 (ebook) | ISBN
  9781781797792 (hardback) | ISBN 9781781797808 (paperback) | ISBN
  9781781797815 (pdf) | ISBN 9781800503823 (epub)
Subjects: LCSH: Music trade--Ireland--History. | Sound recording
  industry--Ireland--History. | Popular music--Ireland--History and
  criticism. | Musicians--Ireland.
Classification: LCC ML3790 .M668 2023 (print) | LCC ML3790 (ebook) | DDC
  338.4/77809415--dc23/eng/20230111
LC record available at https://lccn.loc.gov/2023001184
LC ebook record available at https://lccn.loc.gov/2023001185

Typeset by S.J.I. Services, New Delhi, India

Contents

Introduction   1
MICHAEL MARY MURPHY AND JIM ROGERS

1   The Irish Arrive: Early Stages in the Music Industry   9
MICHAEL MARY MURPHY

2   1930s Ireland: Law and Order, Business and Nationalism   28
MICHAEL MARY MURPHY

3   The Global Music Industries and Ireland   41
JIM ROGERS

4   The 1950s: Elvis and Ireland's Catholic Pop   61
MICHAEL MARY MURPHY

5   Horslips: Advancing DIY and Enterprise in the Irish Music Scene   69
MICHAEL MARY MURPHY

6   U2: Local and Global   76
MICHAEL MARY MURPHY

7   How Teenagers and Students Shaped Ireland's Culture   90
MICHAEL MARY MURPHY

8   Enya: '…not created by the record industry'   107
MICHAEL MARY MURPHY

9   The Corrs: '…genetically engineer the perfect pop group'   119
MICHAEL MARY MURPHY

10   *Riverdance*: Creating Profitable Local Culture   132
MICHAEL MARY MURPHY

11 Boyzone: 'Search is on for an Irish Take That' 146
   MICHAEL MARY MURPHY

12 Westlife: 'He's got to be kidding me' 158
   MICHAEL MARY MURPHY

13 U2, the Virgin Prunes and Graphic Art 168
   MICHAEL MARY MURPHY

   Conclusion 177
   MICHAEL MURPHY AND JIM ROGERS

Bibliography 190
Index 209

Introduction

This is not a history book, at least not in the conventional sense. Instead, it aims to highlight some of the key *forces* that shaped the industry of popular non-traditional music in Ireland. More specifically, it aims to illuminate our understanding of some of the *individuals* – and their motivations, personalities and skills – who made major contributions to that industry. Since the introduction of recorded music in the late 1800s, a small number of crucial individuals have enabled Irish acts to find global success. Their enterprise didn't just shape the careers of Irish music acts; in very meaningful ways, it transformed both Ireland's culture of music and Irish culture itself.

Those individuals, both women and men, didn't work with an overall unified vision. Often, they worked with few resources and little power compared with the might of the global music industry. Yet they still managed to deliver Irish acts that reached the highest peaks of achievement in the industry. They worked effectively and with enterprise and innovation. In fact, their enterprise, effectiveness and innovation were arguably better than that offered by the centralized global music industry. These music entrepreneurs didn't always pull in the same direction as the powerful forces in Irish culture and enterprise. Because of this, it might be useful to see them as outliers. And when we see them as outliers, it enables us to see what a difference people *anywhere*, given the right circumstances, can make in guiding music acts to the highest level of commercial, musical and cultural success. If this is a book about power, it is about how power can be found in unexpected places. The history of many of Ireland's successful music exports provides insight into the power flows that help to shape the global music industry. Clearly, understanding those power flows requires examining not only the nature of *music* but also the nature of the *enterprise behind the music*.

While pop music can conjure up the idea of *play*, most acts that succeed are familiar with work, dedication and perseverance – even if they're not, then the people who are responsible for creating opportunities for those acts certainly are. This book aims to examine the nature of the work that goes into delivering a local act to the global industry. Specifically, we want to identify the *early* enterprise behind a number of Irish music artists. Who helped those Irish acts? In what ways did they help them? Sometimes, we also want to ask *why* they helped. This means thinking about the nature of work in the music industry.

Governments, individuals and organizations often consider the question: how does a country become successful in the lucrative global pop music industry? Currently there is a short answer to that question: *be like Sweden*. But, clearly, not every country can behave like Sweden, and its current pop triumphs are due to a very specific set of circumstances that have been well scrutinized (Johansson 2020). The calibre, creativity and market instincts of Swedish songwriters and producers have been a particularly strong element of this success. Although, as Ola Johansson has expertly documented, Sweden's ascent includes specific economic, cultural and geographic factors. These include the overall 'malleability of Swedish culture' that has resulted in a willingness to embrace outside trends (2020: 10). In addition, the spatial organization of the country's music industry and its situation as a small, cosmopolitan country in Western Europe (2020: 1) have been to the country's advantage. Enhancing these factors, even before the recent wave of workers in the Swedish pop music industry, the country had a pre-existing sophisticated music industry structure with a strong knowledge and skills base. Now it boasts a DJ community that is integrated with a talented songwriter-producer cluster (Johansson 2020: 4) which delivers global hits.

It is also worth acknowledging the pop music success of Iceland. For a country with a population of just over 300,000, it has delivered an admirable number of acts, including The Sugarcubes, Björk, Sigur Rós and Emilíana Torrini, to the global marketplace. However, as Johansson points out, it has failed to produce an equal level of 'globally interconnected commercial songwriters and producers' (2020: 19). That is something Sweden has achieved..

Historically, the global pop market has favoured acts from the US and the UK, so artists and decision-makers from other countries might be encouraged by Sweden's achievement. That said, the global music industry is highly competitive, so Sweden's success means that there are fewer places in the charts for acts from other countries. That is worth remembering when we examine some of Ireland's most notable pop exports later in this book.

Over time Ireland has enjoyed considerable success in the global pop charts. The Clancy Brothers, Ruby Murray, Van Morrison, Val Doonican, The Bachelors, Rory Gallagher, Gilbert O'Sullivan, Thin Lizzy and Horslips all racked up substantial sales from the 1950s and into the 1970s. The burst of energy that accompanied punk and new wave brought artistic and commercial success to The Boomtown Rats, The Undertones, Stiff Little Fingers and, most strikingly, U2. The voices of Irish women were varied and individual, and claimed airwaves and charts internationally with artists such as Dana, Sinéad

O'Connor, Enya, The Cranberries and The Corrs. Irish pop and rock competed in the highly competitive world of commercial music with acts including Boyzone, Westlife, B*witched, Therapy? and, post-2000, Damien Rice, Kodaline, The Script, Imelda May, Hozier and Picture This. The current generation of new Irish artists shows huge potential and diversity and includes Gilla Band, Murder Capital, Fontaines DC, Lankum, Denise Chaila, Tolü Makay, Kojaque, Pillow Queens, Vulpynes, God Knows, Jafaris, Soulé, Kynsy and the chart-topping Inhaler. Irish artists have also found places in highly successful UK acts including The Saturdays and One Direction.

Each of those successes have been the result of a combination of specific music and enterprise factors. Ireland's music has received the attention of some excellent scholarship; however, it is worth restating that Irish popular music studies has been an undeveloped field until recently. The point was forcefully made by Mangaoang, O'Flynn and Ó Briain (2021: 10), although thankfully their edited volume greatly enhances our knowledge of many aspects of Ireland's popular music. That said, some very insightful and illuminating work has been published. A number of full-length books, some by prominent Irish music journalists, have helped to document Ireland's mainstream rock scene. Starting with Mark J. Prendergast's (1987) book, *Irish Rock: Roots, Personalities, Directions*, this valuable work has continued with volumes from Clayton-Lea and Taylor (1992), O'Halloran (2006), Huston (2009), and Clayton-Lea (2012). Maybury and McNulty (2008) undertook insightful work on the less commercial aspects of Dublin's music; Brocklebank and Molony (2013) scrutinized the creative surge of the new wave and post-punk scenes. McAvoy (2016) documented the long span of rock music from Cork, while O'Neill and Trelford (2003) documented punk in Northern Ireland.

Scholarly work has also been very helpful to us as we approached the behind-the-scenes aspects of Ireland's music. Some particularly valuable books that guided us included Gerry Smyth's (2005) *Noisy Island: A Short History of Irish Popular Music*, Sean Campbell's (2011) *Irish Blood, English Heart: Second Generation Irish Musicians in England* and the collaborative *Beautiful Day: Forty Years of Irish Rock* (2005), by Campbell and Smyth. John O'Flynn's (2009) *The Irishness of Irish Music*, Noel McLaughlin and Martin McLoone's (2012) *Rock and Popular Music in Ireland: Before and After U2*, and *Music and Identity in Ireland and Beyond* (2016), edited by Mark Fitzgerald and John O'Flynn, are key texts to any scholar of Ireland's music industry. The publication of Noel McLaughlin and Joanna Braniff's (2020) *How Belfast Got the Blues: A Cultural History of Popular Music in the 1960s* indicates that Irish popular music scholarship continues to deliver high quality analysis.

While fully acknowledging the value of the previous work in the field, to examine the Irish music industry we took what we believe to be a novel approach. To our knowledge, no book exists which examines the individual enterprise behind several music acts from a specific country. While this book doesn't claim to be a theory book, it has been influenced by the approaches taken by three music industry scholars. Broadly speaking, we are working in an area that is informed by research into the music industries of particular countries (Johansson 2020); examinations of the nature of work in the music industry (Jones 2012); and studies of the distinct ways that the for-profit music industry operates (Stahl 2013).

As the music industry theorist, Michael L. Jones, has persuasively argued: 'Making music is an activity that occupies musicians; selling music goods is an activity that occupies music businesses' (2012: 2). That is not to say that high-achieving popular musicians don't possess business acumen. Often, they do. The circumstances, business opportunities and resource management of any act should be considered to understand how some acts 'made it'. The worthy acts, including forgotten Irish ones, that never 'made it' commercially are a driving force in our attempt to examine how the music industry works. Perhaps understanding how the industry works in practice can steer new acts towards better opportunities. That said, there are no simple lessons: as Jones highlighted, 'the industrialisation of music is a complex whole' (Jones 2012: 3).

That complex industrial process provides listeners with a simple pleasure. To many, including the authors, the enjoyment one gains from music is absolute. If there is a particular joy in sitting in a room in Ireland listening to music that was made there, another key point made by Jones should be considered: that the music industry is a 'process' not a place (Jones 2012: 3). When you take this to its logical conclusion, the idea of an 'Irish music industry' is not as simple as it seems. This means that an underdeveloped 'music industry' in any country, or a music industry that is not helpful to local acts, can, at times, be bypassed by musicians who can access the right type of supportive enterprise. This might give hope to musicians in any place that feels far away from Los Angeles, New York, London or Stockholm.

While we acknowledge another of Jones's key points, that music companies add value to what musicians do (Jones 2012: 4), in this book we also want to investigate other individuals and groups that add value to the work of musicians. Here, the work of Matt Stahl has been particularly helpful. He strongly argues that the modern 'pop star' represents a 'double figure'. They 'enjoy exceptional autonomy in their work, as well as a strong property interest in the songs they record' (2013: 1), yet 'typically work under unequal contracts and must hand over long-term control of the songs and albums they produce to their record companies' (2013: 2). Since acts signed with major firms must work within 'stable structures of authority and subordination, of property creation and appropriation' (2013: 3), we feel that it is important to identify where acts receive assistance from the not-for-profit do-it-yourself (DIY) music scene. If the global corporate music industries do not deliver what music fans want, it is worth knowing that sometimes their tactics can be challenged by members of the DIY music community, as we will highlight in Chapter 7, 'How Teenagers and Students Shaped Ireland's Culture'.

In many parts of this book, we are following Ola Johansson's method of examining media texts, mainly archive newspaper articles, which allows 'the reconstruction of relevant events, social processes, and networks' (2020: 44) with probably as much accuracy as a series of interviews with the participants. That said, we have included first-person interviews where we felt this added clarity or relevant details that were lacking from the published accounts. This shouldn't suggest that we are providing definitive accounts of 'what really happened'. As the French sociologists Michel Villette and Catherine Vuillermot (2009) clearly identified, modern stories of iconic business success are often constructed with a view to enhancing reputations. Different types of narratives are produced by different people with different aims and intended audiences. Yet, by equipping musicians and entrepreneurs with the best possible reconstructions of the key events, social processes, networks, resources and decision-making behind historical success stories, perhaps they can find what they need to succeed in a complex industry. At the same time, those lessons could be useful for academics, students, policy makers and anyone else who wants to know how the music industry works in practice.

It is clear that the Irish are passionate about their music. The phrase 'I can't imagine a life without music' has been used by Irish artists including Mary Black (Scott Cain 2004). The Irish don't just use words to appreciate music; they also use their money. Only 27 countries spend more per capita on music product than the Irish (IFPI 2020: 131) – they spent $71.2 million on digital and physical music in 2019. For physical sales of music – CDs and vinyl – they are in the Top 20 globally.

Ireland has been very valuable to the global music industry in two significant ways. First, the Irish have bought music in large quantities from the music industry. Second, Ireland has produced acts that have sold huge quantities of music globally. Between them, Enya, U2, Van Morrison and The Cranberries have sold more than 100 million albums in the US alone (RIAA). Remarkably, only ten bands have sold more records than U2 in the US market.

To understand how Irish music acts succeed in the business, we need to understand that business. In particular, we need to understand the people and situations that advance the careers of music acts, especially in their fragile, formative stages. Understanding the industry can help to answer another key question: how do Irish acts get noticed and nurtured during the early stages of their careers?

It is important to place each of those acts in their own context: to appreciate the local and global factors that helped to shape them; to recognize how social, political, economic, legal, technological, artistic and even ethical factors influenced them. When you examine the 'secrets behind the success' of Irish acts, you will notice two things. First, every act has a unique set of circumstances. Second, Ireland has produced a startling variety of successful acts. In other words, there is no one simple pathway from the local scene to the world market. Most of this book is comprised of case studies which highlight the local ingenuity in the industry of music, but we also explore some of the historical factors that helped to shape Ireland's *local* music culture and even the *global* industry of music. The success stories answer some questions and invite more.

From the late 1800s to the 1930s, Ireland was economically underdeveloped and then dealing with the reality of newly won independence from Britain on part of the island. At the same time the global music industry was developing into a successful and sophisticated modern economic and cultural force. The Irish in Ireland were largely absent from this early pivotal growth, yet the Irish diaspora in America engaged with the industry of music in multiple ways. In this book we examine that diaspora's activities in the recorded music industry, the live performance of music and the music publishing industry. In Chapter 1 we highlight how their activities impacted on Ireland (and its culture) and on the global music industry.

In the 1930s, the dominant forces in Irish society exerted influence over music events and community leisure. This has been well documented. In Chapter 2 we examine specifically how district judges shaped leisure, and pleasure, in Irish towns. This will help to answer two questions. What kind of legal and cultural landscape did young independent Ireland make for itself in the 1930s? Did this affect the way that the Irish socialized and enjoyed life?

Every country takes a different approach to the global music industry. Equally, the global music industry impacts on each country in different ways. In Chapter 3, we examine that dynamic and constantly evolving relationship. This helps to place the local music activities in the context of a rapidly changing industry that has serious implications for Ireland. In a very real way, as we explore in Chapter 4, the 1950s ushered in a major cultural shift. Young consumers, with their passion for music, became an influential economic and cultural force. But this was not an instant and universally embraced shift. Influential forces battled against each other over this youth power. We examine the place of Irish culture in this cultural battle. If Elvis and rock and roll reflected a dynamic, youthful economy in the US in the 1950s, what did Ireland's popular music of the time reflect?

These questions help to illuminate the distinctive, and unusual, ways through which Ireland's music industry developed. It was not a straightforward linear process. Multiple forces pulled it in different directions. Our case studies of successful Irish artists examine the ways that creative and supportive local enterprise helped these acts. One of the most influential group of entrepreneurs in Ireland's music industry history was the progressive trad-prog rock band, Horslips. In Chapter 5 we examine how a group of creative spirits, with a love of modern counterculture *and* Irish traditional music, generated a new path for local bands in the early 1970s.

In a very real sense Horslips ushered in a transformational 'youth power' approach to Ireland's industry of music. It was an approach that also stimulated the growth of the local scene during the 1970s, 1980s and 1990s. What is remarkable about the Irish situation is that university students, and do-it-yourself music entrepreneurship, were behind some of these key developments. Chapter 6 examines the early grassroots activity that sustained and supported U2 in their development phase. Their global success is impossible to contemplate without that local activity. In all likelihood, it saved them from signing the type of music industry contract that could have cost them countless millions of dollars or euros in the long term.

Some of the individuals involved in Ireland's music scene approached music as a counter cultural activity rather than a profitable pursuit. Chapter 7 examines this process to understand how a group of teenagers, with practically no music industry experience or funds, organized concerts for bands, including Green Day and Fugazi.

Chapters 8, 9 and 10 examine the early local stages in the development of three of Ireland's significant cultural exports: Enya, The Corrs and *Riverdance*. We explore how an introverted female singer from Donegal was shepherded to express herself in the early 1980s and went on to transform the landscape of global pop music. This is particularly important because the global music industry has yet to deliver a similar success story in Enya's field. Like Enya, The Corrs developed in a distinctive way in their home country before their eventual success. We trace their development as they expanded their fanbase into countries spanning the globe. Their achievements were not as straightforward as their sales figures, or public image, alone suggest. Following this we ask:

how did a mother in Dublin, who was taking time out from her media career, find a way to dream up, develop and bring to the market a touring extravaganza that generated millions of dollars? The *Riverdance* success was not pre-planned, or anticipated, but indicated how Irish enterprise could adapt quickly to opportunities. The production itself was a mixture of local enterprise and creativity and drew on a skill set of a variety of artists. It is notable that international firms were initially reluctant to invest in *Riverdance*. It is almost impossible to calculate the sums they could have earned with more belief and foresight.

In Chapters 11 and 12 we examine two internationally successful boy bands, Boyzone and Westlife. We address the question: how did Ireland produce boy bands, in one of the most competitive areas of pop, and succeed at the highest level in Britain and in other markets? In particular, we examine the type of groundwork that was undertaken by the group members themselves. Again, this highlights how, in the Irish case, young creative people used entrepreneurial skills to advance their careers, at least initially. Furthermore, through these examples we consider how the economic and cultural situation in Ireland impacted on the band members.

Finally, in Chapter 13 we examine the ways in which behind-the-scenes creative workers can be influential in the local music scene. These workers, Steve Averill in this case, are often intermediaries between the local scene and the global for-profit music industry, and they can serve that scene in a variety of roles.

When we examine these specific case studies of enterprise in the Irish music scene, it makes sense to identify some of the key factors in the growth of the global music industry itself. Music and enterprise in any country develop in the context of cultural and social factors. As the popular music scholar, Martin Cloonan (1999: 205), concluded: 'the location and regulatory strength of one's Nation-State' is a key determinant of any individual's popular music environment. This can be seen in one of the key texts in popular music studies, Malm and Wallis's (1992) *Media Policy and Music Activity*. The book clearly illustrated how the music industries in countries including Jamaica, Kenya, Wales and Sweden developed in ways that reflected the influence of local power groups. In any country, or even region, the enterprise of music is strongly influenced by cultural and political forces.

1 The Irish Arrive: Early Stages in the Music Industry

The enterprise behind Ireland's music should be understood in the context of Ireland's demographics. Ireland may be a small country on the western fringe of Europe, but thanks to its migration patterns a large population of people with Irish ancestry can be found internationally. In fact, Ireland's diaspora helped to shape *both* Ireland's music *and* the global music industry in very significant ways. At times the global music industry designed products for the larger Irish American market rather than the smaller domestic market in Ireland. Naturally, this had implications for the recorded music that was available to the Irish both at home and abroad. The US music industry developed mass-manufacturing and mass-marketing abilities towards the end of the 19th century. At the same time, in 1890 the Irish-born population in the US numbered 1.87 million. Ten years later, in 1900, over 3.3 million second-generation Irish Americans were resident there (Kenny 2000: 184).

One of the highest-selling artists in the US of the era, John McCormack, had the great fortune of commencing his career when the music industry was growing rapidly, and a ready-made audience for Irish products existed in the US. The man responsible for signing him to HMV was later quoted:

> No one was keener to welcome an Irish tenor [to the record label] than I, since I was alive to the commercial possibilities among the Irish Americans, who showed the most idolatrous worship of their bards. (Moore 1977: 92)

But even while some major global firms were actively shaping the recorded music of Ireland, Irish individuals were shaping the global music industries. As we will demonstrate, this can be seen clearly in the industry of music publishing where the Irish successfully campaigned for the rights of music composers and lyric authors.

In the summer of 1907, in the County Cork market town of Youghal, on Ireland's southern coast, a man called Murphy purchased some sheet music. His selection was typical of the music enjoyed in homes and churches in the country at the time. He bought the hymns 'Abide with Me' and 'The Star of

Bethlehem', and the melancholic tear-jerker, 'The Promise of Life'. He returned the following day and bought even more music from the shopkeeper. But Murphy wasn't buying the music for himself. He was acting on behalf of the law, and the law was acting on behalf of the global music industry. Murphy was a local police constable. In his sworn evidence in court (*Cork Examiner* 1907) he testified that the sheet music was contraband, or to use the preferred term of the music industry and the newspapers for over a century, the work of *pirates*. The Youghal shopkeeper was found guilty and fined. The case proved that in 1907 the London-based music industry could protect its commercial interests with the assistance of the local police in Irish towns. A recent Act of Parliament had given the police this power and they were happy to use it; the activities of Irish policemen at the time were governed by laws made in London.

The Musical Copyright Act of 1906 had been introduced to Parliament as a Bill and was known as the T.P. O'Connor Bill. It was the great leap forward that music publishers had dreamt of. But not everyone was celebrating. Naturally, the sellers of bootleg sheet music were disappointed, but so too were the people who felt that the publishers were a 'rich and powerful' group who didn't act in the best interests of the public. Intriguingly, as the historian of copyright legislation, Isabella Alexander, has documented, one argument at the time was that the music publishers colluded to make music too expensive for most people (Alexander 2007: 643–45). However, the success of the Bill is a reminder that 'small groups … can influence the law in their own interest' (Alexander 2007: 626).

At the time, however, there was cross-party backing for the music publishers: the Bill was sponsored by members of the Liberal, Conservative and Labour parties. The law meant that small shops in Britain and Ireland could be raided by the police for selling illegal copies of sheet music. If this seemed like the power of London reaching into rural Ireland, it is worth noting that the law had Irish fingerprints all over it. The Act was named after the Irishman who had championed it, T.P. O'Connor, who was the only member of the Irish Nationalist Party to win a seat in England, when the electorate of Liverpool had elected him. One of the Bill's other sponsors was John Redmond, the leader of the Irish Parliamentary Party. It didn't always happen, but this time the Irish nationalists were on the side of the property owners.

There is an interesting international element to the debate, too. In the 1870s and 1880s, some of the 'pirates' were US entrepreneurs who were acting within the laws of *their* land. It wasn't until 1891 that the US recognized British copyright. Until then, if you thought an English song, protected by copyright in its homeland, might find a market in America, you could publish it there. Even better, you could then sell your 'bootleg' copy in England (Alexander 2007: 627–28).

Securing legislation in Britain which protected their interests was obviously a big victory for the music publishers. But accomplishing this in the US would be a far greater achievement. Soon after the passage of the Musical Copyright Act of 1906 in Britain, T.P. O'Connor travelled to the US. The purpose of his trip was to take part in meetings about how to advance the cause of Irish independence. Yet, fortuitously for the music industry powerbrokers, and for the music publishing industry, his visit was also a chance to advance the cause of *their* businesses.

At one 1906 banquet honouring T.P. O'Connor, and what the Irish politician had achieved for music publishers in Britain, an eminent figure in Irish American politics sat on his right-hand side. His name was Victor Herbert, and at the time he was one of the best-known music figures in the US. He was later remembered by US newspapers as 'America's foremost librettist' (Batchelder 1924), but in 1906, inspired by T.P. O'Connor's legislation, he was absolutely determined to get US lawmakers to protect *his* interests. O'Connor and Herbert had a lot in common: both were ardent Irish nationalists, and by a quirk of fate, both were passionate advocates of composers' rights. By 1916 Herbert was the national president of the Friends of Irish Freedom (*Irish Standard* 1916) in the US, and was using his celebrity status to argue against the US involvement with Britain in World War I. He actively cheered for a German victory and wrote in one US newspaper:

> ...for what I believe to be the best interest of mankind in general, and Ireland in particular, she [Britain] is now fighting against foes whom she cannot frighten or cajole, and in my judgement from the outbreak of the war it has seemed inevitable that the British Empire is doomed and that again we are going to live in a world where there will be liberty and freedom and where the weaker peoples will not have to live in constant dread that their countries and their rights are to be taken from them. (*Irish Standard* [Minneapolis] 1916)

The career and public statements of Victor Herbert show how music, business and politics intersected in the early 1900s. As Marion Casey (2017) has documented, Herbert is a case where 'nativity, identity, diaspora and nationalism can intertwine' in complex ways. While many of his biographies claim he was born in Dublin, probably swayed by his personally authorized CV (Gould 2008: 96), Casey states 'although he never set foot in Ireland, he confidently proclaimed being Irish all his life'. But it is in the music industry that he is most fondly remembered. As his biographer, Neil Gould (2008), has documented, before Herbert's long legal battle to win rights for music authors, sheet music was the only source of revenue for music composers. Thanks to Herbert, composers later

> acquired the right under federal law to royalties for public performance of their work for profit, to phonographic royalties, and later, by extension, to royalties from radio, television and film use of copyrighted works. (Gould 2008: 216)

The revenue that flowed, and continues to flow, to US composers, thanks to Herbert and his legal allies, is considerable. He was one of the founders of the American Society of Composers, Authors and Publishers (ASCAP) who collected over $1.32 billion (Matthews 2021: 5) from music copyright work in 2020 alone. While the achievements, on both sides of the Atlantic, of Herbert and O'Connor on behalf of musicians, composers and the wider music industries were sizeable, this should not be attributed to some natural instinct of the Irish, and Irish Americans, to protect the rights of the creative community. Instead, they show that despite Ireland's economic backwardness in the early 20th century, individuals from Ireland and its diaspora often contributed in significant ways to how the global music industry developed. If the Irish lacked opportunities for enterprise at home, they could find them elsewhere, and when they did, they could alter the cultural life and the industry of music both at home and abroad.

Ellen O'Byrne and the Foundation of the Irish Music Industry

At the time that O'Connor and Herbert were successfully having laws changed to benefit songwriters, the record industry was growing in influence. The global recording industry was shaped by technological and marketing innovations and the speed and success of these had a dramatic effect on domestic Irish culture. The overseas expansion of the early recording firms followed a pattern identified by Dave Laing. He argued that European and US manufacturing industries developed geographically in accordance with 'the regional empires or regional sphere of influence' of the world's major national powers (2013: 33). Industrial concentration and established trade routes equipped the gramophone firms for rapid global prominence. In addition, the 1901 'cartel' agreement between the Gramophone Company in Britain and the Victor firm in the US effectively reduced competition by dividing the world market into two separate 'spheres of influence' (Laing 2013: 33). For any country – and in Ireland's case, one with a complicated relationship with these major powers – the impact was sudden and comprehensive.

At this time, both radio and gramophone records were achieving large sales and increasing their global reach. Robert W. Witkin (2003: 121) identified the performance by Dame Nellie Melba on 15 June 1920 as the defining moment that 'proved that radio could be successful'. She sang in French, Italian and English, in the first broadcast to be transmitted to both sides of the Atlantic simultaneously. This global success was not a fluke. Read and Welch (1959) provided striking evidence of the resources deployed by the major radio firms. In 1924 the biggest of them, Victor, spent $5 million on advertising. It was the largest single advertising budget of any American corporation (1959: 216).

While the global music industry was bringing 'foreign' culture to Ireland, it was also bringing a sense of Irish culture to the world. John McCormack was one of the most successful artists of the era, but he wasn't the only representative of Ireland being recorded. Between 1899 and 1942, approximately 40 companies released recordings of Irish music in the US. Tim Brooks (1978, 1979, 2002) vividly illustrates the Irish content in American recordings during the industry's early years; however, it should be noted that almost three-quarters of these were on three major labels: Columbia with 40 per cent; Decca with 18 per cent; Victor with 16 per cent (Dillane 2002: 114). The amount of material recorded in the US, and the underdeveloped music industry in Ireland, led to Méabh Ní Fhuartháin's (1993) assessment that the major developments in the field of Irish music during the first half of the 20th century occurred in the US.

However, in terms of content, Aileen Dillane (2002) concludes that 'most early recordings of "Irish" music had little to do with traditional Irish dance music practices' (2002: 111). Irish music was just one repertoire category in the marketing-driven, profit-oriented recording industry. As a result, Irish music was shaped by commercial considerations rather than any consistent desire to 'preserve', or even honour, Irish music. Irish cultural interest groups, powerful as they may have been domestically, lacked the ability to steer the global representation of Irish music culture. In fact, the impact of the gramophone on Ireland was striking, although as both Hillary Bracefield (1998) and Fintan Vallely (2008) concluded, this was not always positive.

> This device froze performances in a mass-reproducible, durable, saleable plastic, and for such limited leisure time as people had, it brought other music 'live', so to speak, into less-well-off homes after the opening 1900s, and reaching out to all parts of the island by the 1930s, with the availability of cheap phonographs and emigrants' money. (Vallely 2008: 123–24)

The gramophone became a device for learning Irish music even as it diverted people from the sounds of regional traditional music-making. Where there had been many local accents and variations in Irish traditional playing, now there was one voice, and it came from America embedded in the grooves of records. The format of the 78 records, which limited content to three minutes, shaped Irish music-making. Musicians in Ireland learned tunes and songs from the recordings made overseas and then performed those tunes around Ireland. But these recordings also had a 'galvanising effect on the development of Irish traditional music in Ireland itself' (Bracefield 1998: 34) due to a lack of locally recorded music. The music historian Mick Moloney (1982: 92) found that, even five decades later, those early Irish music records were still influencing the way Irish tunes were being played. Three-quarters of the songs being played in one Chicago setting in 1977 had been learned from gramophone records.

The commercial logic of the industry's major labels decided what Irish music should be recorded. But demand appeared to ebb as the novelty wore off. As Roxanne O'Connell (2013) documented, the 1920s peak production of 'ethnic' recordings, including Irish ones, was never repeated; by the 1940s, the majors had ceased issuing 'Irish' records completely and the only remaining small firm in the field, Celtic Records, failed to secure a long-term business model. If Irish people wanted their version of Irish music to be preserved and promoted, they would have to do it themselves.

One small independent label in New York, O'Byrne-DeWitt, accepted that challenge. Atypically for the era and the industry, the founder was a woman. Ellen O'Byrne had a family name that was more typically spelled and pronounced O'Beirne in the west of Ireland. She was born around 1875 in County Leitrim and emigrated aged 15. In New York she married a Dutch immigrant, Justus DeWitt. Together they opened a shop in Manhattan 'despite initial protests from the companies involved' (Ní Fhuartháin 1993: 55); the objections apparently stemmed from the prominence of a woman in the venture. While Justus maintained the accounts, Ellen successfully 'explored new and enterprising avenues' (1993: 55) for the business. The shop sold musical instruments – accordions were a prominent item – and the new cylinder recordings of music also found space on the shelves. According to Susan Gedutis (2005: 149), O'Byrne-DeWitt 'may be credited singlehandedly with founding the Irish recording industry'.

O'Byrne-DeWitt seemed to embody the values of both old Ireland and modern America. Ellen was socially modest *and* financially successful, and she applied her enterprise skills and vision to capture and preserve a version of Irish culture. Her achievements ensured that Irish music was taken seriously in the early 1900s. Importantly for Ireland, the entrepreneurial activities of Byrne-DeWitt proved that small companies could find a niche in the global recording music industry.

In 1923, a number of US newspapers published a feature on O'Byrne that presented her as a self-made success story (see, for example, Van Der Grift 1923). Readers were informed that she had arrived from Ireland with nothing except 'a love [for Irish music] and a little bundle of clothes'. Now she was a business-owner whose property was valued at $200,000. By today's standards she'd be acclaimed as a multi-millionaire. Naturally, her success in America had implications for her family in Ireland. In the well-established pattern for emigrants, she had paid for her brothers and sisters to leave Ireland and join her in New York. As the newspaper stories recounted, this was in dramatic contrast with her situation in 1911 when O'Byrne was 'stranded with $100 in her pocket and a young and hungry son clinging to each hand'. With the last of her cash, she had founded a shop and diligently applied herself to the twin responsibilities of being a working mother and a small-business owner. She was quoted: 'Until my boys went into long trousers, I made every bit of their clothing'.

O'Byrne, by all accounts, was an astute businesswoman and the newspapers reported how she had cleverly accepted government-issued Liberty bonds during the war in payment for goods when customers were short of actual cash. She used the profits from the shop to buy the building from the landlord. Later, she bought the property next door as well as three houses on Staten Island and five vacant lots suitable for development.

O'Byrne's perspective as a successful businesswoman had elements of a folksy 'how to' manual:

> Don't gossip
> Do something useful every minute
> Use good English. It gives people a better impression of you.
> Read books that deal with thrift and with successful men and women.
> Save. But save judiciously.
> Be kind. It pays.

Some of her wisdom, though, sounded hard-won and specific: 'Don't try to get rich quick, but if you've got an idea fight for it. I had an idea the world wanted an Irish music store, but I had to fight every step of the way.'

If O'Byrne's success story was, for the media, a way of defining the idea of the American dream, it mattered even more for Irish culture. Firstly, she was a female Irish entrepreneur and an American success story. But even more importantly, she was someone with the means and the ability to actively curate her idea of Ireland's musical heritage. Although the article doesn't mention it, O'Byrne's shop at 1398 Third Avenue was one of, if not *the* first, shop in New York selling exclusively Irish goods. Naturally, it became a focal point for the emigrant community. With knowledge of both her customers and the range of records available, she spotted a gap in the market. People wanted Irish music.

If the major labels wouldn't treat Irish music seriously, O'Byrne would find artists and tunes and get them recorded and distributed (Gedutis 2005: 150). In 1916, she arranged for the Irish reel 'The Stack of Barley' to be recorded on accordion and banjo and sold hundreds of copies of the disc. Her son later recalled the process:

> My mother owned a record store in Manhattan, and Irish people were always coming in and asking for old favourites, like *The Stack of Barley*. Well she'd no records to give them because there weren't any. So she sent me up to Gaelic Park in the Bronx to find some musicians. There was always music there on Sundays. Well I found Eddie Herborn and John Wheeler playing banjo and accordion and they sounded great. So my mother went to Columbia [record company], and they said if she would agree to buy five hundred copies from them they would record Herborn and Wheeler. She agreed... (Moloney 1982: 90)

Irish traditional music was being recorded, and, in a real sense, being *made* in the US. O'Byrne may have educated herself to speak better English to help her to succeed in the US, but some of her business moves were the actions of an ardent Irish nationalist. She changed the name of the shop to the Sinn Féin Music House, and when her label released the patriotic ballad, 'Kevin Barry', she included the message: 'Dedicated to all the Fenians living or dead' (Spottswood 1990: 2781).

Ellen O'Byrne's serious approach to Ireland's music contrasts dramatically with many of the musical representations of the Irish during this time. As Moloney (1982) identified, there were four general categories of Irish music being recorded: 'stage Irish' with the racist tropes and stereotypes; European-classical-influenced music; traditional tunes; and hybrids which mixed elements of the other three. It is notable that O'Byrne avoided the buffoonery of the 'stage Irish'. This was Irish culture being made credible and curated by the Irish themselves.

O'Byrne's releases weren't all political or topical. In fact, you can hear the template for the next five decades of Irish popular music, including the showbands, in her records. There were jigs and reels as well as sentimental songs by the masculine tenor voice that became a hallmark of global Irish culture. You could teach Irish geography by just using the placenames in her song titles: Castlebar, Galway, Mullingar, Clare, Down and Innisfail. There were fun songs and sentimental lyrics about fair maidens, small village Ireland and longing. Above all, there were songs about what it meant to be Irish, and songs about how people wanted Ireland to be.

Sadly, O'Byrne didn't live long to further the cause of Irish music. One of the great what-might-have-been questions of the Irish music industry is what she could have achieved with a longer career. After her death in 1926, her son took over the business and, although he enjoyed some success with Irish recordings, he never eclipsed the firm's early years. But Ellen O'Byrne's contribution should never be forgotten; she was a major force in starting the Irish recorded-music industry. At its inception it was a do-it-yourself, female-led, emigrant, Irish-nationalist enterprise. While Ireland, and its diaspora, have since produced some very notable record labels, they have never dominated the music market in Ireland in the long term (Murphy 2021). In a sense, O'Byrne's legacy has never yet been properly fulfilled. That is a good reason for more to be done to understand, document and learn from the history of Irish record labels. But it wasn't just in the industries of recorded music and song publishing that the Irish were being effective. While O'Byrne was influencing the direction of Ireland's record industry, and T.P. O'Connor and Victor Herbert were guiding the global music publishing industry, one family of Irish emigrants were helping to shape the live music industry in the rapidly growing city of New York.

Migration and Conditions

It almost sounds like a joke or a myth, but the law governing music copyright in the US was prompted by one Irish American walking into an Irish American restaurant and hearing his music being played. What T.P. O'Connor had achieved for songwriters in Britain, Victor Herbert achieved for their counterparts in the US. The legal case that finally established that songwriters and composers had a legally enforceable right to be paid when their music was performed in public was *Herbert v. Shanley Co.* In 1917 it made its way through the legal system all the way up to the Supreme Court. It is notable that the case bears the name of the Irish Shanley family, and it proves how the Shanleys, recently arrived immigrants, quickly became a prominent part of New York's urban entertainment. Initially the Shanley brothers were victorious in the courts. They argued that the music was background entertainment, and there was no extra fee for it, so they were under no obligation to pay the composers. Upon appeal, though, Herbert won the case and established the legal precedent that forced hotels, restaurants and, eventually, radio stations, to pay a fee for the music heard in their premises.

The story of the Shanley family, from County Leitrim's Mohill and Dromod districts, illustrates why the young Irish fled Ireland when they could. It also provides an example of the geographic and social mobility in the immediate post-Famine period. It is a story that vividly illustrates the gulf between life in Ireland and in America and indicates why New York mattered to the Irish, and why the Irish mattered to New York. The account of one Shanley family member (Shanley 1990–91) provides details of their lives beyond the newspaper stories in which they were celebrated during their first years in the US.

In the late 1850s, Margaret Faughnan married Michael Shanley. Both grew up during the Famine and saw hardship at first hand. They had eight sons and two daughters, who were sustained by sales of their mother's handcrafted lacework, as well as by a small family-run grocery store and pub, typical of small villages in Ireland. In addition to keeping the family's livestock, Michael was also entrusted with getting the best prices for neighbours' cows and pigs when the time came to sell them at markets or fairs.

While the north of Ireland had benefited economically from the Industrial Revolution, the south had floundered, and counties in the west, including Leitrim, were particularly hard hit. But the Shanley family had the type of enterprise skills required in basic subsistence-level economies. Those skills provided individuals and families not only with a basic income but also with opportunities. The family needed those enterprise skills more urgently when Michael died from pneumonia in 1871. Margaret was now a widow with 10 children under the age of 13. The eldest son, John, when he came of age, took over the running of the small family farm. Every one of the other nine children left. Tom Shanley, the second-eldest son, enhanced his enterprise skills, as much as you could in rural Ireland at the time, by serving as an apprentice to a small drapery business in Carrick-on-Shannon town.

When the time came, a family cow was sold to pay for Tom's fare to America. He followed a well-established pattern, and his emigration changed the family's circumstances dramatically. Young Irish individuals who could afford the boat fare to the US faced an anguished decision, but often there was only one logical choice. Economic migrants need to find places with better opportunities and the US in the second half of the 1800s provided this for the Irish.

This period of large-scale Irish immigration came at a time when the United States was a country in a demographic flux. It was experiencing a huge growth spurt as settlers, with government help, claimed land from wilderness and the native American population. The new arrivals were helping to develop and transform the country. In some of its major cities, these new arrivals came close to outnumbering the native-born population, many of whom were only a generation or two off the boat themselves. The 1860 census records that 47.2 per cent of New York's population was foreign-born; a decade later it was still very high at 44.5 per cent (Gibson and Jung 2006: 89–91). The figure was even higher elsewhere: 48.4 per cent in Chicago, and 49.3 per cent in San Francisco. If a large percentage of the population were recent arrivals, even more had a foreign-born parent. In 1870 the population of New York state was 4,382,750. Of this total, more than 3,360,000 were either foreign-born, or had a parent born abroad (Walker 1872: 299).

While the story of the Irish in the US has been well-documented in parts, some key points are worth highlighting. As Linda Dowling Almeida (2013) has illustrated, the pattern of Irish emigration was different from the norms of other immigrant groups. In the 70 years between 1850 and 1920, four million Irish arrived in the US. Unlike other ethnic groups who tended to spread out in the vast country, the Irish remained in the cities. They generally married other members of the Irish community. They became a very visible, and not always welcome, group in the major cities of the northeast.

The Irish had been arriving long before this significant 70-year flow. George Washington had ordered a celebration of St Patrick's Day in Morristown, New Jersey, in 1778 and had given his troops a day off (Rogers and Anderson 2013: 25–26). Despite the stereotypical idea of Irish immigrants as Catholic, a sizeable number of the early arrivals were Protestant. As more Catholic immigrants arrived, Protestants from Ulster, to differentiate themselves, increasingly identified as 'Scots-Irish' and integrated efficiently, some into the White Anglo-Saxon Protestant (WASP) power group, with large numbers spreading throughout the southern states.

The Irish emigrants of 1850–1920 were primarily Catholic, and the US was their most popular destination. They were impossible to miss in New York where, by 1855, 34 per cent of the voters were Irish (Dowling Almeida 2013: 79). Yet, even in this major period of emigration, there was a noticeable downward trend. In the 1840s, half of the arriving immigrants to the US were Irish; in the 1850s just over a third. By the 1890s, one in ten new arrivals were from Ireland. When immigration quotas were introduced in the 1920s, the Irish were restricted to 18,000 annually. During the 1920s, for every single Irish arrival more than 15 immigrants arrived from other countries.

One startling factor set the Irish apart from other ethnic groups. Almost half of those fleeing Ireland were young women. For other nationalities, a greater proportion of their immigrants arriving in the US were male. US census figures identify this trend (Gibson and Jung 2006): on average, for all nationalities, 117 men arrived for every 100 women during 1870; by 1890, 121 men travelled for every 100 women; by 1910, it was 131 men for every 100 women. Yet the Irish lost almost as many women as men to the emigrant ships. For most ethnic groups, men emigrated in search of opportunities, while women remained in familiar home surroundings. In her account of female Irish emigrants of the era, Diner (1983) documents just how unusual their circumstances were. German immigrants included a sizeable percentage of women, although at 41 per cent it was lower than it was for the Irish with their 50 per cent (1983: 31). Among southern Italian immigrants, 21 per cent were women; for Croatians the figure was 13 per cent; for Greeks 4 per cent. The only immigrant population that came close to the Irish pattern was the Jewish community who were often fleeing murderous hostility in Eastern Europe. That said, the Jewish figures included a large number of children, 28 per cent of the total; for the Irish, children were a mere 5 per cent of the total. Diner concludes that the Irish migration represented 'a mass female movement'; significantly 'no other major group of immigrants in American history contained so many women' (1983: 30). The Irish generally didn't emigrate as families, they travelled alone across the Atlantic and they arrived single. As Janet Nolan (2009: 77), the leading historian of Irish women emigrants, concludes: 'Irish America has foremothers as much as forefathers'. Evidently, Ireland was no country for young women.

The Irish also arrived poor; 'poorer than other immigrants' (Diner 1983: 107) of the time. They were leaving a severely impoverished country, and they had few material resources when they arrived to start their new lives in the US. Towards the end of the 19th century over 60 per cent of residents of New York's alms-houses were Irish, and a US government report documented how the Irish were statistically overrepresented in prisons and charitable institutions. Swiss immigrants had the second-highest rate of paupers per population (Diner 1983: 108), and one in every 200 were destitute. For the Irish it was double that, one in every 100. In those circumstances the Irish suffered an appalling mortality rate (Nolan 2004: 50–51). In 1874, a higher percentage of the Irish in Boston died than any other ethnic group. The infant mortality rate meant that 23 babies died for every 1,000 born. That said, it was even higher in Leeds and Manchester. The Irish emigrated from poverty into poverty.

The Irish typically worked with their hands and feet, or they didn't work. The jobs they were offered were generally at the bottom of the social ladder. Conditions were often treacherous, and the Irish accepted jobs shunned by other ethnic groups and the native-born. Because of the physical dangers, Irishmen had a high rate of death in industrial accidents (Diner 1983: 41). What type of work was needed as urban American expanded? The answer can be seen in modern histories as well as in the newspapers of the time. Those accounts also tell us a lot about the type of people who used that labour. In the 1830s, during the digging of New Basin Canal connecting Lake Pontchartrain with the Mississippi river, slave owners decided that the work was too dangerous for their slaves. The Irish would have to do it instead. It is estimated by T. J. English (2005: 48–49), that between 3,000 and 30,000 Irishmen died during the project from cholera, malaria, yellow fever and overwork.

Less than a decade later, the local newspaper, the *Times-Picayune* of New Orleans, published an article that revealed a lot about both the Irish and the people who controlled labour in parts of the US. Daniel O'Connell, the champion of Irish self-determination, had recently made a speech which was published in the *Freemans' Journal* and later reprinted in US newspapers (*Niles Weekly Register* 1843). The *Times-Picayune* reported on the reaction to O'Connell's words. He was quoted decrying that slaves in the US 'are treated not as human beings, but as the brute beast that expires, and then ceases to have any other existence'. His remarks were rejected as 'insulting to the character of the American people ... [and] the humanity and sense of obligation that are the characteristics of the Southern people'. In fact, the conditions of the slaves were contrasted with employment conditions across the Atlantic:

> ...the absence of restraint, the appliance of comfort, and the social enjoyments of the slave here are freedom, luxury and enjoyment, compared with the conditions in the mines, and the other operatives of Great Britain. (*Times-Picayune* 1843)

There, industrialists saw no irony in using the words *freedom* and *luxury* to describe the conditions of their slaves. The message was barbaric, and there was a subtext. The Irish were welcome to work, in the most dreadful conditions, but they shouldn't expect better conditions for themselves or other workers.

The dangers of the type of labour that Irishmen undertook contributed to Irish women outnumbering Irish men in many cities. It was hardly surprising that, when they could get them, the Irish swelled the ranks of public service jobs in police and fire departments as well as on building sites. In Boston in 1890, only one in ten of the Irish had white-collar jobs (Kibler 2015: 35). For Irish women, too, the work was low status. In 1920, 43 per cent of white, female foreign-born domestic servants in New York were Irish (Lynch-Brennan and O'Rourke Murphy 2014: xix). Women from other ethnic groups frowned on the idea of working in another woman's home. Yet, very quickly, the Irish women in the US dramatically transformed their own fortunes.

The Shanleys: An Irish Success Story

It is difficult to imagine the culture shock for the new arrivals from Ireland during New York's urban expansion. They came from small Irish villages and towns and had to quickly adapt to their new circumstances. Tom Shanley from Leitrim did just that, and he played a role in making New York a truly cosmopolitan city. According to the family history (Shanley 1990–91), by 1880 he was a buyer for the Ehrich House of Fashions, earning $10,000 a year plus bonuses, as well as a prestigious annual business trip to Europe. He was married with three children. He had paid for three of his brothers to join him in New York where they also found work in the services industry. Barney was a maître d' in the prestigious Union Square Hotel, while Patrick and Michael were waiters in the city.

The four brothers learned quickly in the city and confidently started their own enterprise. Importantly, they had also made friends in New York, and one of these proved particularly valuable. John Jacob Astor was one of the wealthiest individuals in the US at the time and possessed a sizeable property portfolio. He had faith that these young Shanley immigrants could build a business. The Irish brothers believed that New York was ready for something new. Dining was socially stratified in the city, people ate with their social peers, so the Shanley idea was somewhat of a social revolution. In the heart of the theatre district, at Sixth Avenue and 23rd Street, they opened a restaurant that was elegant and relaxed, where people of varying social classes could dine and spend time together.

It is tempting to conclude that recently arrived emigrants were more likely to take a risk on this innovative idea. In any event, the four US-based Shanley brothers quickly funded the transatlantic fares of their four younger siblings, Peter, Andrew, James and Annie. By 1901, the Shanleys had three prominent establishments in the city and their business was a major force in making dining a cross-social-class activity. Despite the luxury of the setting, Shanley's didn't attempt to imitate European fine dining, despite the snob appeal of continental cuisine among well-heeled Americans. In their Irish American business, the food was identifiably American. Only the wine and champagne were imported, although when they did buy imported goods, they bought them in bulk. According to accounts (Shanley 1990–91: 16–20), the restaurants were uncorking 150,000 bottles of champagne a year. This made them the city's biggest buyers of champagne; the sparkling drink alone earned them a million dollars annually. On one occasion, they bought half a million dollars' worth of wine in a French auction. In 1919, a Hearst newspaper baron ordered champagne for the entire restaurant to celebrate the return of US troops from World War I. He ran up a bill for $50,000.

The scale of the business was impressive. The restaurant on 43rd Street could accommodate 2,000 diners. One thousand people could be seated in the main dining room, and 300 in the grill room. The kitchen beneath the restaurant was a full street-block long. The wine cellar and storage area beneath this were almost the same size. The dining-room walls were decorated with expensive English oak panels, 100ft long and 30ft high.

Newspapers praised the new dining establishments. The *New York Times* (1906: 24) boasted how the city now had 'just as one had in the old days in Paris, as they say in French, an "embarrassment of riches"'. New York was now home to world-class eateries, and they were serving American-sourced food. Writers recalled that 'its silver shone. Its waiters were all Irish, and the service was flawless' (Heffernan 1932: 6). This was no place for Irish small-talk and witty banter; the service philosophy for waiters was drilled into the staff: 'Be pleasant, be smart, be prompt and be gone' (Shanley 1990–91:18). There was something multinational, modern and yet still Irish about the business. The food was American, the wine was French, but the tablecloth was Belfast linen embroidered with the Leitrim family's crest.

In a gushing full-page article, the *New York Times* (1906) celebrated the dining and socializing revolution in which the Shanleys were a major force. To the newspaper, these restaurants set the city apart: '... there are few first-class hotels in this country outside of New York', they boasted. Shanley's was certainly good for the newspaper, which it frequently paid to advertise its food and entertainment. Small wonder, then, that the *Times* boasted that the city's food was now suitable for the '*cosmopolite*' who can dine on Shanley's 'planked steak with vegetables or planked fowl with truffles and vegetables'. A meal at the Irish-owned restaurant was an 'artistic creation and a luxury' (*New York Times* 1906: 24).

In his historical analysis of New York's nightlife, Lewis A. Ernberg (1984) concluded that leisure businesses like the Shanley's revolutionized US culture in an important way. By 1920, women had finally been allowed to vote in US elections and Shanley's played a role in challenging the restrictions on women's behaviour in public. This wasn't just the tokenistic fraternizing of wealthy socialites with underground figures in the speakeasies, where the most expensive lawyers could generally smooth things over for both groups. This was a genuine breakdown of barriers of class and gender, although, notably, not race.

Cabaret entertainments were a significant factor in the shift away from Victorian values, with their rigid definitions of acceptable behaviour, to a more carefree way of living and socializing. To Ernberg, this encouraged the 'expanding consumer economy, offering powerful visions of liberation'

(Ernberg 1984: 259). If the American ethos is liberty, choice, freedom and fun, the Shanleys from rural Leitrim delivered that to New Yorkers during a key moment. Their cabarets were some of the most celebrated and innovative of the era.

As Shanley's grew, it no longer simply offered food and a place to see and be seen, music was on the menu too. The restaurant was a key part of the industry of music. In 1918, the *New York Times* included ads for a 'twenty-act cabaret' at Shanley's; even the afternoon luncheon service included music. By 1920, the Shanleys were boasting that they served their own signature dish, 'Pear Shanley' and just as importantly they were advertising that even their lunch meals were now accompanied by live music (*New York Times* 1920). They were in the entertainment business, 'sparkling entertainment' as they described it. Dining at Shanley's was a very public social event. In 1922, Shanley's was advertising the *Shanley Revue* featuring Thelma Harvey and the Big Beauty Cast (*New York Times* 1922: 18). This American style of cabaret was closer in spirit to variety shows than to the more raucous and bawdier Berlin cabaret of the 1920s, which, as one historian noted, had a sense of 'anti-romanticism' (Kosta 2009: 131). Shanley's use of music, on the other hand, was bringing a sense of romance to the dining experience.

Shanley's cabaret shows often featured women with a clearly demonstrated sense of self. The successful iconic female cabaret acts clearly had opinions and apparently enjoyed their freedom of expression. As Shanley's developed its reputation for variety and vaudeville entertainment, it encouraged its customers to do more than listen. In the early 1920s, the Shanleys were urging New Yorkers to 'Join in the Dancing' (*New York Times* 1921).

The 1906 *New York Times* idea of luxury and cosmopolitanism was still rooted in rigid, stratified Victorian sexism. While women were welcome in the fine establishments, when it was time to select the food 'they rely so much on the vaunted superior judgment of man'. It would take a social revolution to shift the entrenched idea that women were dependent on, and subject to, men. Shanley's was at the forefront of that struggle. Shanley's didn't just deliver cabaret to mainstream American, it helped to shape its values.

Just how free and easy was New York's urban environment at that time? You can sense the clear suspicions and prejudices about women who entered restaurants on their own in 1907 from newspaper reports of the time. Probably in response to the refusal of Delmonico's restaurant to admit Mrs Cornelius Vanderbilt to its main dining room, the *New York Times* reported on restaurant attitudes and policies. What does it say about the culture of a 'cosmopolitan' city if a married member of the country's wealthiest family couldn't dine alone in a public place? The newspaper noted the 'unwritten rule' of the city's restaurant trade. Unescorted women would be ignored in the hope that they would leave without a fuss. There was some notion that a 'lady' would be admitted, although the managers of the Knickerbocker and Rector's seemed to have difficulty defining precisely the type of women who could be classified as a 'lady'. Sherry's only wanted women who 'looked well and behaved well'. The Astor would only admit women before a certain time in the evening, while Delmonico's openly discouraged unescorted women at any time. Thomas Shanley's response to the question of whether a woman could dine alone in his restaurant was politic:

> Well, far be it for any man to discuss such a delicate subject. But when a lady comes in here, it is not for an Irishman to treat her otherwise. (*New York Times* 1907)

The Shanleys didn't just talk about equality for some women, there is evidence that their business practices were also inclusive. Bernard Shanley, one of the founding brothers, died in 1901 and the *New York Times* (1905) later reported that his widow, Rose, 'continued in partnership with the brothers' before opening her own restaurant. The Shanleys didn't just give women seats in the restaurants and places on their stages, they treated them as business partners.

The Irish Rising Socially

Tom Shanley believed that enterprise was a way for the Irish to overcome their economic circumstances. His thoughts during the early 20th century were later reprinted:

> What can a nation of poor people do for themselves? As long as the Irish stay poor they are defenceless. Let the young and enterprising go forth to where there is money and opportunity, and send some of their plenty home to those who simply can't get away. If they live a better life, they'd be able to have more self-respect and then take care of the British in no time. (Shanley 1990–91: 17)

There is no doubting his belief in enterprise. He opened his first New York restaurant in 1889, and by 1901 the family were running three restaurants. His earnings were used to fund the 'chain migration' that was a feature of Ireland's developing diaspora. Shanley's restaurants were opulent and luxurious, yet they provided opportunities for fellow Irish immigrants who arrived at the bottom of the social ladder. They trained over a thousand Irish waiters

(Shanley 1991), and work experience there opened significant job opportunities afterwards.

Ethnic groups can only advance themselves when they have opportunities, and Shanley's offered many, though mainly for men. The Irish tended to stick together when they arrived in the US. While pay and conditions were better outside the city, few Irish domestic servants chose to work outside it (May 2011: 51), even though many of them had been farm labourers and were well-suited to agricultural jobs beyond the confines of US cities. There was a tragic and practical reason for the Irish staying in the first city they landed in (Rosenwaike 1972: 41). Sadly, their money only paid for the transatlantic voyage, and they lacked the funds to leave the cities.

Their visibility as a group meant that they were part of how the general population classified the Irish and other groups who shared aspects of their identity. The visibility of the Catholic Irish, as well as other Catholic communities including Italians, meant that in New York Catholicism was identified with 'the lives and rituals of the immigrant working classes' (May 2011: 30). But during the early 20th century, Irish women underwent one of the most dramatic changes in circumstances of any social group in the US. Irish women grasped the opportunity to escape from poverty. In fact, in most cases, Irish women were socially more upwardly mobile than their brothers and achieved white-collar work a generation before Irish men. As Nolan (2004: 4) has argued, 'Irish-America's remarkable female-driven group mobility has been overlooked'. Education was the key to this upward social mobility.

Historically the Irish at home had been under-educated; in 1850 just over half could read and write (Nolan 2004: 10–14). But they benefited from an education drive undertaken by the British government. In 1831, state education was introduced to Ireland, four decades before it was available in England and Scotland. With an emphasis on 'literacy, numeracy, orderliness, cleanliness' (Nolan 2004: 12), it was a valuable education for young women with limited prospects in Ireland. The new programme was clearly a success and, by 1911, 90 per cent of the Irish were literate. As Diner (1983: 140–41) documented, education, for the Irish, was a way out of poverty, and for Irish girls in particular and in many locations. During the 1860s in Waltham, Massachusetts, for every Irish boy who graduated from high school, four Irish girls graduated. In Trempeleau, Wisconsin, the Irish were the only ethnic group that sent more girls than boys to school.

Once they were educated, many Irish women enrolled as teachers and educated Americans while bettering their own economic standing. In many cities, a high percentage of teachers were Irish. One girl's school alone, St James, run by the Sisters of Mercy order, had produced over 400 Irish teachers for

Chicago by 1911. In the city's public schools, more than a third of the teachers came from the Irish community (Clifford 2014: 110). In San Francisco, almost half of the teachers had Irish surnames (Nolan 2004: 2). In New York, some neighbourhoods could boast that two-thirds of their teachers were Irish. The previously uneducated had become the educators when other opportunities for social advancement in the US were limited for recently arrived Irish women. But as Ellen O'Byrne had proved, Irish women could achieve the elusive American dream. Most of them achieved this in undramatic ways, but the overall impact on the Irish was dramatic.

In his autobiography, the musician Johnny Cash (1997: 53) wrote of a local teacher who gave him singing lessons. The songs she sang included 'I'll Take You Home Again Kathleen' and it is not a great leap to imagine that she was Irish. At any rate, a female teacher in Arkansas in the 1940s was teaching Irish songs to a future iconic American musician. Thanks to hard graft, ingenuity and the culture industries, the Irish and their culture had come a long way in a few decades.

2 1930s Ireland: Law and Order, Business and Nationalism

By the late 1920s, America had made it possible for Irish entrepreneurs to found businesses like Shanley's restaurants and O'Byrne's shop and record label. But how would the newly independent Irish Free State deal with the music industry? This was, after all, an industry that, to some, threatened to swamp the local Gaelic culture, which was being revived and promoted by the Irish government as an expression of *true Irishness*. Finding a balance between global and local culture was a public obsession in Irish life for decades. Some individuals, although they were relatively unknown, had a huge say in how Ireland navigated between the local and the global. One of them, District Justice Goff, even managed to make Irish morals an international talking point.

In 1922, soon after independence, Bartholomew Goff was appointed by the Irish government to be a judge, one of the legal guardians of the nation. His nationalist credentials were impressive. The local and national newspapers during his lifetime and shortly after his death (*Cork Examiner* 1922; *Irish Independent* 1957; *Meath Chronicle* 1957) reported on his lengthy association with the Gaelic League, his membership of Sinn Féin's national council, and his participation in the 1917 elections as well as his harassment by the British authorities. With his legal background and nationalist credentials, it is easy to see why he was entrusted with helping to guide the country into the modern world whilst protecting its native culture. A Roscommon man, he was born in 1879, studied law in University College Dublin (UCD) and qualified as a solicitor in the year of the Easter Rising, 1916. Less than three years later, his ardent nationalism and dedication to independence resulted in his arrest at his Sligo law office. He was imprisoned and served two months. After his release, members of the British military raided his office, confiscated his documents and eventually forced him out of his practice. He was known to conduct court business in Irish when he could.

Goff was one of the active and visible guardians of both Irish law and morality, and in his rulings it is possible to sense his anxiety about protecting Ireland's culture. His perspective can be understood in the context of Eileen Hogan's (2010: 57) conclusion that 'fears of foreign cultural corruption and the liberalization of sexual mores were articulated through intensive campaigning, led by the Catholic elite'. It is clear from the evidence that Goff was in a position to use that fear to advance his own notions of morality. As Hogan also argued: 'the broadcasting service and the dance halls represented key sites of formation of Irish national identity' (2010: 57).

Tapping into the widespread national concern about music from overseas, Goff used his courtroom to crusade against it. He put his judgments in a historical and social context, and the headline, '"ADDICTS" OF JAZZ: People Not Normal: Justice's Views' (*Donegal News* 1931), summed up his outlook. This report of his rulings on an application for a licence to hold a dance included his views that we were living in 'post-war times' and 'terrible things [have] happened during the last 14 or 15 years – with a large number of people who have been subject to exceptional influences'. To people with the power to shape the landscape of culture in Ireland, like Goff, popular music was a clear and present danger:

> We are dealing with a kind of dance which has been described by one of the gramophone manufacturers as dancing to savage rhythms ... [it] is, I am afraid, associated with the arousing of certain base passions, and is associated in that way in the minds of a very large number of people who are not normal. (*Donegal News* 1931: 6)

He railed against modern industries of mass communication:

> I am afraid that the influence of this jazz dancing, and the influence of the cinema have been very bad; that they have made a terrible number of people abnormal, and that these people, whom I call jazz addicts, have lost control of themselves. (ibid.)

The loss of control, diagnosed by Goff, sounded like a form of demonic possession:

> In fact, you will see them on the streets, in the railway carriages, and on the tramway cars, and they cannot keep quiet. Their bodies are being moved about and are swaying to some imaginary jazz rhythm. (ibid.)

Unsurprisingly, he refused to grant permission for the dance. The conservative national newspaper, the *Irish Press*, naturally celebrated Goff's verdicts. So did other moral groups. The executive committee of the Irish Association for the Prevention of Intemperance amplified Goff's opinion that the law was too soft. They quoted his view on low moral standards: 'the law was not free from blame' (*Irish Press* 1937a: 2).

Goff provided the answer to the question: what did the moral guardians want and what did they want to prevent? When taking a hard-line Catholic position, he also found common cause with the Protestant authorities in Northern Ireland. He argued strongly for Sunday restrictions on entertainment. He admired the draconian laws in Northern Ireland where, he argued, 'they were much more advanced than we were with regard to the opening of licensed houses on Sundays' (*Meath Chronicle* 1937: 7). His idea of 'advanced' was different from the views of Irish publicans and many of their customers. However, the conservative moral guardians didn't have it all their own way. Even in the 1930s challenges emerged to their power and control. By then, trade groups such as the Licensed Grocers and Vintners Association were pushing back against the repressive measures. To them it was bad for business, and they called Goff out on his strict judgments. They claimed in print that he relied on dubious 'information supplied by third parties, not on facts stated in court' (*Irish Press* 1937b: 4).

The Church and Justice

In the 1930s the Catholic Church in Ireland and its allies campaigned very actively for ultimate power over dancing in the country. One feature of their campaign was an anti-commercial argument; 'close supervision' didn't just mean keeping couples apart physically, it often meant financial control, by the Church, of dancing. The *Connacht Tribune* editorial wondered:

> ... is Ireland to lose her pride of place as the home of the most chaste women in the world? ... Dance halls and the pictures [cinemas] with their alien and exotic standards are blamed ... [dangers could befall those] who haunt the ensnaring atmosphere of the commercialised dance hall. (*Connacht Tribune* 1934: 8)

Elsewhere, one clerical campaigner, Fr Devane (1933), agitated against these 'commercialised country dance halls'. He claimed that 'police and court records give irrefutable testimony to the intimate connection between them and the alarming growth of sexual offences' (1933: 10). The *Irish Press* published the Lenten letter of the Bishop of Ossory:

> The social life which not so long ago formed the central attraction of the home and the family circle of relatives and friends has now been removed to these public places of commercialised, expensive amusement with their attendant evils. These places create artificial expensive tastes in many directions and raise standards of amusement which a poor country and a Catholic country can very well do without. (*Irish Press* 1934: 7)

Foreign Affairs

On 29 June 1935, the editorial in the *Drogheda Independent* described the type of country it wanted Ireland to be. The newspaper contrasted the current modern, public celebration of church rituals with the anti-Catholic Penal Laws, enacted from the 1690s, which had driven the religion underground. The author praised the recent Corpus Christi celebrations. The modern rituals were proof of:

> how widespread and how earnest is now the public cultus given in this dear old Catholic Land to the Holy Eucharist ... this glorious National Act of Faith. (Editor 1935: 6)

The editors also celebrated Goff's dancing pronouncements, but warned:

> now the vogue is the stuffy dance hall, where jazz or some other foreign monstrosity replaces the grand old Irish dances which our fathers and mothers used to enjoy in the good old days. (ibid.)

This was a pointed type of nostalgia. The editors were arguing that some aspects of Irish culture had been in better health before independence. Was there a more damning conclusion? Young people and jazz seemed to be a bigger threat to Irish culture than the British had been.

To truly control the industry of dancing in Ireland, the church needed allies in the Irish courts. They found them in men like District Justice (DJ) Goff, and his public judgments provide a clear example of how the relationship between the Catholic hierarchy and the law played out in practice. From early in his career as the District Justice for County Louth and County Monaghan, Goff made it clear that he worried about dances. In 1926 he was quoted in the *Drogheda Independent*: 'those all-night public dances are the curse of the country' (6). More than a decade later, in *The Liberator* (1938), he preached that jazz dancing was 'a definitely harmful form of amusement, and has a definitely bad moral effect' (13).

Goff didn't feel he was alone in his crusade against any dancing he disapproved of. On many occasions, he used his courtroom to argue that Ireland's culture should be guided by the Catholic clergy. In 1928 it was reported nationally that he had refused a licence for the Louth Hunt Ball to serve alcohol. The applicants had argued that alcohol was only going to be served with meals, and no bar would be open. Goff wasn't having any of it. Not only did he rely on the Church's view, but he defended the clergy against any accusations that they were out of touch with ordinary Irish people and their pastimes. The *Irish Independent* (1928) reported how Goff acknowledged that 'he was influenced by what was said and preached by the clergy and the hierarchy as to the evils of these occasional licences at dances' (8). To anyone who claimed that 'the clergy are not men of the world', he was quoted:

> The clergy, who are constantly hearing confessions, ought to have a very great insight into the evils of human nature, and the things which give rise to those evils. (ibid.)

Goff only wanted dances that suited the clerical-led rhythm of Irish life (*Irish Independent* 1935b). Absolutely no dances were to be held during Lent or Advent, or during the times of the local church retreats or missions. Saturday night dancing was prohibited along with dancing on the eve of Church holidays. He also made it very clear who should be in charge of arranging dances in Ireland. He ruled that dances in the countryside could only continue after 11pm if they were one of three types: well-established dances; 'genuine Irish dancing' with céilí bands; or parish hall dances 'where clergymen apply and accept responsibility' (*The Liberator* 1938: 13). While dances were occasions for people to mix in public gatherings in a relatively relaxed way, they were also a way for entrepreneurs to make money, either for themselves, or for charities. But Goff clearly wanted the keys to the industry of dancing in Ireland to belong to the clergy. In a very real way, he wasn't just shaping cultural life; he was shaping economic life.

In 1939, it was reported nationally that he had issued a £3 fine for an unlicensed *home* dance. The *Irish Press* headline told its own story: '70 Boys And Girls At Barn Dance In Court' (*Irish Press* 1939a). But some of Goff's comments were even more revealing: 'the whole thing was an outrage on the regulations of the Bishop of the diocese for dancing'. Here Goff seemed to be serving Church, not State. He consistently acted with deference to the clergy. Despite his reported 1935 statement (*Irish Independent* 1935a: 10), 'I am not out to kill dancing', he clearly only wanted certain types of dance to be enjoyed in Ireland. Here again, he was following the clergy and cited a bishop claiming: 'the dancing craze was approaching the dimensions of a plague'. Goff was resolute: it was 'up to the court to curtail them' and apparently, he knew how to do that. He ordered that dances had to be alcohol-free, with no one under 18 admitted, and had to finish by 11pm. In addition, at least one-quarter of the dances had to be Irish and absolutely 'no sitting out' was allowed. Goff's banning of 'sitting out' suggests that he wasn't concerned only with what happened when people were dancing together. Sitting out referred to taking a rest from the dance, and its supervisors, outside. This was about more than dancing. This was an effort to control behaviour off the dancefloor. For Goff, socialization should be done where it could be watched:

> People should sit in the hall in [the] presence of other dancers if they want to sit down and rest or talk. (*Cork Examiner* 1935: 4)

Amongst other things, Goff was worried about people who used cars. To him, they were 'motor hawks', swooping down from afar on their prey. These men, to Goff, 'make it a practice to attend country dances for very improper purposes, and very often they succeed in ruining simple country girls' (*Irish Independent* 1935b: 12). As for Goff's battles against 'foreign' dancing, his public statements indicate that he eventually lost faith in his ability to steer the country towards Irish dances.

In June 1931, full of optimism, he demanded that Irish dances should make up one-third of any night's dancing, and the remainder should be 'old non-jazzy dances' where possible (*Meath Chronicle* 1931: 6). But by 1937 he seemed to have had a change of heart. He stopped refusing licences to halls that ignored Irish dances. After years of organizers being forced to include Irish dances, times had changed. He was quoted: 'Nothing can be done by the Courts to save Irish dancing' although his regret was evident. The local Garda (policeman) seemed to know what had happened when Goff had forced Irish dances on organizers. He was quoted as stating that Irish dances, when 'not done properly ... were little more than semi-jazz' (*Liberator* 1937). But the debate about suitable dances wasn't over. In 1940 the central council of the Gaelic Athletic Association (GAA), by then the country's most powerful sporting organization, praised Goff's efforts and slammed the organizers of 'old-time waltzes' because they were 'absolutely foreign' (*Irish Independent* 1940a: 4). It wasn't just modern dancing that was under attack, it was something as apparently innocent as old-fashioned waltzes.

Goff may have surrendered in this battle to force dancers to do Irish dances, but he was still at war over Ireland's morals. During the 1940s he railed against Ireland's moral standards, and, in particular, the morals of young people. He was quoted in 1940: 'Is the position that we must satisfy this dancing craze of more or less depraved young people?' (*Irish Independent* 1940b: 7). But if Ireland's youth were depraved, Goff knew why. He blamed the parents:

> Parents nowadays are not taking the slightest interest in their children ... They allow them to go to 'the pictures [cinema]', which are primarily pagan in character. (*Irish Press* 1943: 3)

These remarks had a context, but they revealed the uneasy relationship between the global cultural industries and the guardians of Irish morality.

At the same time, Goff was urging the Irish justice system to get tough on its youth: 'Boys May Still Be Birched, D.J. Warns'. His remarks in Dundalk

Children's Court were part of his campaign against a 'very foolish and faddist attack on birching'. In a letter read out at a Gaelic League meeting in 1941, Goff argued that he was being prevented from doing his moral and cultural duty. This time he didn't blame the parents of Ireland's youth, he blamed the current 'spirit' of the country.

> I would like to help our language and dances, but unfortunately, District Justices can do little because of interference by the Circuit Court and the lack of proper spirit among the people in practically every part of the country. (*Irish Press* 1941: 8)

Goff was not just criticizing the people and the Circuit Court, the law itself was at fault. To him, 'the blame should be put on the [Criminal Law Amendment] Act'. But by this time, even some of Goff's closest allies were openly questioning his draconian dance decisions. The 1935 *Drogheda Independent* editorial had previously cheered him on; by 1941 they felt he was going too far. In response to the GAA's ban on 'foreign' dances of all forms, the paper quoted an unnamed GAA club official. He claimed that if the organizers of public dancers were forced by the courts to include Irish dances, they would have to shut their hall 'because not more than five per cent of the patrons could, or would, perform the Irish dances'. The paper enthusiastically noted the fashion for events which mixed waltzes with Irish dances. This was 'a good alloy combining the best from abroad with the best at home'. The cultural value of the waltz was praised, and its originators, the Austrians, were given the ultimate accolade: 'a people who have been called "the Irish of the Continent"'. But the newspaper's challenge to Goff was clear, and it was barbed. The types of ban the judge imposed:

> would not tend to raise the general cultural standards of our people by depriving them of the opportunity to appreciate the artistic achievements of other races, some of whom have a longer tradition in this respect than ourselves. (Editor 1941: 2)

Even worse, the newspaper felt that Goff was driving Irish dancers into the hands of the promoters of the jitterbug and the tango, although that is hard to imagine in the average Irish village. Readers were reminded that Goff had viewed such entertainment as 'jungle music'.

It is clear from the historical records that powerful groups in Irish society decided what music Irish people were allowed to dance to. But those views were subject to change. They were inconsistent. Ideas ranged from a total fear of anything foreign, to more nuanced views. Power groups in Ireland deployed the argument that best suited their purposes at any particular moment. Because of these inconsistencies it is important to identify how words and ideas came to be defined in Ireland. Here, Goff's case is very revealing. In 1940, as winter gathered in and locals looked forward to pre-Christmas entertainment, District Justice Goff had other ideas. He decided to reduce the number of late-night dances by a third, he increased admission prices to 'jazz' dances, and demanded mandatory weekly Irish dancing in every hall. This was part of his continuing crusade to foster local Irish culture and to protect the Irish from foreign influences. He was worried that two of the towns in his area of jurisdiction, Dundalk and Carrickmacross, had been 'jazzified'.

But what exactly did *jazz* mean in 1940s Ireland? Goff was asked to define it during one court session. The session made the front page of the *Evening Herald* (1940) newspaper. His answer revealed very little about dancing and a lot about the fear of alien influence on Irish morals. To Goff, jazz was 'the thing popularised by the Jews in America; it was English and American of the worst sort, and was of savage origin' (*Evening Herald* 1940: 1).

Goff was determined in his crusade against jazz. He repeated his claim that enjoying this music was a form of mental illness, and that jazz, and anything he associated with it, ran counter to Irish Catholic values. Anyone in favour of these dances was 'going against the wishes of the bishops as regards the national spirit and morals ... Time and again they had denounced this mania' (ibid.).

Would Goff and the other guardians of Irish morality have been so obsessed with stamping out waltzing, and what they felt was 'jazz', if they knew what was coming? It is an impossible question to answer, but by taking extreme positions, these people risked making themselves irrelevant, and out of step with mainstream everyday Irish culture. In one case, Goff's judgment was so out of step with global culture that it drew international media attention to, and revulsion against, Ireland's moral attitudes.

Irish Kiss, Global Scandal

In one very significant case, Goff proved that Ireland's reputation was influenced by what happened in its regional courts. Local attempts to control Ireland's youth by men like him could have international consequences. He was fixated on keeping Ireland culturally isolated from anything that he judged to be outside of domestic Catholic standards. He was quoted in September 1935 as saying:

> Things take place in other countries which do not take place in this country; but other things, I am sorry to say, which do not take place

> in other countries are frequently seen in Ireland. (*Irish Independent* 1935c: 12)

Here Goff was referring to 'shameful embracing in public places'. He had a solution, though. If he discovered such a case, 'he would impose the maximum penalty of one month's imprisonment'. Goff was anxious to bring a couple of public embracers before the court, so he didn't wait until a couple was found, he sent people out looking.

The judge had sometimes felt constrained by Irish laws in his moral crusade. But in 1935 Éamon de Valera's government handed him a gift. Section 18 of the updated 1935 *Criminal Law Amendment Act* provided Goff with an opportunity to police social activity. The law was strict but also open to interpretation:

> Every person who shall commit, at or near and in sight of any place along which the public habitually pass as of right or by permission, any act in such a way as to offend modesty or cause scandal or injure the morals of the community shall be guilty of an offence under this section and shall on summary conviction thereof be liable to a fine not exceeding two pounds or, at the discretion of the court, to imprisonment for any term not exceeding one month.

In October 1937 Goff grasped an opportunity to wield the Act. While the *Irish Press* (1937c) October headline, 'Embraced in Public', didn't appear to flag any scandalous activity, that's not how Goff and his local allies felt. The case involved a local young man 'who embraced a girl friend in public'. Members of the Blackrock Vigilance Committee reported the 'incident'. For their alertness and actions, Goff proclaimed that the group 'was to be highly commended'. On many levels the case didn't seem to be particularly significant. It was even argued, in the young man's defence, that 'the boy was respectable and had had one or two more drinks than he should have'. In addition, 'there was nothing whatever *immoral* in what had happened' (*Irish Press* 1937c: 13, emphasis added). Because nothing immoral had taken place most judges would have either dismissed the case or dealt with it leniently.

In fact, before the 1935 Act, no charge *could* legally have been made. Even Goff, at first, appeared to judge that the case was not particularly outrageous. He was quoted as saying that 'there was no criminal misconduct'. He decided to dismiss the case against the boy provided he gave a £2 donation to the St Vincent De Paul charity and paid the court costs.

The boy had escaped the judgment of DJ Goff. But what about the girl? If the case did not 'injure the morals of the community', was it worth pursuing?

Goff was empowered by the other aspects of the Act. Had the couple's embrace, now that they boy had been treated leniently, 'offended modesty' or 'caused scandal'? If it had, and scandal and modesty can be defined in many ways, then the girl could be in trouble. When Goff claimed that 'what had happened was calculated to give scandal', it was clear that she was in trouble with the law. The local Garda testified that 'he couldn't say that the girl had any drink. The man seemed to have drink taken...'. That appeared to claim that if the boy was drunk in public, the girl wasn't. However, in court, Justice Goff asked: 'What type of girl is she?' before being told that there was no record of her ever being in trouble before. Despite the boy being effectively pronounced legally innocent, the girl was charged 'with committing an act of impropriety in a public place'. The *Irish Press* (1937d: 9) reported on her fate and DJ Goff's judgment was quoted: 'I will order her one month's imprisonment.' It was an extraordinarily harsh sentence and some of the court reports provide background to the decision and to life in small-town Ireland. The boy's defence (*Irish Press* 1937d: 9) was that he had been 'carried away by "the appearance and get-up" of his partner' who was 'on holiday from England'. The local vigilance group members had immediately notified the priest as well as the local Gardaí.

But there was more to the judgment than might appear. Goff acknowledged that the girl, Julia Clarke, lived abroad, in Scotland, so she was unlikely to serve her jail sentence. In fact, he cautioned against appealing to the British government to extradite her. How likely was it that they would have sent a British resident to serve a month in an Irish prison for the crime of kissing? Goff knew this, and his judgment was a means of ridding Ireland of people like Clarke. Knowing that she faced a month in prison if she ever returned, she was effectively banished from Ireland.

Outside of Ireland the judgment was met with shock. The *Irish Times* (1937) quoted a *London Star* article:

> It shows how far Ireland has travelled back on the road to Salem, Massachusetts. The District Court Judges who were scandalised by the girl's kiss would be at home in the company of the grim Puritans of 'The Scarlet Letter'. Freedom appears to have brought gloom instead of happiness to the Irish temperament.
>
> Now they have a law which makes it a crime 'to offend modesty or cause scandal'. There was never a charter of repression so widely drawn as that. We hope that it is not yet an offence to kiss the Blarney Stone in public. (*Irish Times* 1937: 8)

From his courthouse Goff responded to the negative international press coverage. He felt that the press reports, rather than his sentencing, could hamper the country's tourist trade, and were 'intended to intimidate the Guards and others from taking action under that section of the Criminal Law Amendment Act' (*Irish Press* 1937e: 2). To prevent the court of public opinion from undermining his views and judgments, if negative articles continued, 'he would ask the Attorney General to put a couple of the offending editors who were within his reach in the dock'.

Goff wanted to suppress the media and prevent them from reporting on his decisions. But it was too late. It was a public relations disaster for the Irish government; newspapers globally sneered at the judgment. Accounts of the decision even made it into a newsreel shown in British cinemas. In 1937 Pathé News filmed Julia Clarke kissing a man, while a narrator retold her story and spoke of this Irish 'crime' and its punishment. Goff had turned a girl who had publicly kissed in Ireland into a film star. It was a short clip, only 14 seconds long, but it depicted Ireland as out-of-step with the world. Whatever control de Valera and his government had domestically, they were powerless to stop the story going viral. This was not just a ruling in a provincial courthouse; it reflected directly on de Valera.

The *Los Angeles Times* (Durling 1937: 28) depicted the judgment as outrageous and highlighted the gender aspect: 'Yes ma'am it seems the woman pays in Ireland, and how!' The *Palm Beach Post* ran a front-page story and condemned the 'lack of proportion, lack of humor and plain intolerance' (Carter 1937a: 1). The newspaper found it even more 'odd' given 'Mr de Valera's own parentage, Irish-Spanish' and concluded that 'enough efforts are being made elsewhere to destroy human spontaneity'. In Oregon, again on the front page, the new Act was described as 'De Valera's Vice Law' (*Klamath News* 1937: 1). Other newspapers spread the story, some made the front page, others included photographs, and the headlines spoke volumes:

'Kiss in Ireland Brings Life Exile', *Wilmington Morning News* (1937)
'LASS Exiled From Irish Free State For Public Kiss', *The Klamath News* (1937)
'Public Kiss Bars Pretty Girl From Ireland Visit', *Waco News Tribune* (1937)
'Kiss Bars Girl from Irish Free State Forever', *Napa Journal* (1937)
'She Got Thirty Days For This. Miss Clarke shows a reporter just what a 30-day kiss was', *The Star Press* (1937)
'To Prison For a Kiss', *Lincoln Star Journal* (1937)
'Scottish Lass and Irish Lad Can't Kiss, B'gad', *The Atlanta Constitution* (1937)
'Coleen is Sent to Jail for Kiss', *Santa Ana Register* (1937)

One widely syndicated columnist wrote about the judgment in particularly disparaging terms. He placed de Valera in ominously disturbing company:

> Why should some dried-up male moralist pounce upon a poor girl, make an example out of her, but let off her male friend virtually scot free?
>
> Enough efforts are being made elsewhere to destroy human spontaneity without courts adding their share. Hitler tried to bar women from using rouge and lipstick and they laughed in his face. Mussolini ordered more and better babies from Italian women and the Italian birth rate has dropped off a little.
>
> What de Valera sponsors is simply a return to dark ages witchcraft and intolerance. (Carter 1937b: 4)

That said, in a way, even the international ridicule of Goff's 'one month for a kiss' sentence served a purpose. It broadcast an image of Ireland as innocent. When rock and roll arrived with swivelling hips to mainstream America in the mid-1950s, many people saw it as a curse. Some of them saw Irish entertainers as the cure. We will examine this in the next chapter.

Goff's vision for the role of the global cultural industries in Ireland may seem extreme when we look back on it. But he should not be seen as a crusading outlier. He reflected what key elements of the Irish establishment believed. As Jim Smyth (1993) argued: 'The Clergy were not against dancing in principle – as long as the dances were Irish ... and the supervision was close' (1993: 51). The supervision embraced both dancing and the business of dancing. Helen Brennan's (2001) account of dancing in the country argues that, following the 1935 Dance Halls Act, which delivered control of dancing to the government, in rural Ireland 'the clergy organised the construction of parochial halls, and thereafter Church and State combined to eliminate the organisation of any dances outside these halls' (2001: 126). To some, the Act didn't go far enough. The 1939 Fianna Fáil Ard Fheis, or party conference, indicated that the legislation so far had been unsuccessful. It had failed to protect *their* interpretation of Irish culture. The Monaghan and Kilkenny delegates proposed an amendment to the Dance Halls Act. It, they asserted, had resulted in the commercialization of dance halls 'which debased their pastimes and culture'. The remedy was to change the law to prevent dances under the auspices of anyone who was not involved in 'the promotion of Gaelic culture' (*Irish Press* 1939b).

In some cultural spheres Ireland effectively sealed its borders against material the authorities deemed immoral. Some books, magazines, plays and films were banned. But not records. It is one of the great unanswered questions of Irish culture: why were all of the other major media banned or censored at times but not records? Maybe the answer lies in how music was used. Public dancing absolutely terrified the Irish authorities; listening to records at home appeared much more genteel, and certainly much less dangerous. Until music went mobile and affordable thanks to mass production, music was consumed in Irish homes as part of a family occasion. By making music consumption a family affair, the record industry proved to be a suitable ally, culturally, of the Irish authorities.

The overzealous policing of dancing in Ireland had a major consequence. It stunted the growth of the domestic music industry, and it meant that Ireland was dependent on overseas record companies. For decades, many of the best of Ireland's music entrepreneurs reacted to the heavy-handed policing of dancing. They emigrated.

3 The Global Music Industries and Ireland

The bulk of this book is dedicated to telling the story of key people and 'moments' that have proven fundamental to helping Irish acts achieve success on the international music stage over more than a century. From the endeavours of Leitrim-born Ellen O'Byrne in recording and distributing Irish music in America in the early 1900s, to more recent superstar acts like U2 and Westlife (with many others in between), the different chapters combine to chronicle how local acts have been delivered to a global arena. As such, the book unpacks and critiques the nature of the endeavours and processes that have ultimately led to Irish acts scaling the heights of the global music industries, and the perception of Ireland as a 'world beater' when it comes to popular music. Here, it is worth briefly considering how we might conceptualize the global music industries, and how they relate to, and function, within a local setting.

The music industry is conventionally understood as an umbrella term encompassing three core sectors of enterprise: the recording industry, the music publishing industry, and the live music industry (Hesmondhalgh 2018; Wikström 2020; Williamson and Cloonan 2007). While traditionally, much academic analysis of the business of music focused predominantly on the recording sector (see Williamson and Cloonan 2007), many more recent accounts have addressed activities and developments across all three domains. In fact, any political economy account of the more recent evolution of the global industry must be attentive to features, characteristics and trends across all three core sectors. This is because the biggest music industry companies on the world stage now function as multi-dimensional actors that generate revenues from a range of diverse activities since the advent of 360 degree, or multi-rights recording contracts over the past dozen years or so (see, for example, Marshall 2013 and Rogers 2013 for an analysis of 360 degree recording contracts).

A comprehensive history of the music industry would demand that we journey back to 17th-century Venice to provide an account of what is widely regarded as the first 'commercial' opera, *L'Andromeda*, produced by Ferrari and Manelli at Teatro San Cassiano in 1637 (Kolodin 1976). We would have to retreat even further to trace the origins of music publishing in 16th-century England, when Henry VIII essentially granted licensing rights to printers to reproduce music texts (Wainwright 2006). The recording industry would only emerge some three-and-a-half centuries later but would quickly become the largest and most lucrative (see, for example, Gronow and Saunio 1999; Negus 1996, among others). Moreover, from its earliest days, the recording industry operated on a transnational basis, with a small number of players rapidly growing to dominate the international landscape (Tschmuck 2006).

In fact, in the 21st century, all three sectors find themselves bearing the characteristics of concentrated ownership. Just three major companies – the Universal Music Group (UMG), Sony Music Entertainment (SME), and the Warner Music Group (WMG) – combine to monopolize the global market for recorded music. The publishing arms of the same three major companies hold sway in the global music publishing market. When it comes to the live music industry, just two operators – Live Nation Entertainment (LNE) and the Anschutz Entertainment Group (AEG) – dominate the landscape. In short, each of the three core sectors of the global music industries is dominated by a very small number of very large organizations.

Such concentration, however, is not a recent occurrence. Rather, it has characterized the nature and form of the music industry for well over a century. Local music markets around the world have consistently been dominated by a handful of international music companies and have been saturated by the products they peddle. If we are seeking to explore possible connections between local music scenes and the international successes of recording artists growing out of that local context, then, it is perhaps useful to offer some historical context to the evolution of the international music industry, and in particular, some key trends that have characterized its development, on a macro-level, over many decades. Here, we will be particularly attentive to the recording sector, the most economically significant sector of the music business over time.

Recent Oligopolistic Trends across the Three Core Music Industry Sectors

The well-worn trends of acquisition, joint-venture and merger remain consistent characteristics of all key sectors across the music industry. Such consolidation maintains a high level of concentrated ownership and serves to buoy and reinforce the market position of the leading corporate actors. Here, let us take a headline-level look at the current composition of the recording, music publishing and live music spheres.

The Recording Industry

Notwithstanding the promise and potential of digital innovations for disrupting the economic dominance of the recording industry's corporate elites, two decades into the 21st century, UMG, Sony and WMG still combine to account for two-thirds of the global market for recorded music (Mulligan 2021). In the Irish market, where the current authors are based, the market share of these majors has on occasions exceeded 90 per cent (Rogers 2013).

Accounting for almost 30 per cent of the global market (with 2020 recording revenues of approximately $6.8bn), Universal is the largest record company in the world (Mulligan 2021). In 2019, it was home to nine of the top ten best-selling artists around the globe (Ingham 2020a). With operations in approximately 60 countries, its 200-plus labels include Capitol and Virgin-EMI, acquired courtesy of its takeover of EMI in 2011. By that stage, Polydor, Mercury, Def Jam, Interscope, A&M, Island and Vertigo had all been assimilated into the Universal family, courtesy of Vivendi's takeover of Seagram's entertainment division. Overall, its labels possess combined rosters of more than 1,000 acts or artists. Until autumn 2021, Universal was primarily owned by French media conglomerate Vivendi, with Chinese technology conglomerate Tencent holding a minority stake. However, in September of that year, 60 per cent of the Universal Music Group was publicly traded on the Amsterdam stock exchange.

With a revenue intake of more than $4bn, which accounts for just over 20 per cent of the global market (Dredge 2020; *Music and Copyright* 2021), Sony stands as the second biggest player in the global recorded music market. Following the decision of the Sony Corporation to extend its interests into content markets back in the late 1980s, Sony subsequently entered the recording industry via its purchase of CBS Records. Having entered a joint-venture arrangement with Bertelsmann's BMG Records in 2004, Sony ultimately established full control of the operation in 2008. This saw Columbia, Epic and RCA brought together as the core labels/groups under the Sony umbrella. Sony currently has operations in 43 territories worldwide, and, as of 2021, owns (or has interests in) 140-plus record labels (directly, or via subsidiaries).

As with the other major labels, the ongoing integration of independent networks with Sony infrastructure illustrates how the lines of distinction between the major and independent recording industry have become increasingly blurred. Already with a vested interest in independent network RED, which handled distribution for more than 60 independent record labels, 2009 saw SME acquire a majority stake in the International Online Distribution Alliance (IODA), an international sales and distribution company that offered digital distribution and related services to record labels and other independent actors in the music and audio-visual domains. The operation was fully acquired by Sony in 2015, and subsequently rebranded as The Orchard. That same year SME also acquired independent heavy metal label Century Media Records, with offices in the UK, US and Germany for a reported $20m (Christman 2015). A year later in 2016, Sony bought Ministry of Sound for £67m (Ingham 2017). By that stage, Sony had also acquired a 50 per cent stake in Simon Cowell's Syco Music label (*Music Week* 2017).

Warner constitutes the third major actor dominating the global record industry landscape and had a revenue-intake of $3.8bn in 2020 (Aswad 2020), claiming approximately 16 per cent of the global market (*Music and Copyright* 2021). Originally formed by Warner Brothers in 1958, and once part of the Time-Warner Corporation, the Warner Music Group (WMG) is, since 2020, a publicly traded company. With operations in more than 50 countries, the group's five 'umbrella' recording labels – Warner Bros. Records, the Atlantic Records Group, Rhino Records, Parlophone and Warner Music Nashville – combine to own some 89 record companies around the globe. When the European Commission ordered UMG to sell a third of EMI's assets as a condition of its 2011 takeover of that company, Warner's subsequently acquired the Parlophone Label Group, which came with a host of artists including David Bowie, Pink Floyd, and part of the Beatles catalogue.

Like Sony and Universal, Warner is also a key distributor for the independent sector and has secured or entered joint ventures with some of the most successful independent companies of recent decades (including Sub Pop and Rykodisc). It currently distributes recordings for approximately 140 such labels through the Alternative Distribution Alliance, Warner's independent music and film distribution company. Outside of this, arguably the biggest independent actor in the recording industry, the PIAS Group, is itself a significant international operator, distributing recordings for more than 100 labels through its 19 offices around the world.

Historically, innovation in the recording industry has often been perceived as occurring primarily beyond the domain of the major labels, with the independent sector described in terms of the research and development laboratory of the industry as a whole (see, for example, Gillett 1970; Peterson and Berger 1990; Longhurst 1995; Negus 1996). Likewise, more recent research (den Drijver and Hitters 2017) demonstrates how independents often operate with moral and political imperatives and motivations, but do not challenge the dominance of the majors. Moreover, as Andrew Mall observes, ongoing changes in the record industries in terms of how music is produced, distributed and consumed 'do not represent discontinuities so much as they illustrate new stages in a long trajectory of the political economy of popular music' (2018: 463). The processes described in these various accounts are often cyclical, with new innovative labels ultimately being co-opted by the majors, which in turn creates a demand for more diverse, alternative content, a demand that is then fed by smaller, independent companies, thus starting the cycle all over again. With such co-optation recurring across the history of the popular music industry, the major labels have (albeit through cycles of high and less high concentration) managed to bolster their market share. Also, finding an independent record company that has enjoyed longevity and sustained itself economically without the intervention of a major label at some point in time (in terms of distribution, marketing and promotion, finance) is extremely difficult to do (Rogers 2013). In sum, despite the proliferation of digital platforms for the distribution of music, the dominant major labels remain almost inevitably intertwined with, and fundamental to, the independent recorded music sector.

The Music Publishing Industry

The domain of music publishing shows similar oligopolistic trends with the sector currently dominated by what are essentially different arms of the same three major actors: Sony/ATV, the Universal Music Publishing Group, and Warner Chappell.

With Sony/ATV Music Publishing completing the acquisition of EMI Music Publishing in November 2018 (Digital Music News 2018), it effectively doubled the size of its catalogue to almost 4.5 million songs, making it the largest music publishing company in the world. As a result, it saw its revenue intake increase by more than 46 per cent the following year to $1.5bn (*Statista* 2020). By 2020, its share of the global music publishing market was approximately 24.5 per cent (*Statista* 2021a). Sony/ATV Music Publishing's catalogue now includes The Beatles, as well as The Rolling Stones, Leonard Cohen, Lou Reed, Queen, and countless others. Starting life in 1955 as Associated Television (ATV), the company was purchased by Michael Jackson in the mid-1980s, and subsequently merged with Sony Music Publishing a decade later. In 2016, it became solely owned by Sony (Ingham 2021a). Over the decades it has acquired the song catalogues of many other labels including Motown, Deutsche Grammophon, Famous Music, Geffen, and Verve. Prior to procuring EMI, the company had already been valued at approximately $2.4bn (Christman 2016). As of 2021, it runs 38 offices across 22 countries around the world (Sony Music Publishing n.d.) and is valued at approximately €2.5bn (Ingham 2021a).

With revenues approaching $1.4bn in 2020 (*Statista* 2021b), Universal Music Publishing is currently the second largest player in the global publishing arena. Founded in 1965 as part of the Music Corporation of America (MCA), it has offices operating in 42 countries and administers publishing rights for catalogues by Elton John, Irving Berlin, Tom Waits, and the Bee Gees, among others. In 2006 it acquired Bertelsmann Music Publishing and, at different points in time, held ownership of Zomba and Rondor. Alone, Universal Music Publishing accounted for more than 23 per cent of the global market in 2020 (*Statista* 2021a).

The third major publisher in the global marketplace is Warner-Chappell, which, as of 2020, held more than 11 per cent of the global market (ibid.), with revenues exceeding $650m (Ingham 2020b). Originally founded as Chappell & Co. in the early 19th century, in its early decades it published works by Beethoven, and the Gilbert and Sullivan operas (Boosey 1931). Warner Brothers entered the domain of music publishing in the 1920s when it purchased a string of existing publishers, including the Remick Music Corporation which had rights to works by the likes of Gus Kahn and George Gershwin. Some six decades later, Warner acquired Chappell, thus forming Warner-Chappell in 1987. It currently has offices in more than 50 countries around the globe and administers song catalogues by artists such as Radiohead, Randy Newman, Eric Clapton, Led Zeppelin, Dr. Dre, and Ray Charles (Warner-Chappell n.d.). In recent years, its purchase of existing companies such as Southside and 615 have seen it extend its catalogue of pop, rap, and country.

So, combined, the publishing arms of the three largest music majors in the world account for almost 60 per cent of the global market. The next biggest players in the field of music publishing are Kobalt and BMG Rights Management who, by early 2018, had a combined global market share of approximately 18 per cent (Christman 2018).

Representing approximately 200 songwriters and artists, BMG owns approximately a dozen other publishing houses, while sub-publishing for many more. Overall, the company saw its revenues grow by 21 per cent in 2017 to a figure of almost $630m and has approximately 6.5 per cent of the global market (*Statista* 2021a). BMG has sustained itself through a series of acquisitions across recent years. For example, it has taken over Virgin Music and Famous Music UK from Sony/ATV, in addition to acquiring a number of independent publishers. These include the Chrysalis Music Group, Crosstown Songs, Cherry Lane Music Publishing (whose publishing portfolio includes such artists as Metallica, The White Stripes and Barbara Streisand), Primary Wave (a company founded by former Virgin and Arista executive Lawrence

Mestel and whose catalogue includes Kurt Cobain and John Lennon) and Talpa Music (who carry songs by AC/DC, will.i.am, Take That, and several others).

With Google and US-based private equity firm MCD Capital as key investors, Kobalt Music Publishing has retained a global market share of 7 per cent across recent years (*Statista* 2021a; *Music and Copyright* 2021). This is aided in part by its 2017 acquisition of SONGS Music Publishing, an independent company which itself had grown to represent more than 150 artists and songwriters in little more than a decade through its operations on both sides of the Atlantic. However, as an administrative music publishing company, Kobalt currently oversees more than 20 music publishing companies, and has repertoires by Bob Marley, Albert Hammond, Prince, and Trent Reznor under its control. Until recently, it claimed to represent some 8,000 artists around the world; however, November 2020 saw Kobalt sell some 33,000 copyrights to British song management company Hipgnosis for a reported $322m (Christman 2020).

So, with millions of songs under their ownership and/or administration and serving as 'parents' to numerous other publishing houses, these five companies alone, combine to account for more than three-quarters of the global music publishing market.

The Live Music Industry

When it comes to the concert industry, there are just two major players who dominate on the world stage: Live Nation Entertainment (LNE) and the Anschutz Entertainment Group (AEG). While these combine to account for some 67 per cent of the global concert industry, LNE alone lays claim to 52 per cent of tickets sold around the world in 2017 (*Statista* 2018). Founded by US media entrepreneur Robert Sillerman in 1996, Live Nation proceeded to acquire a series of venues and promotions companies across the US and Canada until its sale for $4.4bn to Clear Channel Communications at the turn of the millennium (CNN 2000). It subsequently evolved as a spin-off of Clear Channel before merging with Ticketmaster in 2009, an alliance that saw the biggest touring agent and concert promoter in the world join forces with the planet's largest ticketing retailer. Rebranded as LNE post-merger, the organization owns, operates or retains an equity interest in hundreds of venues, small, medium and large around the globe. With the significant expansion of the global concert industry in the 21st century, LNE events and revenues have likewise grown. The year 2017 saw its global revenues grow by 24 per cent to $10.3bn (and more than double the 2014 revenue intake), with 86 million tickets sold for LNE events that year (*Variety* 2018). That involved LNE staging more than 30,000 concerts across 40 countries. As the global market leader regarding touring and concert promotion, ticket retailing and other related activities, LNE's evolution illustrates a fundamental change from the traditional structure and organization of the live music industry in that it has now become vertically integrated. Moreover, the international music festival circuit has increasingly fallen under the control of LNE with the company's website currently indicating that it has promoted some 144 such events across North America, South America, Europe, Asia and Australia between 2017 and 2019 (Live Nation 2019).

To emphasize LNE's domination of this domain even further, Ticketmaster's acquisition of the Frontline artist management group in 2008 (which came under full ownership of LNE in 2011) now means that LNE companies manage the careers of more than 350 of the recording artists who play in their venues across the world. With 22 offices spread across North America, Europe and Asia, AEG is the second biggest player in the global live music market. Owning or controlling more than 150 venues around the globe, it promotes in excess of 10,000 concerts annually, and owns or promotes some 40 festivals (AEG 2019).

The Global Music Industries and Ireland

Over the decades, Ireland has evolved as a significant location on the global music industry map. A somewhat crude but nonetheless useful barometer for marking its evolution comes in the form of the *Hot Press Yearbook* – a music industry directory, published on an annual basis, containing listings for individuals, bands and businesses active across all areas of the music industry in Ireland, as well as actors across the range of ancillary sectors servicing the music industry. When first published in 1979, the directory had six recording studios listed, notwithstanding that there were in reality more in existence at the time. By the early 2000s, the number of such facilities listed had mushroomed to in excess of 120. In fact, the 2020 *Hot Press Yearbook* carries listings for more than 6,000 separate businesses operating across the music sector, as well as broader related entertainment, promotion, audio-visual, PR and technology domains, as well as information on official bodies and legal and financial services related to the music industry (*Hot Press* 2020).

At a glance, music industry activity in Ireland appears phenomenal. On one level, this reflects a number of things. Primarily, the sheer level of activity in and around music has proliferated – in terms of creative, technical and business endeavours. Moreover, the costs involved in setting up a band, label, recording facility and so on have radically diminished. There is more music, more access to resources and facilities, and more access to information and services. Concomitantly, there can only be greater levels of expertise within and around the industry as it operates in Ireland. For example, take one particular domain of activity – recording. Facilities such as Windmill Lane, Bow Lane and Westland developed international reputations hosting such renowned international artists as U2, David Bowie, The Rolling Stones, Ed Sheeran and countless others. It was within this environment that many local technicians and engineers learned their trade – working with some of the most successful acts on the planet. As such, numerous Irish engineers and technical crew are in a position of knowledge and expertise.

Additionally, at different points in time, specific milestones appear, on the surface at least, to make Irish artists and audiences stand singular on the world stage. For example, in 2001, the year the domestic market for recorded music peaked, Ireland stood as the 23rd largest market in the world (IFPI 2002). By 2008, albeit in a contracting global market for sales, it stood at number 21 in the world, at a value of $143m (IFPI 2009). Despite significant technological change across the 21st century, much reported disruption emanating from online file-sharing, and the occurrence of a deep financial crisis that saw Ireland subject to austere economic policies, in terms of recorded music, consumption remained comparatively high, relative to 'most other countries' (Deloitte/IMRO 2015: 31). In terms of generating content, 2001 saw Irish recording artists combine to sell a staggering 56 million album units in the global marketplace, making Ireland the eighth largest exporter of recorded music in the world (Music Board of Ireland 2003). Earlier, through the CD boom of the mid-to-late 1990s, when the global record industry enjoyed a decade of super-profits, Ireland was the fourth largest producer of hit records in the European Union (Strachan and Leonard 2004). More recently, given the successes of Imelda May, The Script, Kodaline and others, commentators (e.g., Byrne 2015) talk in terms of the 'Hozier effect', just as, back in the 1980s, the 'U2 effect' made Ireland the focus of the A&R world.

Also, with a population of under five million, our commitment to attending live music also sets us apart. For example, in 2011, despite Ireland being in the throes of an acute economic recession, Dublin's 3Arena was the fifth most attended concert arena in the world that year (and the third in Europe). That year alone, this Live Nation venue saw 670,846 concert-goers attend more than 80 shows, each of which grossed in excess of $1m (Deegan 2012). By comparison, New York's Madison Square Garden saw a mere 616,874 enter through its doors. We are not only one of the largest concert-going audiences in the world, but we also lay claim to the biggest live act in the world. U2's *360* tour (2009–11) remains (at the time of writing) the highest-grossing concert tour in history, taking in more than $736m across some 110 shows

– averaging an astonishing $6.7m per show (*Billboard* 2011). This involved playing to almost 7.3 million people. Their three other stadium tours of the new millennium (*Elevation*, *Vertigo* and *The Joshua Tree*) combined to gross a figure well in excess of $800m (Allen 2017, 2018; Gunderson 2005).

So, in terms of facilities, consumers and artists, there is much that makes Ireland stand out. As many journalistic and official reports attest, we are 'punching above our weight'. The bottom line appears to be that as a collective group of people, we are very important to the business of music. However, here it is worth taking a moment to briefly consider how revenues generated within the Irish market for music are distributed; and also to identify the fundamental actors shaping the success of those Irish artists who 'make it' on the international stage.

As we have seen above, the global market for recorded music is (and was historically) highly concentrated. While the share of the global market controlled by major labels has, broadly speaking, averaged around 70 per cent over recent decades, these companies have often performed even better in the Irish context, at times accounting for up to 92 per cent of sales in that market (Rogers 2013). The vast majority of revenue generated within Ireland is expatriated to the global centres of production and distribution. Moreover, Irish acts that succeed in the global marketplace are invariably on labels owned or distributed by the major transnational companies. As the Irish arm of the majors cannot guarantee releases outside of the Irish market for acts they sign, these artists are almost invariably signed to the UK or international office of the company. While the international offices of the major labels generate music that the Irish offices are generally bound to distribute and promote in the local market, there is no such flow of locally generated recordings moving in the opposite direction. Moreover, the share of the domestic market enjoyed by Irish artists (including those signed to major labels outside of Ireland) has, in relative terms, been quite low (O'Flynn 2004).

As illustrated above, the music publishing industry is also highly concentrated. If we take just one aspect of this, the domain of performing rights, Ireland makes for a particularly interesting case study. Performing royalties are (in theory) generated for songwriters and composers each time their work – their 'intellectual property' – is used in the public domain. Various royalty collection societies around the world collect and administer such performing rights and royalties on behalf of the artists they represent. Since gaining independence from the UK's Performing Rights Society in 1995, the Irish Music Rights Organisation (IMRO) has seen its revenue intake grow significantly. From a figure of approximately €16m in 1996, revenues increased to €38m in 2010, falling back to more than €33m by 2017 (see various IMRO Annual

Financial Statements, 1997–2018). However, reflecting the globalized nature of the domestic market, well in excess of 80 per cent of this can get expatriated in any given year (Rogers and Cawley 2016). So, while, for example, Irish radio generates close to three million airplays a year for recordings to a domestic audience that listens to more than three billion hours of radio (Deloitte/IMRO 2015), the vast majority of content is international.

In the live music arena, reflecting broader international trends, LNE is firmly established as the key player in the Irish context in terms of venue ownership, concert promotion and ticket retailing. It co-owns Dublin's 3Arena, the country's largest indoor concert venue, as well as the Bord Gáis Energy Theatre. As of 2018, Live Nation, in a joint venture with Gaiety Investments, finally took full ownership of MCD Productions, Ireland's largest music promoter. Demonstrating the size of the live music market in Ireland, MCD was the eighth largest concert promoter in the world in 2017, with more than 1.6 million people attending their shows (Pollstar 2018). The country's other high-profile promoter, Aiken Promotions, itself featured at number 43 on the same list, courtesy of its operations in the UK. When it comes to ticketing, like many other territories, through Ticketmaster, LNE holds prime position in ticket retailing in Ireland.

Bringing Ireland to the World, and the World to Ireland in the 20th Century

Over recent decades, numerous reports and commentaries highlight music as a key driver of economic growth in Ireland (e.g., Coopers & Lybrand 1994; Simpson Xavier Horwath 1994; Stokes Kennedy Crowley 1994; Burke 1995; IBEC 1995, 1998; FORTE 1997), and very much part of the Celtic Tiger, knowledge-based economy from the mid-1990s to mid-to-late noughties (e.g., Music Board of Ireland 2003). Moreover, in the wake of the deep global economic crisis from which the world is still emerging, and which produces profound consequences for Ireland, music, in the context of broader copyright industries, has been trumpeted as fundamental to recovery and growth at a national level (Deloitte/IMRO 2015, 2017).

Such reporting celebrates the uniqueness of this popular cultural form in the Irish context, and consistently flags the scope and potential of the Irish music industry. Ireland is lauded as 'punching above its weight' in terms of the scale of its exports to the global music market, and the relative size of the domestic market for music. From Thin Lizzy and the Boomtown Rats in the 1970s to artists such as Kodaline, Dermot Kennedy, and Hozier in the 2020s, there is an unbroken line of major international recording acts emanating from Ireland. Successive state and/or industry reports talk of strategies for nurturing raw talent and fostering commercial innovation so as to ensure the hotbed of musical creativity that has been cultivated can realize its optimum potential and fulfil its purpose. In crude terms, there is something in the water here that makes us distinctively good at 'this sort of thing', and we have to act now (usually in terms of the investment of public funds, tax incentives, and stronger intellectual property rights protections) to continue delivering our inordinately high number of world beaters to the global stage. Such assertions are supported by various statistics that show how Ireland grew to become one of the most prominent exporters of recorded music on the planet, thus outpacing many much bigger countries; and also a significant consumer market for music, again comparing favourably to other, larger economies around the world (see, for example, Music Board of Ireland 2003; Strachan and Leonard 2004; Deloitte/IMRO 2015, 2017; Pollstar 2018).

Based on all of this we might readily hypothesize that, for instance, Ireland produces a lot of people who are very talented and who go on to attain a high level of success, and that we are very good at exporting this success. We are thus encouraged to conclude that Ireland must possess, at least to some degree, a reasonable infrastructure for developing and harnessing such talent and advancing its exploitation; and that Ireland has a very developed music market, and significant benefits to the domestic economy accrue from activities in this sector.

In the following section, we briefly probe some of the key changes that have occurred in the domestic music industry in decades gone by that, on one level, might serve to help explain this apparently unbridled success, but on another level, problematize and contradict this image. While far from a comprehensive overview of the evolving environment for popular music in Ireland, we have chosen to highlight a number of key developments.

Bringing the International Record Industry to Ireland

In the context of the international economic crisis that took root in the 1970s and ran through the 1980s, the wider political-economic domain underwent radical transformation. With emphasis on deregulation, privatization and the intensified foregrounding of free-market ideology as the cure for all of society's ills, neo-liberalism took root at the heart of policy regimes around the world (see, for example, Harvey 2005, 2011).

Within this, capital's response to this period of economic turmoil can, in part, be characterized by a significant shift in investment strategies towards services sectors (see, for example, Hesmondhalgh 2018). As Hesmondhalgh illustrates, the de-regulation of broadcasting and telecommunications helped set the context within which culture and information became increasingly important sites of economic activity. Within this, for example, the spheres of radio, television and advertising expanded rapidly around the globe. This, in turn, meant more spaces for recorded music to colonize. In short, markets for cultural and creative industries were undergoing radical enlargement, with more sites for the promotion and monetization of music opening up for music rights owners. Ireland was not immune to the picture of change evolving across the broader international landscape. With successive governments pursuing a liberal agenda, it would mature across the late 20th/early 21st century as one of the most globalized countries in the world (see various AT Kearney reports and KOF globalization indices; also see O'Toole 2004; Inglis 2008). Simultaneously, the country would also gain a reputation as a major success story in the global music industry. In terms of commercial accomplishments and cultural reach, this was the era within which U2 would become 'bigger than Guinness and George Bernard Shaw' (Van Nguyen 2017). A subsequent unbroken string of Irish acts would penetrate right to the heart of major international markets for pop and rock across the decades to follow. Moreover, as we illustrate below, Ireland would become a nation of avid music consumers and concert-goers.

One specific act of parliament from the late 1960s would be the key to Ireland, and Dublin in particular, developing a reputation as a major centre of production for the recording industry across the decades that followed. Section 2 of the 1969 Finance Act makes a specific provision for residents of the State to enjoy exemption from income tax on royalties derived from 'a work or works generally recognized as having cultural or artistic merit' that they are deemed 'to have written, composed or executed'. In effect, songwriters and recording artists now had a new tax haven. While offering significant incentives to international recording artists to take up residence in Ireland, it was also the ultimate catalyst for initiatives such as Windmill Lane Recording Studios.

In the early 1970s, figures from the literary world such as J.P. Donleavy and Richard Condon had taken up residency in Ireland to avail of this regime (Smith 1975). As the decade progressed, the opportunities the Act provided for players in the music business became apparent to some. Up to that point in time, in terms of studio facilities, there was Eamonn Andrews Studios, and also the smaller Trend Studios, as well as Lombard, Keystone and a few others that, to date, had catered largely to the showband scene. Windmill Lane first opened its doors in 1978. Founder James Morris initially moved to London in the early 1970s as a recording artist, to make the album *Davey and Morris* with collaborator Shaun Davey for York Records. This would prove to be Morris's only venture as a musician, and after training and working as a film editor in London, Morris returned to Ireland in the mid-1970s to set up his own company – James Morris Editing. However, his observations from his earlier experiences in the music industry pointed to the possibilities of developing a music recording facility in Dublin. As Morris explains:

> I knew that, in those days, if a band in the UK had a hit, the first thing that they were advised to do was to leave the country for tax reasons ... But they also had to make a follow-up record. So we knew that there was good business to be had by studios outside of the UK for UK bands. That was the extent of our market research! We built the studio on that basis, and Windmill Lane, down by the Gas company, was just about the only place in Dublin we could find at that time that was cheap enough and big enough for us to build a recording studio ... And it worked. Our theory proved to be correct ... Bands came here ... It had nothing to do with Ireland, but with the UK tax system. (Morris 2014)

The 'handiness' of Dublin – English-speaking, and only an hour across the sea on a plane – made it the ideal location for British bands looking to save on a tax bill. Simple Minds, Kate Bush, Elvis Costello, Def Leppard, David Bowie, Lisa Stansfield, and a host of others would subsequently record in Dublin. In essence, Windmill Lane signalled the reversal of a tide, with acts now coming to Ireland to record, and moreover, Irish acts staying at home to do so. Morris's college friend Paul McGuinness would bring U2 to Windmill Lane to record their first five albums. Moreover, with a post-production facility and a recording studio under the one roof, Windmill was positioned to benefit from the evolution of music television across the 1980s and 1990s. For Morris, it was 'the confluence of the music strand with U2 and MTV' that ultimately grew the studio's brand on the global stage.

Shortly before the launch of Windmill Lane, Westland Studios (then under the name Lombard Studios) was also opened in Dublin. Owned and managed by Tom Costello and Brian Molloy who grew out of the earlier showband scene, Westland would claim Bob Dylan, Thin Lizzy, The Cure, and Bryan Adams among its clients in the years to follow. In the 1980s and 1990s, Bow Lane Studios would also host Def Leppard among others. In short, Ireland had become a place to work and/or live for some of the biggest names in the global recording business, with Irish recording facilities becoming international brands in their own right.

Developing Music on Radio in Ireland

Up to the 1970s, the Irish broadcast media landscape was limited. Within this, space for music was at a premium. While BBC Radio 1, Radio Luxembourg, and a range of prominent pirate stations from outside Ireland were listened to by younger Irish audiences, Radio Éireann remained the only domestic broadcast outlet for promoting records. However, as a public service station, it effectively sought to fulfil an 'all things to all people' remit, so music formed just one aspect of the broadcaster's overall output comprising news, current affairs, drama, education, religion, science, children's programming and a host of other genre categories. The slots for music were thus slim. By the early-to-mid 1970s, weekly music columns had started to be published in the *Evening Herald* and *the Evening Press*, but that, combined with the slender opening on Radio Éireann, represented the entirety of indigenous media space available to exploit.

From the late 1970s onwards, this picture began to change quite radically. By the end of that decade Ireland would have its first dedicated national music radio station. Across the 1970s, the emergence and growth of pirate stations such as Alternative Radio Dublin and Big D had offered significant promotional opportunities to record companies operating in Ireland. As the decade progressed, with pressure mounting on the political establishment to legalize the pirates, a decision was taken to set up a second national station devoted to youth – RTÉ Radio 2 (subsequently 2FM). A decade later, and in keeping with broader international trends in terms of the de-regulation of broadcasting, Ireland would have its first national and local commercial stations. By 2020, in addition to 2FM and the range of digital stations delivered by RTÉ, the picture would include (in terrestrial radio), 31 licensed local commercial stations (with music forming the primary output of most urban stations), three national commercial stations (two of whom are primarily music-based), and a host of community stations. As such, broadcast space for music has expanded exponentially over the past four decades, with 81 per cent of the adult (15 years+) population listening to radio on a daily basis (JNLR 2020).

However, a recurring issue for Irish artists across the decades has been access to Irish airwaves. Lobby groups such as the *Jobs in Music* campaign and *Fairplay for Airplay* have, at different points in time, promoted the plight of home-grown talent to broadcasters and legislators alike. Illustrating the point, a December 2016 article by *Irish Times* journalist Jim Carroll indicates that at 2FM, only one Irish track featured in the top 20 most-played songs on that station across the year (Carroll 2016). At national commercial station Today FM, the figure was two. At multi-region commercial station 4FM, it was zero.

For those Irish acts that do manage to get play-listed, being signed to a major label and having already achieved international success appear to be a prerequisite. As Carroll illustrates, singer-songwriter Soak, who that same year won the RTÉ Choice Music Prize, received only nine airplays on 2FM across the entire 12-month period, placing her at joint 1,477th in the list. Moreover, of the top 50 most-played songs across Irish radio as a whole in 2013, just six were by Irish artists (PPI, cited in Barry 2014). However, all six tracks were accounted for by just two major acts – The Script and Kodaline.

While closer scrutiny of playlists indicates that the percentages vary from station to station, such statistics appear very out of line with the guideline of 30 per cent Irish music recommended for all applicant radio licences by the Broadcasting Authority of Ireland (BAI) – the State-funded regulator of the independent broadcasting sector.

In the 1990s, the successful European Commission legal challenge to the Irish Radio and Television Committee's (IRTC, now Broadcast Authority of Ireland, BAI) application of a minimum quota of home-produced music as policy means that this 30 per cent figure merely acts as a 'guideline' rather than a rule (see, for example, Smyth 1996). In the wake of this legal ruling, the IRTC subsequently conceived a much broader definition of Irish music content that was towards a cultural rather than economic end, and a quota has been deemed to be appropriate in the context of Ireland by the relevant European bodies. The definition of Irish music as agreed by the European Commission is worded as follows:

> Any music which contributes to a distinctively Irish contemporary music culture by engaging with lyrical themes that deal with the history of Ireland, the contemporary realities of life in Ireland today ... or which contains, reflects or develops on established Irish musical forms.

Such a definition is, in essence, so broad as to be of little practical value. There is much music that can fit the Irish music definition, but has no relationship with the Irish recording industry or even the broader Irish music industry. An example is the theme tune from the movie *Titanic*. It was sung by Celine Dion who is French-Canadian, and recorded by a US record company. Because it related to a historical piece, it technically would have fitted the above definition of Irish music. Yet it did not have an Irish artist, it was not recorded in Ireland, it was not written by an Irish writer and those had been the three primary points of focus of the then-IRTC in getting a quota accepted at European level. What all of this means is that there need be little positive discrimination by Irish broadcasters in favour of home-produced repertoire in order to satisfy regulatory requirements. As such, domestic airwaves are dominated by international content, and becoming an established act on the international stage appears the only real route to the airwaves for Irish bands.

Promoting Training for the 'Irish Music Industry'?

Since the 1990s, a number of lobby groups have emerged urging government to implement measures to support the music sector. As we illustrated at the outset of this chapter, this has led to a drip-feed of 'official' reports which point to the distinctive achievements of the 'Irish' music industry.

These reports also repeat, ad nauseam, calls for copyright reform that, they claim, are fundamental to enhancing opportunities across the sector for Irish artists and companies. The logic advanced is that '[b]ringing copyright legislation up-to-date is an essential pre-requisite to a strategy for developing the Irish music industry to its potential' (Simpson Xavier Horwath 1994: 3). Clearly in the strategic vision's line of sight was the objective of fostering 'indigenous creative output' (2). The report prefaced its 14 proposals on copyright reform with the aim that Ireland 'be seen as a copyright friendly country … as one basis on which to attract international investment in the Irish music industry' (33). Moreover, an IRMA/PPI consultation paper (2014) notes that core copyright industries in Ireland generated a turnover of €18.65bn in 2011, and gross value added of €4.6bn representing 2.93 per cent of GDP. This paper emphasizes that '[T]his value is heavily dependent on copyright protection' (2014: 3). So, reinforcing copyright protection is deemed core to bolstering the music sector, and sustaining and augmenting its contribution to the Irish economy. However, as we illustrate below, the primary beneficiaries of music copyright in Ireland are not domestic actors. While this does not make Ireland an exception by any means, the extent to which the domestic market is dominated by global companies and rights owners is extremely high.

Moreover, such official reporting has consistently called for state intervention in terms of training and education for the music industry in the context of developing domestic music industry infrastructure, and its contribution to the local economy (IBEC 1995, 1998; Forte 1997; Music Board of Ireland 2003). Within this context we initially witnessed the development of such initiatives as the 'Rock School' at Ballyfermot College of Further Education, which since the late 1980s has evolved to offer a range of courses in music performance, production and management. The 1990s also saw funding for such initiatives as Musicbase and, subsequently, First Music Contact. The former was an Arts Council funded popular music information and education centre; the latter a free support and advice service for musicians and bands, again funded by the Arts Council of Ireland up to the present day. Subsequently, we have seen the emergence of a range of third-level programmes around careers in music and the music industry across various institutions (both public and private) including Dundalk Institute of Technology, Dublin Institute of Technology, BIMM Dublin, and Cork Institute of Technology, among others. For some industry commentators, such initiatives serve to provide upcoming artists and prospective industry professionals with an awareness of the mechanics of the music business, and to enhance the do-it-yourself approach to developing a career in the industry. Former Polydor representative and long-time music writer and journalist Jackie Hayden argues:

> Those initiatives are hugely valuable in a way that is almost impossible to quantify. If you have government money put into that area, and even if it never produces a single hit record, it still is a huge input into education in Ireland, never mind culture or music or anything fanciful like that. But it is teaching people basic skills. There are a whole range of social skills, technical skills and business skills ... simple things that some people might not have any other way of learning ... (cited from Rogers 2013: 143)

What Does This All Mean?

Across recent decades, Ireland itself has become a global brand in the context of the music industry. The domestic landscape for popular music has evolved beyond recognition since the 1970s. With some of the biggest-selling acts in the world emanating from Ireland, and many more international superstar acts using the country as a place to record and live, it is renowned and celebrated as a music industry success story. However, in terms of those who live and record here, it has, until relatively recently, served as a tax haven. While much official reporting on the industry (see, for example, Music Board of Ireland 2003; Deloitte/IMRO 2017) points to the benefits of developing Ireland as a centre of record industry production in terms of employment for technical crew, equipment hire and so on, the fact remains that the majority of profits emanating from recordings produced here remain outside of the country.

Broader processes of political-economic development have contextualized and shaped how the music industry has developed across time and space. In fact, when it comes to Ireland, the music industry finds itself evolving in a particularly globalized economy (see various AT Kearney reports and KOF globalization indices; see also O'Toole 2004; Inglis 2008). Just one example illustrating this, as we have seen, relates to the saturation of Irish radio with international content, and the significant problems faced by Irish artists in accessing Irish broadcast media space without the intervention of a transnational music label.

The contradictions implied by the poor showing of indigenous industries relative to the phenomenal success of Irish artists abroad is 'consistent with the designation of Ireland as the most globalized state in the world' (O'Flynn 2004: 53–54). So, while Irish audiences have evolved to constitute significant consumer markets for live music events and recorded music products and services, and while Irish artists have long-since triumphed in the international arena, again, the benefits (economically at least) are largely claimed elsewhere.

All of these factors combine to mark a sizeable shift in the roles and interests of major record labels in the 21st century. Furthermore, they have helped to maintain the dominance of the global labels in the Irish market and facilitate the ongoing expatriation of much locally generated revenue. The overall success of this restructuring process is illustrated by the revenue figures illustrated earlier for all three major labels.

Conclusion

Here, we have briefly considered the macro-level organization of the global music industry and how it features in the Irish context. In essence, it is a story of takeovers, mergers, joint ventures and other forms of alliances, to a point where power in all core music sectors is intensely concentrated on a worldwide scale.

In summation, it is worth considering a couple of stark statistics that highlight the polarization of wealth across the music industries and illustrate the dominance of a (relatively) small number of global acts and labels. As detailed above, all three core sectors of the global music industries remain highly concentrated in terms of market share, with a small number of large companies still wielding control. Within this, we can note that some years as few as 1 per cent of 'superstar' acts account for 77 per cent of revenues generated by the global record industry (Mulligan 2014). Moreover, just 5 per cent of acts account for 85 per cent of revenues generated by the global concert industry, with the top 1 per cent taking 60 per cent of the proceeds (Krueger 2020).

Considering all of this, a quote from Irish writer Gareth Murphy comes to mind, which perhaps most succinctly and concisely describes the Irish situation:

> Ireland doesn't have a music industry in the real sense, but rather the musical equivalent of a *comptoir*, the colonial term for a trading post that facilitates the outflow of raw materials to foreign factories and the import of products back in. (G. Murphy 2015)

The accounts that follow – which offer penetrating insights into the moments that defined the emergence and flowering of Irish acts on the global popular music stage – must thus be considered in that light.

4 The 1950s: Elvis and Ireland's Catholic Pop

When the *History Channel* presented ten defining moments that 'changed America' (Gillon 2006), a 1956 appearance by Elvis Presley on the *Ed Sullivan Show* was included. Presley made three appearances on the show during a four-month period, and his mass-marketing campaign was so successful that some historians concluded that 'he defined an era' (Gillon 2006: 224). Certainly, his international success brought rock and roll music to previously unseen popularity, but his appearances on the *Ed Sullivan Show* served a very important purpose for Ireland too. The television show dramatically contrasted American youth culture with Irish culture, and it did so with the most sophisticated and powerful medium of the time.

The economic and demographic differences between Ireland and the US were stark at the time. In 1956, teenagers in the US had a combined income of $7 billion and spent $75 million of that on vinyl records (Gillon 2006: 205). At the same time, Ireland's economy was in crisis. Disturbingly, gross domestic product (GDP) growth rates between 1939 and 1958 were only 1.1 per cent annually, the lowest of any European country (Ó Gráda 2008: 3). As rock and roll music was spreading around the world, so were the young Irish. Proportionally, emigration was at levels that had not been seen since the 1880s (Ó Gráda 2008: 7).

In the US a moral panic accompanied Elvis's rise in popularity. Often the anti-Elvis crusade was just as inflammatory and wild as the young singer was supposed to be. Shortly after the second *Ed Sullivan* appearance, inhabitants of Iowa could attend a public lecture on 'Moral Insanity and Elvis Presleyism' (*Des Moines Tribune* 1957: 3) while newspapers published sensational and ignorant accounts of the new music:

> Some say jazz had its origin in a Negro humming in a whiskey jug. Rock and roll is even worse. They both contribute to the noise and confusion of this machine age... The savage beat of the tomtoms is for savages. (Wilson 1957: 30)

Some of this bile and dread came from religious sources who were able to springboard on Elvis's popularity to promote their own causes. One unnamed New Jersey pastor devised 'Ten Commandments for our Teen-Agers' which included: 'Thou shalt not bow thy knee to "Elvis" ... God alone is worthy of thy worship' (*Clarion Ledger* 1957: 36). One of the most-quoted, anti-Elvis media statements after the second *Ed Sullivan* appearance came from the Rev. William Shannon. His *Catholic Sun* newspaper column was amplified by mainstream newspapers who reprinted his words:

> Presley and his voodoo of frustration and defiance have become symbolic of our country and we are sorry to come upon Ed Sullivan in the role of promoter ... [the] Presley influence [is] a plague, a threat to tomorrow's youth ... It is to be read between the lines of our stories of gangs and car-thieves and vandals ... It is universally disheartening to the priests, sisters, brothers and good parents who train our fine children in the solid principles of morality, to have this training threatened by the lewd contortions and base appeal of this invincible bellower. (*Post Standard* 1957: 16)

It is notable Shannon didn't just dislike Presley's music, he felt that Elvis undermined authority figures. He placed this in the context of a Catholic environment where priests and nuns (sisters), as well as other religious personnel (brothers) guided America's youth. The language of this 1950s 'culture war' in the US echoed DJ Goff and the Irish authorities in the 1930s. But there was a key difference. In the US the demands and influence of commerce could sometimes triumph over censorship. In Ireland, that wasn't the case.

Fr Shannon's argument pitted authority against reckless liberals who were undermining values, and he included Ed Sullivan with the latter. But Ed Sullivan was no fool and he was acutely aware of the American cultural landscape. His popularity depended on it. He was the second of nine children born into a second-generation Irish-Catholic family (Nachman 2009: 108), and the very idea of a family was essential to his TV show. In Gerald Nachman's account, it was 'Sullivan's mission to construct a family audience'; crucially, 'The Family was regarded as the glue that holds the country together' (2009: 199). This meant that if Sullivan wanted to broadcast Elvis, he also had to broadcast something that would *counteract* Elvis and his wild youthfulness. He found it in Ireland.

Maybe today The Little Gaelic Singers from County Derry would be looked at as an oddity. Even in Elvis's time they looked out of date to America's youth. But they were still a sign of the times, and they indicated clearly that the Church in Ireland was confident in its relationship with the record industry.

The Little Gaelic Singers emerged from the intersection of Catholicism, commerce, culture and the music industry, under the guidance of their very skilled music director, James MacCafferty. He had been a member of various music groups in Northern Ireland, one of which, The Ten Columbians, was a very early example of the showband genre. While most accounts of the showband industry credit the Clipper Carltons as the showband originators, The Ten Columbians had been putting on a showband-type show since 1946 (MacCafferty n.d.). MacCafferty had also performed for the large number of servicemen based in Northern Ireland during the war, including gigs in the local Apprentice Boy's Hall.

MacCafferty clearly understood a wide range of entertainment types, but it was with The Little Gaelic Singers that he achieved his greatest international recognition; their self-titled debut album was released by Decca in the United States, and they appeared on *The Ed Sullivan Show* on three occasions. The impresario Albert Morini specialized in bringing ethnic acts to the US and he undertook a search for an Irish children's choir (*Ulster Herald* 1956). He found the choir, who had been acclaimed at the Derry Feis that year, and had already been recorded by the BBC.

The first US tour of The Little Gaelic Singers took place in 1956, but it wasn't a conventional tour by rock or pop standards. In fact, it was successful thanks to a considerable amount of DIY activity by Irish American Catholics. This community engagement was acknowledged by the music industry as contributing to the success of the tour: *Billboard* (1956) magazine commented on how the series of concerts was 'another example of disk sales increased by a personal appearance tour'. More distinctively, the public involvement by the Irish American Catholic hierarchy was also recognized as contributing to the financial success of the tour. The group received very meaningful personal endorsements from US cardinals, so it is fair to say that it was Catholic action that brought them to their date with Elvis.

It was natural that the group of Derry orphans would appeal to the large Irish American community. But the degree and nature of the community support went beyond just purchasing tickets. In most cities, a local Irish Catholic community group participated in the organization, and potential profits, of the concert. For example, the Reading, Pennsylvania show was arranged in conjunction with the Junior Catholic Women's Club, with proceeds aiding the Catholic Interracial Centre. This 10-week tour took place at a time when American society was engaged in an ongoing debate about the morality and legitimacy of the newly emergent 'rock and roll'. Television heightened the moral tension. Elvis Presley was the most prominent proponent of this new style of popular music and The Little Gaelic Singers were unwittingly drawn into the debate. Presley's first appearance on the *Ed Sullivan Show* on 9 September 1956 has been acknowledged as a milestone in the mainstream acceptance of both his persona and the rock and roll genre. His second appearance on the national show consolidated this reputation and the commercial potential of rock music; it also coincided with the debut broadcast of The Little Gaelic Singers. The Irish choir, with their implicit narrative of innocent youth, under the stewardship of Catholic clergy, were unsurprisingly linked in the media with Irish identity myths of naivety and purity. In Connecticut they were described as 'radiant and enchanting youngsters from the Emerald Isle' whose concert was 'appropriately sponsored by Division No 1 Ancient Order of Hibernians' (*Meriden Journal* 1961: 6). To critics of Presley and rock and roll, they were positioned as the antithesis of the modern America phenomenon. The obedience of the orphans apparently contrasted with 'rebellious' American teenagers.

Bauman et al. (2012: 5), while examining the impact of television and mass media in the era, suggest that The Little Gaelic Singers were booked to appear on the same show as Presley 'apparently to add some generational balance': young well-mannered Irish orphans appealing to parents horrified by American teenage devotion to Presley. Apart from the *Sullivan* show, The Little Gaelic Singers also enjoyed other sophisticated modern mass-media promotion.

Decca Records' albums by the children promoted them in a way that reinforced the idea of Irish innocence. The cover art for the second Little Gaelic Singers album, *From Donegal to Galway*, featured two toy dolls in 'Irish costume'. The dolls appeared in front of a map of a united Ireland while a smoking pipe rested against a green hat with a silver buckle. *Billboard* (1957: 34) magazine described it as 'one of the strongest display contenders of the week'. In the weeks leading up to St Patrick's Day, images like this represented Ireland with a cultural and musical landscape radically different from modern America.

Recently, Ireland has reassessed aspects of its history, and the reality of Irish orphans and their lives have come under scrutiny. While most of Ireland's adult emigrants during the 1950s went to Britain (Ó Gráda 2008), The Little Gaelic Singers weren't the only children from Ireland crossing the Atlantic during the 1950s. As Moira J. Maguire (2002) documented, 'hundreds' of healthy children were sent out of Ireland to adoptive homes in the US from the 1940s to the 1960s. Until 1952 all that was required from the adoptive parents was a signed affidavit that the child would be brought up as a Catholic. At times, virtually nothing was known about the adopting couple's 'background, home life or financial position'. It was a human movement carried out with 'silence and secrecy' (Maguire 2002: 390). That secrecy was punctured when the *New York Times* published a photograph of six children arriving from Ireland in March 1950. In response, Dublin's influential Archbishop John Charles McQuaid, rather than the government, ordered the temporary suspension of the movement of orphans from Ireland. The movement of these children was made legal with the 1952 Adoption Act, where 'religion was the defining issue', and for Maguire this resulted in a 'callousness that seemed to characterise the overseas adoption scheme' (2002: 391–92) and didn't 'halt the exodus of children or enact measures to protect the civil and legal rights of children who were removed from the State' (2002: 399).

The idea of the Church as the natural and ideal guardians of Irish youth was reinforced by Decca Records. The sleeve notes to The Little Gaelic Singers' album *From Donegal to Galway Bay* claimed that:

> one of the most unforgettable experiences in Ireland today is to visit Nazareth House ... Its upkeep is made possible by public donations from the people of Derry and of the neighbouring Counties. Americans, too, have helped to support Nazareth House, particularly the personnel of the US Naval Base at Derry. (Little Gaelic Singers 1957)

By this account, Ireland wasn't a country to invest in, it was a country in need of charity. And the Catholic church was a key force in how and where, and for what ideological purposes the donations were spent. In a meaningful way, the hierarchy benefited from the sustained idea of Ireland being backward.

Mass media continued to enable the images of 'backward' Ireland to be generated and communicated. Ed Sullivan contributed to the representation of Ireland in other clichéd ways, apart from hosting The Little Gaelic Singers. The noted harpist Mary O'Hara (2012) recalled her appearance on the television show in 1957. She was anxious that the presentation wouldn't be 'an embarrassing stage-Irish one' and remembered:

> to my horror I saw them [the Ed Sullivan staff] carrying on two giant cut-out shamrocks ... I was dumbfounded when I was asked to sit with my harp on one of them. (2012: 102)

An Irish wolfhound dog was placed on the other shamrock. O'Hara felt that the stereotypical images continually identified with the Irish had a negative effect culturally. To her, the shamrock became tainted:

> When it is perennially associated with leprechauns, shillelaghs, green beer and Delaney's donkeys, I feel it is a prostitution of the

> true image of our beautiful country and of its ancient culture ... Celtic Ireland has a wealth of art treasures of rare beauty and craftsmanship, much better for representing a nation than the kitsch elements of pub-culture. (ibid.)

Three years later, Sullivan's show influenced Irish pop culture in a major way. He booked a group of New York-based folk singers for his show and gave them significant airtime. The knitted Aran jumpers of The Clancy Brothers and Tommy Makem instantly, and almost permanently, defined the visual look of Irish folk music. While folk music had some level of support in Ireland, it had never before been exposed to this level of mass marketing and media reach. The band had been financially supported by the Guggenheim family heiress, Diane Hamilton, in New York, but the *Ed Sullivan Show* appearance took them to a whole new audience.

The raucous balladeers of the 1950s and 1960s, including The Clancy Brothers and The Dubliners, are recalled fondly in Ireland's popular music history. But it is worth remembering that during this time the Church, and its orphanages, were enjoying the good graces and mass marketing techniques of major international recording firms. Ireland's image was being projected by the increasingly sophisticated global media, but it was a nuanced and multifaceted image, and included rousing singalongs as well as Church-controlled choirs. It was stimulated by a two-way-flow of representations between Ireland and countries with sophisticated culture industries.

There is another aspect of the Elvis moral panic and America's anti-rock and roll crusade that shows where Ireland and its music belonged culturally. It highlights that such moral panics and crusades are often more nuanced and complex than they appear; the battle lines are often not clear. For example, there were still traces of 'old Ireland' in the pop charts as Elvis made his ascent to stardom. In 1959, one Irish song remained in Top 10 popularity charts in the US, alongside Elvis and his modernity. Over four decades after it had been composed, 'Danny Boy' was still in the Nashville Top 10 (*Tennessean* 1959). The sound of 'old Ireland' still had fans in America while teenagers were screaming for Elvis.

In fact, it was a song that Elvis knew and performed. Ireland's music was part of the repertoire of this modern icon. His army sergeant recalled how the singer performed for his military colleagues; away from home, the songs they wanted to hear weren't always his pop hits but Irish songs including 'I'll Take You Home Again Kathleen' and 'Danny Boy' (Hopkins 1977). The latter was the favourite song of Elvis's father. During his declining years, on his final concert tours where the singer often looked bewildered and in need of rest, he would stop his show and point to one of his background singers who would break into the familiar sound of 'Danny Boy'. Elvis and rock and roll hadn't replaced or eliminated Irish songs, but they had made them feel like the music of their parents, or the soundtrack of the lost, lonely and homesick.

Of course, it wasn't just the American mass media which represented Ireland as a country of pleasant, innocent young people. The Irish were perfectly capable of playing that role themselves. In the crowded international pop music industry, it often made sense as a performance strategy. Ireland's much televised popular culture moment of the early 1970s invoked a style very similar to The Little Gaelic Singers. Dana, who won the Eurovision Song Contest in the first year of that decade, reinforced the image of Ireland's entertainers as wholesome and innocent. She appeared in the finals wearing an outfit that resembled a traditional Irish dancing costume. Her skirt may have been shorter, but in many respects, it resembled the stage outfits of The Little Gaelic Singers in the 1950s.

For some people, Dana's outfit and presentation echoed the 'quaint' costumes of The Little Gaelic Singers, but it is worth remembering that those outfits had brought them to share TV opportunities with Elvis. Certain aspects of Dana's career and presentation demonstrated the gulf in the 1970s between the underdeveloped local music industry and the sophisticated world of commercial pop. When she won the Eurovision, she was being managed by a local schoolteacher who was still working at his day job. Sadly, her Eurovision win was accompanied by a public dispute with the song's writers that could possibly have been avoided with savvier personnel management. Yet it was clear that Dana's performance of a version of Irishness was marketable internationally. Buoyed by sales in Northern Ireland, her Eurovision song even went to number 1 in the UK. While she did achieve another four Top 20 singles in the UK, there is a sense of lost opportunity and lots of 'might have beens' about her career. The Eurovision certainly gave her a global platform, but she never capitalized on that high profile and momentum. It is notable that the next Eurovision winner after Dana to go to number 1 in Britain became the embodiment of sophisticated, modern Europop. ABBA's global commercial breakthrough in 1974 showed the chasm between Ireland's mainstream pop and the world market. It was almost as wide as the gap had been in the 1950s between The Little Gaelic Singers and Elvis.

Dana's national celebrity status reveals something about the relationship between the Irish pop industry and other power groups. The Irish news headlines of the time showed the continuing comfort level the church had with local pop. Her public persona was embraced by the Catholic hierarchy: 'Bishop wishes Dana luck' (*Sunday Independent* 1970a: 3) before the contest, and

'Bishops greet Dana in Derry' (*Irish Independent* 1970: 22) afterwards, are not the sort of headlines you would expect to find in most other European countries at the time. Yet they indicated how comfortable Ireland's Catholic hierarchy were with the field of pop music. While the Church of Ireland bishop had been a member of the welcoming party in Derry, most of the clergy featured in Ireland's pop world were Catholic. In the year of Dana's Eurovision triumph one local celebrity priest, Father Michael Cleary, branding himself as 'The Singing Priest', released his debut album for the Release record label. From 1977 a group of priests had performed on stages throughout the country, appearing in cabarets and at fundraisers for Catholic charities. Originally branded as 'The Holy Show', the performers were then billed as 'The All-Priests Show' and enjoyed popularity for decades. Ireland's pop industry gave the clergy opportunities to be forces behind the scenes, and also to be 'stars' and personalities. This was not just local fun; the commercial height of the *priests on stage* movement came when three Catholic priests even made the UK Top 5 with their self-titled album, *The Priests* (2008), on Sony records. It is evident that mainstream Irish pop music was conservative and in line with establishment values.

Recent academic work has been successful in examining where pop music challenges to conservative Ireland emerged from. The writing of Aileen Dillane (2021) on Sinéad O'Connor and Ann-Marie Hanlon (2021) on Zrazy are particularly helpful examples of this. Pop music, in the Irish case, didn't travel in a straight line to the current situation where voices that would have once been seen as left-of-centre are now enjoyed by large audiences.

With this in mind, it is hardly surprising that after Dana's UK chart-topper it took almost a decade for Ireland to get back to the number 1 position there. When it came, with The Boomtown Rats, the performance mode seemed a world apart from The Little Gaelic Singers and Dana. The Rats' achievements were aided by a new generation of counter-cultural music entrepreneurs, as we will explore in later chapters.

5 Horslips: Advancing DIY and Enterprise in the Irish Music Scene

Polly Devlin's account of her childhood in rural County Tyrone, *All of Us There*, first published in 1983, is a startling document of Ireland's cultural transformation. The 2003 edition of the autobiography includes an introduction by the celebrated novelist, Emma Donoghue, who identifies themes in the book. Most strikingly, she notes that Devlin's recollections of the 'rigorous suppression' of sexuality in 1950s Ireland 'amount to an indictment of Irish culture'. This was a childhood populated by abusive priests and punishing nuns and 'the cruelty of adults to children, in a culture that equated the sound of children laughing with "being bad"' (Devlin 2003: xii).

The culture of 1950s Ireland, described by one reviewer as 'almost that of the 18th century' (Devlin 2003), feels a world apart from the realms of fashion or rock music. Yet in the 1970s the Devlin children, now grown-up, were significant Irish figures in global fashion and rock. By 1979, Polly Devlin, then a London-based journalist, was a curator of global commercial culture and had edited *The Vogue Book of Fashion Photography*. In the same year, her younger brother, Barry, a member of Horslips, was being lauded for his contribution to rock music. The *Irish Press* review of the group's National Stadium concert noted:

> the on-stage dominance of bass player Barry Devlin ... Devlin ruled on stage. He moved, rocked, postured, cajoled and exhorted ... [Horslips] turned the Stadium into a quivering mass of demented humanity. (MacRuairi 1979: 4)

Again, this was a far cry from the County Tyrone upbringing during which the musician recalled that the local parish priest 'hated the thought of pop music, so the chances of hearing anything vaguely modern were zero' (Cunningham 2013: 14).

In the late 1970s, Dublin newspapers also noted that Horslips brought rock to small towns including Nenagh (County Tipperary) and Bawnboy (County

Cavan). Away from Ireland's cities, they 'still hold the attendance records in many rural ballrooms' (Spain 1979: 7). One rural newspaper correspondent wrote emotively of his own personal experience with Horslips and the local venues. He described 'the often cruel and always fickle nature of the dance hall ... the only God-forsaken place to begin the mating process' (*Western Journal* 1979: 18). He placed Horslips in the context of the country ballroom's usual offerings.

> Here was a group who were manifestly more different and infinitely more accomplished and pleasing than the standard Country and Western Cowpunchers who were threatening to keep musical Ireland in the Dark Ages with their terrible regurgitated versions of United States Country Music Songs. (*Western Journal* 1979: 18)

While Ireland may not have been the centre of the fashion or rock music industries, the Devlins had proved that Irish people could be fashionable and could rock. In 1979, Horslips were touring to promote an album, *The Man Who Built America*, that eulogized emigration and separation. Unlike the songs about Ireland written in America in the early 20th century, Horslips were writing songs about America while staying at home. Ireland had come a long way.

Enterprise and Subculture

Music subcultures have been the site of some of Ireland's most innovative and surprising business enterprise. Some of this activity is based on ideological principles, particularly the punk movement's deliberate opposition to major-label corporate practice. But most of this enterprise is 'do it yourself' by necessity. Young artists, including those who want eventually to sign with major labels, require ways to get noticed, build an audience or generate revenue from their art. The music scene is a place where young people can use enterprise and creativity to raise their profile. It is also a place where savvy use can be made of the cultural divide between the mainstream and subculture. This youthful combination of enterprise and creativity is evident in the case of Horslips. While the band were unquestionably musically ground-breaking, their business enterprise was just as innovative. They conducted their affairs in a way that proved that an Irish rock group could live and work in Ireland *and* control key areas of their art and presentation. In fact, their collective enterprise, or self-industry, helped to usher in a modern era on the local music scene, and showed that Irish rock didn't have to be completely dependent on established labels.

Thanks to their creativity, musical ability and business savvy, Horslips became part of Ireland's mainstream rock. But it is worth remembering that they emerged from a music subculture, and in Ireland music-related subcultures were frequently viewed with hostility by the establishment. Horslips, with their hybrid of Irish tunes and modern rock music, played by long-haired and frequently bare-chested young men, were clever enough to use the tension between Ireland's establishment and its youth to their advantage.

In 1971, the year of Horslips' first public performances, national newspapers covered the supposed threat posed to Ireland's values by the hippies and other youth subcultures. Ireland's open hostility to the hippie movement was evident in newspaper headlines. In April the *Evening Herald*'s front-page headlines included: 'Skinhead gangs battle at new community hall' (Denieffe 1971) and 'Cardinal raps sex obsession' (*Evening Herald* 1971). According to the report, the first two threats mentioned by the cardinal were 'Western society's motiveless murders' and 'hippies'.

Hippies had been treated as a threat by the Irish establishment since the late 1960s. They were also useful for debates about other varied threats to Irish culture. 'Town stages a hippy boycott', ran one *Connacht Telegraph* front-page headline in 1969. This story concerned the island of Dornish, which had been purchased by the Beatle, John Lennon, four years earlier. He had visited the island with Yoko Ono and then made it available to what the locals referred to as 'hippies'. At a town hall meeting, it was agreed that local businesses in Westport would refuse to serve the hippies. In addition, any business that provided hippies with goods or services was to be boycotted. This was represented as a struggle between local Irish values and outsiders. A local hairdresser, Larry Hingerton, was quoted as saying, 'We will form an anti-hippy organisation to keep them away', while the restaurant owner Michael O'Beirne said: 'I returned from London to get away from the permissive society there'.

It is hardly surprising that the local hairdresser was opposed to hippies; with their long hair they represented a direct threat to his livelihood. Other opposition to the hippies came from women's groups and the clergy. The Westport Guild of the Irish Countrywomen's Association (ICA) didn't mince their words: 'Our message to the hippies is loud and clear – Keep out, because we mean business' (*Irish Press* 1969: 3). The countrywomen soon found useful allies in the anti-hippy crusade; the local boxing and cycling clubs joined them (*Mayo News* 1969: 1). Tellingly, the local Catholic curate, Fr Kilkelly, used the crisis to request legislation for controlling drugs. The Westport council unanimously adopted a motion calling on the Taoiseach to control not only drugs, but also aliens.

Against this media backdrop, Horslips, with their noticeably long hair, began their publicity campaign. The group had formed almost by accident. A television advertisement for Harp lager needed a pop group to appear in one scene. Some of the male staff at a Dublin advertising agency thought they met the requirements, and they stood in (Barry 1979). They enjoyed the experience and decided to see what would happen if they made music together. Television provided them with another major boost when a friend, Aine O'Connor, introduced them to an RTÉ producer who wanted a music group for a new six-part series, *Fonn*. This was a clever bilingual pun. Fonn is the Gaelic word for sound, but it is pronounced 'fun'. While the group members had also provided the music for a version of *The Táin* in the Abbey Theatre, the first announced Horslips concert performance was in Navan. A local newspaper, the *Drogheda Independent*, had published a dedicated music column since 1967, but it had recently been championing Ireland's rock groups rather than the showbands. It provocatively positioned the upcoming Horslips gig as part of a cultural battle between old and new Ireland. The concert was to be Navan's 'first heavy rock' night featuring Horslips' 'rock-ceili sound that has yet to be categorised' although the band's posters advertised 'Horslips funky ceili':

> Questions will be asked about how it could be allowed. Accusations of a cultural sellout will be hurled ... by the president of the local preserve-our-Irish-heritage-at-all-costs society. But it's coming. (Gee 1970a: 20)

If inviting the Irish heritage preservationists to view Horslips as a threat was provocative, it was a tactic that gained their attention. The gig was cancelled. The *Drogheda Independent* rock critic used this to highlight Ireland's city/country divide. He quoted the gig's Dublin lighting operator:

> Navan is only 20 miles from Dublin but it looks like it is 30 years behind. I think their attitude is slightly startling. We are certainly going ahead with our plans but they will not include Navan for a few years anyway. (Gee 1970b: 22)

Horslips' local notoriety in Navan, for a show that didn't take place, was leveraged into a national news story. They used the non-gig to highlight a divide between old conservative Ireland and the modern culture that Horslips belonged to. The *Sunday Independent* (1970b) ran a story with the headline 'Group is angry with Curate'. The local priest was 'not available for interviews', so the band got to tell both sides of the story. According to the band the concert was cancelled on short notice after the manager of the Church-owned hall objected to the posters promoting it. These featured a picture of the group superimposed on a large pair of apparently female lips, a poster deemed by the curate to be in 'gross bad taste' for an event that was 'immoral and designed to seduce the girls of Navan'. Jim Lockhart of Horslips was quoted:

> Obviously, we protested and told him that we had gone to a lot of expense; but he told us that there were 20 good men and true in Navan who would not allow their daughters to be seduced by this class of entertainment. (*Sunday Independent* 1970b: 3)

Horslips had become a national news story without even playing a full concert. Now they were perceived as modern, rebellious and anti-authoritarian – perfect traits for a rock band. The message was clear: the young media-savvy bands might be barred from church halls, but they were going to challenge the conservative rules.

Horslips' early activity was pure do-it-yourself. When they did engage a manager, it is notable that he respected what the band members could contribute not just musically, but also in the business sense. He was later quoted: 'My contribution was to ensure that every decision was made by the band' (Cunningham 2013: 65). The collective decision-making of Horslips and their manager, Michael Deeny, transformed the local landscape of popular music in Ireland. They proved that a locally based rock group could thrive and even become part of the mainstream culture.

One of the key figures in Irish cultural analysis, Roy Foster (2018), wrote that the 1960s were one of the 'fast-forward eras in Irish history ... when old moulds were broken, and a change in consciousness seemed to presage a new kind of future'. Pop music was a vibrant element of that fast-forwarding of Irish culture in the 1960s. Ted Carroll, who was later instrumental in Thin Lizzy's management and London's Chiswick record label, promoted youth gatherings, while local underground rock venues supported rock music to an extent. The impressive *Teenage Express* magazine published by Ken Stewart was launched and circulated. This was young Ireland finding its voice in a very notable way; Irish youth no longer waited for their turn to speak, they published and promoted their own views in their do-it-yourself media. Later, this practice became an intrinsic element of punk and new wave culture in Ireland.

However, it is arguable that the change of consciousness of 1960s Ireland wasn't explicitly expressed in a sustained way in youth culture until Horslips emerged in the early 1970s. Their combination of music, enterprise and sophisticated promotion did not just 'presage a new kind of future', it delivered it to Irish doorsteps. Earlier, the Belfast and London-based Solomon firm, with Van Morrison and Them, proved that Ireland could successfully deliver rock music to the major global markets. But Horslips did something even more remarkable: they proved that an Irish rock band could penetrate those global markets from an Irish base.

In the early 1970s, local newspapers supported and amplified the profile of both Thin Lizzy and Horslips. Rock music was no longer solely part of city culture. It was finding a home in rural Ireland and readers around the country were being kept up to date on its progress. The *Longford Leader* (Mooney 1972) heralded Horslips' achievements in delivering their debut album to the market. Since Ireland lacked the desired recording studios for a major rock production, the band had rented The Rolling Stones' mobile studio and had installed it in a County Tipperary mansion. If there was an upside to the country's economically deprived state of affairs in the early 1970s, it was that large country homes could be rented at relatively affordable prices. Horslips commissioned an Irish-born producer, Alan O'Duffy, to record the album. Being based in Ireland didn't mean they were cut off from the global industry of rock. While mixing the album over three days in London, it was reported that they spent time with French superstar Johnny Halliday, Bobby Keys (the saxophonist who played with both Buddy Holly and The Rolling Stones), Jim Horn (who performed with Duane Eddy and Frank Sinatra), and most notably, Led Zeppelin's Jimmy Page. Regardless of how much time the band actually spent in the company of these legendary musicians, in terms of mythmaking Irish musicians were now mixing with rock royalty.

The recording in rural Tipperary was unprecedented in Irish rock. Jim Lockhart was quoted:

> It was a bizarre session. Friends and strangers were arriving every day to wish us luck and some of them stayed on, sleeping in armchairs and sofas. There were even some car-loads of 'straight' sightseers having a look at the freaks!! (Mooney 1972: 11)

This was a home victory for internationally competitive do-it-yourself creative enterprise, and the band members were hands-on participants in most aspects of their career. The marketing of the first album was also enterprising. Steve Averill, a member of the Dublin rock community, remembered:

> nobody as a band had ever thought of, or had ever used, big advertising hoardings for the release of a record. The first day it was released you walked down the street and suddenly you had six of these 60' by

> 40' posters on a wall, each with an individual member of Horslips on them. The impact was incredible. I thought, 'Wow, somebody's actually doing something from a local point of view and doing all they need to do to make themselves stand out'. (Averill 2018)

This was no mere local hype either. The clever marketing resulted in large sales in Ireland. Steve Averill recalled:

> I was working in Golden Discs and I have never remembered an album leave the shop in such quantities. We had boxes under the counter and people were coming in every two or three minutes and buying albums. For an Irish band, for an independent band who'd done everything themselves, that was pretty amazing. (ibid.)

Having a graphic designer (Charles O'Connor) in the band helped. The Horslips debut, *Happy to Meet – Sorry to Part* (1972), came in a fold-out, die-cut cardboard sleeve shaped like a concertina. This was new Irish music, a fusion of the old and the modern, and it was sophisticated and savvy and offered no apologies. Horslips were confident cultural entrepreneurs.

Horslips' accomplishments were many. While their success was notable, their influence on Irish rock was perhaps even greater. They proved that a locally based rock group could compete not just in Ireland but internationally. They accomplished this initially with their DIY label, OATS, and later with major labels abroad. In doing so, they demonstrated that Irish rock musicians could participate meaningfully in their own careers. *The Man Who Built America* (1979) was an album about emigration by a band that had managed to stay at home. This set the tone for Irish rock acts who followed them, and the members of Horslips continued to influence the development of Irish rock in highly significant ways.

6 U2: Local and Global

In September 2014, U2 collaborated with the Apple corporation and released their new album exclusively, and free of charge, to iTunes users. Two months later, *Rolling Stone* magazine asked the band's singer about what it described as 'an instant, noisy, sometimes kinda-hysterical backlash' to the release (Hiatt 2014: 57). Bono responded:

> In America you look up at the mansion on the hill and you say, 'One day, if I work really hard, I might get to live there'. In Ireland, particularly in Dublin, you look at the mansion and you say, 'One day, I'm going to get that bastard'. That's a great preparation for life on the internet. (Hiatt 2014: 57)

It is interesting that when Bono represented the difference between local Irish culture and America's celebration of success, he feels Dublin's 'school of hard knocks' provided a good training for the globally interconnected culture of the 21st century. This invites some key questions. What was U2's early experience with their local music scene? How were they supported or hampered? What allies did they find, and how did they impact on the band's development?

This is particularly important because the *Rolling Stone* article represents the two worlds in almost binary-opposite terms: the centralized music industry of major labels, stars and plentiful resources; and the local scene with limited resources. The magazine depicts U2 now within the concentrated, yet powerful, centre of the global music industry along with their many collaborators, both musical and entrepreneurial. These include their former and current business managers and their business allies including 'Steve Jobs [former Apple CEO] ... [who] was a close friend' (Hiatt 2014: 58). Their achievement as 'the biggest band left on Earth' (Hiatt 2014: 54) provides them with a lifestyle complete with 'a vintage Epiphone Casino guitar' (Hiatt 2014: 56), Bono's 'Maserati sedan' and personal assistant (Hiatt 2014: 57) and their villas on the French Riviera, 'bought for $3 million ... apparently worth far more now' (Hiatt 2014: 61). In direct contrast to this world, the band's early days are recalled: 'driving around in an orange VW Beetle, the Edge's mom, [Gwenda Evans] at the wheel – "she was our first roadie" – with rolls of wallpaper advertising U2' (Hiatt 2014: 57). While no magazine story, or even book, can tell the full story of any artist, the magazine – by identifying the band's friends and business allies, and the crossover between them – highlights the collaborative culture of the music industry. In both the local music scene and the centralized music industry, the band have benefited from collaborating with allies, from the guitarist's mother to some of the world's most powerful corporate titans.

How U2 Stayed at Home

By 1985, Irish rock music was being feted nationally and globally. The industry indicators of commercial success were evident: by February two U2 albums, *War* and *The Unforgettable Fire*, had sold in excess of a million copies each in the US. By July that year, the band had another million-seller, the mini-album, *Under A Blood Red Sky* (RIAA certifications). To understand how U2 became so commercially successful, their early career needs to be placed in the context of the assistance they received from entrepreneurs in the local music scene. While it was a British label, Island, which released their records and successfully promoted them, it was the Dublin music scene's distinctive characteristics that sustained them until they signed with Island.

Barbara Bradby (1989) wrote of the need to examine the sociological reality behind the success narrative of U2. She rejected the simplistic explanations that are often given for cultural production. Clearly, artistic output is a product of a collective activity. U2's early trips to London provide an insight into the value of a local supportive network. Bono, in the official U2 account, depicts how in April 1979 he travelled to London in an attempt to attract media interest; the singer was accompanied by his girlfriend, Alison Stewart. In fact, she played a significant role in the business trip – she financed it. As Bono later recalled: 'Ali paid for all this, by the way, I had no money' (Bono et al. 2006: 76). The local media provided another source of financial support: *Hot Press* magazine reportedly offered to pay him if he reviewed a London gig for them (Graham 1989: 35). During the excursion, they met with Phil Chevron from The Radiators from Space whom Bono described as 'very helpful'; 'he pointed us in the direction of a couple of music journalists he thought were good' (Bono et al. 2006: 76). One of the journalists recommended by Chevron played a major role in raising the young U2's profile. *Record Mirror*'s Chris Westwood, was, according to Bono's account, 'extremely generous', 'he was the most encouraging of them all'. Westwood even wrote a front-page cover story on the band in the 10 November 1979 issue. This enhanced their reputation and was a huge source of prestige for an unsigned Dublin band.

To capitalize on this momentum, and to try to make more influential friends, the band planned another London trip in 1979. This time it wasn't just Bono and his girlfriend: the band were going to perform. Because U2 and their manager themselves couldn't afford the costs, the trip was going to be funded by the London industry-insider, Bryan Morrison (Bono et al. 2006: 84). He had negotiated a publishing deal with the band's manager; in return for a share of their future song-writing royalties, he was going to pay the band approximately £3,000. U2 had accepted the deal because they 'were so desperate' (Bono et al. 2006: 84). But just before the London trip, something profound happened, and the implications are almost incalculable. According to U2, Morrison had phoned the band and had reduced the amount he was willing to pay them to £1,500. It was a small amount of money, but it had massive financial implications for all of them. The Edge summed up the transaction:

> We were going to sell our publishing rights for a pittance for the next twenty years or something. It was a pretty crap deal and, at the very last minute, knowing that we had this tour booked, he made it worse. So we basically told him to stuff it up his arse. (Bono et al. 2006: 84)

The band desperately needed to get to London. Momentum is vital in the commercial music industry. U2 were booked to play concerts in London, and had invited key London gatekeepers, including A&R scouts from major labels, to see them, so the band frantically searched for alternative ways to fund the trip. Their manager, Paul McGuinness, recalled: 'I borrowed some money from Seamus Byrne and Tiernan MacBride, who were film colleagues'; the remainder was borrowed from the band members' parents (Bono et al. 2006: 84). The importance of this financial wrangling has never been adequately explored in the context of U2's success narrative. Depending on what percentage of the band's royalties he was acquiring, the loss in revenue to Morrison was probably, in the long term, worth tens of millions, and perhaps even more.

The £3,000 that Morrison was offering the band for the publishing share was instead provided, without strings, by the band's supportive local Dublin network, which, by doing so, saved them from signing away a portion of their song-writing royalties. Because these types of deal are generally for the life of the copyright, Morrison's attempt to save about £1,500 had cost him tens of millions. It was one of the greatest mistakes in the history of popular music.

DIY: Steve Averill Subverting the Core-to-Periphery Flow from the Outside

Phil Chevron clearly helped U2 by providing introductions to key London industry gatekeepers that resulted in a music magazine front cover. This wasn't the only assistance the band received from members of The Radiators from Space. In a small music scene like the one in Dublin, getting support and advice from other bands could make a significant difference. Before this, The Radiators themselves had benefited from the supportive network available to *them* in Dublin. Their initial development was aided by both Horslips and Thin Lizzy and their allies. Their early recordings were financed by Eamon Carr from Horslips and Jackie Hayden from CBS (Ireland) and had attracted the hip Chiswick record label to the band (Hayden 2012). Subsequently, Chiswick's London-based, Irish-born, proprietors, Ted Carroll and Roger Armstrong, had supported the band financially. In turn, The Radiators became part of a supportive network available to the next wave of Irish bands.

Steve Averill from The Radiators played a number of key roles in the early development of U2. The band's first interview in *Hot Press* magazine was published in April 1978, when Bill Graham perceptively highlighted how the local scene, the site of collaborative and co-operative, as well as competitive activity, was tightly networked, in part because some influential individuals played multiple roles within it. He wrote:

> ... moreover, in the small world of Irish rock, roles get duplicated. Besides being a fan, one ends up as some species of friend and adviser. (Graham 1979: 9)

Graham was referring to himself; he was both a journalist as well as a fan and an adviser to U2 and other bands. Similarly, previously, before he became their full-time manager, Fachtna O'Kelly had been both a journalist and an adviser to The Boomtown Rats. In his U2 article, Graham described Steve Averill as a 'mentor (though not a manager)' to U2 (Graham 1979: 9); U2 were already building their own supportive network within the local scene.

In their official self-representation, *U2 by U2* (Bono et al. 2006), the band acknowledged the importance of Averill to their development. He is credited as 'the man responsible for U2's graphic output from their first poster' (Bono et al. 2006: 351). This alone would make him a significant figure, yet his involvement went beyond his graphic design and aesthetic input. Adam Clayton, who had initially acted as the band's manager and was a highly active networker on the band's behalf, is quoted:

> Steve Averill was the son of a friend of my parents ... he had been in The Radiators From Space ... he was someone who knew the ropes ... probably ten years older than us ... I would walk over to his house ... His wife would normally give me coffee or something to eat and we'd listen to music and talk. It's amazing now when I look back,

> a guy that age talking to a teenager for a few hours on his night off after he'd been at work. That was a very generous thing to do … He started to suggest that we think about what we wore, told us we needed to get some photographs done and he subsequently designed our first poster … (Bono et al. 2006: 44)

Averill also recommended changing the band name from The Hype, as they were then called. He even provided them with a specific name, U2 (Bono et al. 2006: 44) and organized their first photo shoot (Bono et al. 2006: 52). He was not just a key contributor to U2; he was also a bridge between them and the Dublin underground DIY music scene. The former Trinity College entertainments officer, Kieran Owens, who featured prominently in the local scene as manager of The Virgin Prunes and The Fountainhead, recalled the creative ethos of that culture. He argued that the 1977 Irish music scene witnessed:

> the beginning of another extraordinary era of self-promoted [music activity], and it was all in the DIY-punk ethos if you like, fanzines… [etc] (Averill 2012)

The Irish fanzine culture has been well-documented by Anto Dillon (2003) and Ciarán Ryan (2020); Dublin had a small number of creative fanzines during the punk/new wave era between 1976 and 1984, most of which were enabled by another recent technological innovation, the office photocopier. Self-financed and self-published, the fanzines provided interviews and reviews and actively encouraged participation in the scene. The first of these in the punk era, *Raw Power*, was issued in March 1977 by Averill. It was inspired by the new English punk fanzines including *Sniffin' Glue*, which was being encouraged by Ted Carroll in London. Averill recalls: 'We saw *Sniffin' Glue* was around and we thought this is a great communications tool for our fans' (Averill 2012). Averill's fanzine embodied and transmitted the DIY ethos. *Raw Power*'s debut issue urged readers:

> And most of all don't sit around doing nothing. If you want to see these bands let them know, if you're in school organise a dance, get them to play. Form your own bands if you don't like any around at the moment. Write your own fanzine so that other people will know that there are others around like them. Don't follow fashions, start your own. But do something positive NOW. (Averill 1977: 2)

Raw Power was quickly followed on the Dublin scene by another stylish and accomplished fanzine, *Heat*, issued in July 1977 by Pete Price and Jude Carr. Averill also made contributions to it. Both publications were well-designed and were arguably more legible and more visually appealing than many of their British contemporaries. They continually advocated the DIY ethic and challenged standard commercial music industry practice and orthodoxy. Averill's multiple roles in the Dublin music community made him a very important connecting node in the local network. He was not only a significant figure as a catalyst and mentor, but also embedded counter-hegemonic, collaborative DIY principles.

The music industry can be better understood when the activities of people behind-the-scenes are included. In many respects, Averill indicates how it is possible to sustain a role in the music scene without possessing musical qualifications. He recalled:

> I also knew very early on from doing guitar lessons that I had no musical aptitude. So, you try to find a role for yourself in that [scene] ... I ended up ... doing light shows for bands and things like that and getting involved in various ways, putting people together. (Averill 2012)

In addition to doing light shows, being a graphic designer, working in the Golden Disc record shop in Liffey Street and publishing fanzines, Averill assembled and was a member of The Radiators from Space. His role of 'getting involved in various ways, putting people together' in Dublin is evident in his role with another Dublin band, The Boy Scoutz:

> I had kind of got involved with The Boy Scoutz and given them the name, put an ad in one of the fanzines and said 'look you girls should be doing it as well'. I got four girls together. I more or less said 'look, I don't want to be Kim Fowley [the manipulative manager of all-female band, The Runaways]. I just want to get you together and I want to step away from the whole thing'. So I did, I let them get on with what they were doing. (ibid.)

Averill was both a commercially minded full-time businessperson and an active, encouraging member of Dublin's supportive network for young artists. He was also active in the more standard profit-driven music industry environment by designing artwork, including U2's, for international labels.

Jackie Hayden... Subverting the Industry Core-to-Periphery Flow from Within

As this case shows, the world of the DIY collaborative music scene often overlaps with the commercial realm of the for-profit music industry. In practice, they do not always represent binary opposites. While U2 were accessing

Averill's subcultural capital from the DIY fanzine world, they were also accessing the networks of full-time music-industry insiders. One of these, Jackie Hayden, was familiar with Averill and, like Averill, had also participated in both the supportive local network *and* the centralized music industry. He had formed a local independent label, Midnite, with Eamon Carr from Horslips and had released music by The Radiators from Space. Generously, the Dublin-based label then allowed the band to sign to Chiswick in London. At the time Hayden held a full-time position with CBS Records. As one of Ireland's few music industry members, he was frequently a judge in talent contests. On one significant occasion he was a judge in a talent show won by U2 in Limerick. One of the prizes, the option of recording with CBS (Ireland), was declined by the band, although they sought Hayden's advice on a number of occasions. He subsequently recalled his early contact with them:

> And I remember Adam Clayton saying to me 'If we turn this [the CBS (Ireland) recording] down does that mean you'll never talk to us again'. I said 'not really, it's not that important. I have a good job and I'm not going to take it personally'. They then kept coming into my office and they would have questions for me. That's really what stands out. They would ask me about the business. They wanted to know things like: How does the record get into record shops? Who decides what gets played on the radio? How do you make money out of songwriting? What's publishing about? You know, that kind of stuff. I presume they were asking other people these questions as well and not just me. (Hayden 2012)

The Limerick talent contest had provided U2 with an important industry contact. It also gave them a 'point of interest' for the local music scene. It was that boast, 'the winners of the talent contest', that prompted Bill Graham to meet the band, according to his recollection in *U2, the Early Days* (1989). Graham then connected U2 with their future manager, Paul McGuinness, a friend from his student days in Trinity College Dublin.

Although the CBS headquarters in London declined to sign U2, despite making a demo recording with them, Hayden was able to persuade the British office to allow him to sign the band to an Ireland-only deal. His promotion of their debut release became a significant element in U2's success narrative and was used to attract more industry attention. Hayden suggested to the band and their newly appointed manager, Paul McGuinness:

> could we do a deal where you sign for the rest of world with another label – none of our business, but stay with CBS [in Ireland]? And the deal was worked out ... (Hayden 2012)

Although CBS international had passed on the band, the perceived success of the single released by the local CBS branch in Ireland attracted the attention of London industry gatekeepers and Hayden's promotion of the single in Ireland certainly contributed to the band signing a deal with Island in London. This was a productive, yet unexpected, flow between the industries in London and Dublin. In the U2 case, the usual centralizing music industry process was short-circuited by individuals and their actions at the local level. Even before this, Hayden and the Irish branch of CBS had supported local talent by releasing singles by Irish acts:

> We were doing that [releasing singles by Irish acts] in spite of the fact that we were repeatedly lied to by CBS UK, who in other respects were very good to work for. They didn't interfere, they would give you a target of monthly sales figures to achieve and a budget and they'd let you get on with it ... But this was happening against the backdrop of the Troubles in the North. (Hayden 2012)

For Hayden and the CBS staff in Dublin, the political situation and violence in Ireland naturally had implications:

> And we had had a number of threatening phone calls to the office which we knew might have been wind-ups. But we were very conscious that here we were making a lot of money in Ireland out of selling records for what people would have assumed was a British company even though ultimately CBS was American. And we thought 'well even as a PR exercise and to be seen to be putting something back into Irish music, it would be great if we only put out a single or something every month to make some gesture'. (Hayden 2012)

The promotion of local acts was designed by Hayden as a relationship-building exercise with Irish music scene:

> I justified making these records out of our marketing budget because this is part of a PR exercise, it is doing us good as well as keeping us from being shot or whatever might have been behind those threats. So, it made sense on a number of levels. (Hayden 2012)

The response from the London office of CBS was less than supportive, however. Hayden and the CBS (Ireland) staff were threatened with dismissal if they continued recording and releasing Irish product. From a corporate point of view, they were misusing funds that had been allocated for the promotion of product that had been selected by CBS's London headquarters. Apparently, the firm's global decision-makers had decided to limit their activities to spending money in Ireland only on product of non-Irish origin.

Hayden described the power-struggle between the London and Dublin CBS office and recounted how the London office reinforced the message to Dublin: 'you don't have A&R (artist and repertoire) function. You have no right to be signing acts' (Hayden 2012). If the Irish branch lacked the ability to sign or release artists, it also lacked meaningful input into the centralized A&R decision-making in England. Hayden recollected during an interview: 'they [CBS London] had completely turned down without any interest as far as I can remember Horslips, Chris de Burgh, The Boomtown Rats and actually just about anyone we'd offered them, they'd actually said no to'. He also recalled promises made to the Dublin staff that if they achieved certain sales-targets, they would be permitted to release local product:

> 'When you get to such and such level then we'll give you a budget'. But when we would get to that level, they still wouldn't give us the budget. So we were very frustrated about this. But we were cocky enough to think 'the company is doing well, what are they going to do? Are they really going to fire us because we put out a single by Reform that cost a couple of hundred quid to make?' (Hayden 2012)

When Hayden did sign U2 for CBS (Ireland) he used his marketing skills and local network to draw attention to the release. He engaged very productively with some of the recently arrived media outlets, including RTÉ Radio 2's *Dave Fanning Show* and *Hot Press*. He felt a limited edition of 1,000 individually numbered 12-inch singles would attract interest:

> Then we hit on the idea of getting Dave Fanning to play the three tracks so the listeners could pick the [A-side of the] record which to us was, basically, a way of getting airplay. ... And I think around that time I'd arranged a cover of *Hot Press* and an ad on the back for the single as well. This was a whole big thing in *Hot Press* who'd previously written about them anyway, Bill Graham was a big fan, Niall Stokes [*Hot Press* editor] was a big fan. Back then if you got Dave Fanning and *Hot Press* aboard what was to stop you? (Hayden 2012)

Via the supportive local network, U2 had found a key ally in Hayden, and that relationship, through both U2's and Hayden's networks in Dublin, brought the band to a wider audience. But even before the band signed with CBS (Ireland) and then Island in London, they had benefited from the other forms of supportive entrepreneurship in the local Dublin music scene.

Advancing 'New Forms of Irish Culture': The Dandelion, Hot Press and the Pirates

U2 also engaged productively with the Dublin music scene's DIY activity in other ways, and even used some of the elements of that DIY activity in their global self-representation. This can be seen in one of their earliest syndicated interviews in the US:

> We used to play in a car park (indoor parking lot) on Saturday afternoons in the city centre. Four walls, roof, floor, 700 people crowded in there at 3.00 in the afternoon. That caused a bit of excitement. (Arar 1981: 48)

The Dandelion Market's mythic status indicates how Ireland's capital city suffered from a lack of professional promoters and regular concerts. The seriously underdeveloped rock music scene required entrepreneurial innovation to sustain it. The Dandelion venue, thanks to its organizer, John Fisher, provided new Irish acts, from both sides of the border, with an opportunity to appear before a younger audience. Bands that played there included DC Nien, The Outcasts, Zebra, The Strougers, and Square Meal. Unlike the few pubs that hosted gigs at the time, there were no age restrictions at the Dandelion because the concerts were alcohol-free events. The city centre venue operated from April 1979 to March 1980 and hosted almost 90 gigs. Its activities were curtailed on occasion by factors specific to Ireland, including public bus strikes and the pope's Irish visit. The gigs were run on a DIY collective basis. As Bono mentioned to the US media (Arar 1981), the bands had to arrive early and help to assemble the stage for the performance; the admission charge was 50 pence which went to the bands (Fisher 2021).

Fisher was part of the new generation of Irish entrepreneurs who were both inspired by, and found, market opportunities in rock music and youth culture. In his account, a journey to England for the Reading and Knebworth music festivals in 1976 prompted Fisher and his business partner, Eoin O'Shea, to address the needs and desires of Ireland's growing youth population. They returned to Dublin with rucksacks filled with rock band badges and opened a market stall, Sticky Fingers, in the Dandelion Market. To attract more customers, they launched a series of weekend concerts at the market. The venue, such as it was, was 'the one vacant area in the market – an enclosed dark, dank shed that housed the power supply for the whole market' (Fisher 2021). Few music fans who attended gigs between 1976 and 1982 will disagree with Patrick Brocklebank's and Sinéad Malony's (2013: 15) observation that Dublin's venues at the time were 'oftentimes makeshift sweatboxes'.

However, the makeshift nature of these venues, and the do-it-yourself enterprise of the local rock scene, did foster a spirit of collaboration between some Dublin bands.

Another significant change in the local scene was the emergence of new media outlets. The magazine *Hot Press*, founded in 1977, was edited by Niall Stokes, who had earlier documented the precarious state of the domestic music scene in other Irish newspapers and magazines. *Hot Press* was socially progressive, very overtly youth-centric and provided extensive and in-depth coverage of local and international artists, as well as political commentary and interviews. In tone and style, it was closer to America's *Rolling Stone* than to the British music weeklies. McLaughlin and McLoone described its launch as 'arguably the most important development in popular music culture' at the time (2012: 120). At the same time other key Irish print media outlets were also taking rock music far more seriously than it ever had been taken before. Local bands were reviewed and interviewed by a wave of young journalists such as Joe Breen at the *Irish Times* and Brian Bell at the *Irish Press*. In fact, U2 and their contemporaries enjoyed press attention that hadn't been available to Thin Lizzy, Rory Gallagher and Horslips. At the same time, new publications like *In Dublin* and *Vox* (2019 reissue, O'Neill, editor) were also treating youth culture seriously. The latter was a fanzine with high production values and featured the more cutting-edge local and international acts. It championed The Virgin Prunes, Stano, DC Nien, and gave early coverage to U2.

Beyond the printed publications, other mainstream media were also important to the young bands of the 1976–1982 era. This was a time when even new and challenging acts could secure major national television exposure. Ferdia Mac Anna was one key individual who was playing multiple roles in the Dublin music scene, and he effectively bridged the gap between the young musicians and the local media. He was the lead singer with Rocky de Valera and The Gravediggers, whose raucous Dr Feelgood/Pirates sound stood out in the new wave scene. He worked with Fisher on his Dandelion market rock merchandise stall, and he was also involved with *In Dublin*, the local listings magazine in the style of London's *Time Out*, which devoted considerable space to film, theatre and music. The magazine was a progressive voice in a conservative country, and it generated a bit of controversy. The Dublin band DC Nien recalled being given the front cover of one issue:

> We were photographed naked and had our genitals airbrushed out. That was our little homage to Kraftwerk because we wanted to look like the robots. So we said, 'we'll make ourselves sexless' and that was where that idea came from. That caused uproar. I actually had

> to go around to my local shops and buy all the copies of the magazine so the neighbours wouldn't see it. (Seales 2012)

Mac Anna was also encouraging other local acts including Stano, who was making challenging post-punk music, although with decidedly unpunk layers of piano and disembodied voices. He recalled how Mac Anna's 1982 *In Dublin* interview with him led to a surge of interest in his work and offers from labels and publishers (Stano 2011). Always on the lookout for venues to host young acts, Mac Anna played in the local community centre in Howth with The Gravediggers (Mac Anna 2006: 199). Soon afterwards he was phoned by Larry Mullen who was searching for venues for U2 to play in. Mac Anna provided him with the promoter's phone number. Soon afterwards, he was hired by the *Late Late Show* as a programme researcher. Interestingly, Mac Anna (2018) recalled being hired because he expressed his disinterest in the programme to the show's host, Gay Byrne.

> ... the reason I got the job in the *Late Late Show* was I said I hated the *Late Late Show* and I wouldn't watch it. I had no interest in it. That's why Gay Byrne gave me the job.

This was the counterculture, in a relatively uncompromising way, altering Ireland's cultural landscape. Representing the youthful energy of the local post-punk music scene, Mac Anna felt he 'had a mission in a way to replace showbands on the *Late Late*, because there were always showbands on it' (ibid.). Today, it seems absolutely out of the question for young avant-garde bands to get on the country's premier family television show. Yet Mac Anna managed to negotiate places for The Virgin Prunes and Steve Averill's band Tell Tale Heart. Despite these counter-cultural victories, Mac Anna had to lobby for U2 to be on the show and remembers encountering resistance to the then relatively unknown band and other youthful acts:

> I remember suggesting that U2 come on, and Gaybo had no interest, he didn't want them because they were young. But then once he met them, he thought that they were absolutely charming. (Mac Anna 2018)

U2, as Bill Graham observed (1989: 10), were skilled at getting people to 'discover' them. The small size of the Dublin music scene meant that bands and managers were accessible. The members of U2, while keeping their distance from some of the other Dublin bands who socialized in the central and upmarket Bailey pub, sought out local band managers to enhance their network and their industry knowledge. Both Billy McGrath (McGrath 2013), who managed The Atrix, and Kieran Owens, who managed The Fountainhead and The Virgin Prunes, recalled U2 attending meetings with them. Owens (2012) even remembered Bono showing up at one of the first business meetings he had with The Virgin Prunes; he apparently wanted to know what Owens could do for The Prunes, and to understand how he did business. Understanding, and being comfortable with, the business side of music was a good training for U2's later career in the highly visible, and volatile, global social media landscape.

While, perhaps inevitably, the majority of the people they sought advice and insight from were men, it is worth noting that it was a female promoter, Elvera Butler, in Cork, who delivered them to large concert audiences before they signed a record deal. With a very distinctive and community-focused way of conducting business, Butler showed that the Cork music scene was populated by individuals with creative and counter-cultural approaches. This was an era when ambitious young entrepreneurs entered the local music industry in search of profits, and some succeeded handsomely. At the same time, others invested their enterprise skill by supporting music talent and building the scene by operating with community-enriching goals. The Irish music scene in the 1976–1982 period was a site of innovation and enterprise; there were many overlaps between it and the worlds of business, counterculture and DIY. The impact of Butler and other individuals who straddled the industry and the scene will be examined in the next chapter.

The era's pirate radio stations were even more counter-cultural, at least in the legal sense, than *Hot Press* or *In Dublin*; their activities were both entrepreneurial and illegal. Worryingly for the Irish establishment, they were also very popular. Although subject to frequent police visits and the confiscation of their equipment, the pirates found an eager listenership in Dublin's youth. By 1979, there were 25 stations on the air, although some had very limited broadcasting range. Like *Hot Press*, the popular pirate stations featured a mix of international and local acts. The best-known stations attracted both significant market share and loyalty; Radio Dublin claimed it had 30 per cent of Dublin's audience (Morash 2010: 187). It certainly had widespread and visible supporters; 10,000 people took to the streets to protest a 1978 police raid on the station (Morash 2010: 187).

While the pirates were not beyond the reach of the law and were eventually suppressed, their enterprise proved that a demand existed for adventurous popular music broadcasting. The national broadcaster responded by launching RTÉ Radio 2 in May 1979. The new service recruited a number of ex-pirates and had an emphasis on, although not a total commitment to, youth and contemporary popular music. This reactive policy is consistent with Morash's (2010) conclusion about the subdued launch of RTÉ's new television channel a year earlier. He felt this 'demonstrated once again the nagging sense that the media provided by the State could not cope with the new forms of Irish culture' (2010: 189). That conclusion can partially be explained by the cultural distance between the Irish establishment and the large youth population. The entrepreneurs who *could* 'cope with the new forms of Irish culture' were young, and a large proportion of them came from the ranks of the elected representatives of Irish university student unions. As we will examine in the next chapter, they formed a very effective bridge between the DIY scene and the music industry and enabled some of Ireland's most notable rock music successes.

7 How Teenagers and Students Shaped Ireland's Culture

Both the Irish music industry, with a profit motive, and the Irish music scene, with a community focus, were guided and driven in crucial ways and at key moments by young people. That is a good reminder that music is an aspect of culture where youth can actively participate, and not just as consumers. A small number of such music-loving entrepreneurs were instrumental in developing Ireland's live music industry during the punk/new wave movement of 1976–1984. They also played a vital role in the early development of both The Boomtown Rats and U2. The Boomtown Rats' Bob Geldof spearheaded the Live Aid concert in July 1985, at which U2 appeared in what the Irish media theorist Christopher Morash (2010: 199) argued was a vital 'sudden shift'. To him, the Irish, culturally, were transformed from 'a feeling of belatedness' to appreciating 'the potential of new media technologies to reverse this feeling of Irish peripherality'. It was a transformation shaped by young entrepreneurs who understood counter-cultural rock. Previously, Irish culture, not only in music, had generally been determined by older men who had firm ideas of what young people *needed*. So, it was a paradigm shift when young people decided what *they wanted*.

This key cultural moment when young entrepreneurs were actively shaping the framework of live music in Ireland can be placed in the context of the post-1976 emergence of punk music and do-it-yourself enterprise. In the Irish case, this had implications beyond the music scene. The Irish author, Dermot Bolger (2021), recalled part of the inspiration behind his book-publishing venture, launched in the Dublin working-class suburb of Finglas:

> Raven Arts Press sprang from the punk explosion of 1977. If young people could start punk bands in sheds without knowing how to play their instruments, it seemed natural for us – with no money or knowledge of publishing, and indeed no actual shed – to start a publishing house as a platform for anyone who felt marginalised. (2021: 265)

The collective proceeded to publish books by authors including Colm Tóibín, Patrick McCabe, Sara Berkeley and Fintan O'Toole.

Part-time Promoters: The Ents Entrepreneurs of the 1970s

The Irish music industry transformation between the mid-1970s and 1985 was underpinned by demographics. The steep increase in birth rates during that period resulted in a larger and younger population. By 1984, almost 40 per cent of the Irish population was under 20 years of age (McDonald 2011: 190). The pop music output of the period was both youthful and successful. In the 1980s, local acts weren't just having occasional pop hits; they were achieving high sales of albums in some of the world's biggest markets. Irish pop music was now part of the national cultural conversation and some of the most important acts were being managed by a new generation of Irish pop entrepreneurs. Very significantly, the Irish acts that achieved the biggest success in the 1980s were managed by Irish managers.

Five of the new Irish pop managers were particularly significant and made a sustained impact on both the local and global music industries: Fachtna O'Kelly, Paul McGuiness, Dave Kavanagh, and the Nicky and Roma Ryan husband-and-wife team. They guided a wide range of Irish acts to international acclaim, including The Boomtown Rats, Sinéad O'Connor, U2, Enya, and Clannad. The range of the acts was considerable, and they communicated a very sophisticated and complex idea of Ireland: introvert and extrovert, ultramodern and drawing from tradition.

O'Kelly was the first of them to bring an act to the top of the British charts. He had been writing news stories for the *Irish Press* since the early 1970s and had inserted reviews of the underground rock scene into the pages of the large-selling but conservative paper. His music taste was counter-cultural, and he wasn't afraid to criticize the Irish music industry establishment. In 1974, he claimed that the showband 'businessmen' had 'done many great disservices to music over the past 20-odd years'. Ireland now had a new generation of music entrepreneurs with their own voice and perspective. He then began advising and managing Clannad before proving that young Irish acts, singing their own songs, could top the British charts. He achieved this with The Boomtown Rats and later managed Sinéad O'Connor. Paul McGuinness managed the hugely successful U2; Nicky and Roma Ryan formed an alliance with Enya, while Dave Kavanagh managed Clannad at their commercial peak. Later, in partnership with Paul McGuinness and the Celtic Heartbeat label, Kavanagh was responsible for marketing the music from the *Riverdance* show. No group of domestic managers has since emerged with anything approaching the success of this five-person generation. Not only was their success unprecedented; up to the current time it has not been repeated. It is also noteworthy that apart from O'Kelly, who moved to London in 1976–1977, they were all domestically based.

The prescient *Hot Press* journalist Bill Graham (1989: 19) argued that from 1977 'a small cabal of graduates' from Ireland's universities 'emerge[d] as the new leadership' of the domestic industry. He listed the prime movers in this group as Niall and Dermot Stokes from *Hot Press* magazine, the music industry accountant Ossie Kilkenny, RTÉ's Dave Fanning, Clannad's manager, Dave Kavanagh, James Morris and Meiert Avis from Windmill Lane studios, and Billy McGrath, who managed bands, produced television shows and later shaped the local stand-up comedy scene.

Graham was intimately familiar with the small group of individuals who represented the 'new leadership' of the Irish music industry. In fact, he was a member of it himself. Irish rock, at this key stage in its development, was helped by a small group of former student union officials from the country's universities elected during the 1970s. They were small in number, yet they pushed the local rock scene in a direction that enabled local acts to develop and find an audience, and they also stimulated the growth in live gigs with important visiting acts. In this way they were a vital force in the modernization of Ireland's culture and media. We will label these university student union innovators as 'ents entrepreneurs'.

Graham recognized early in his student days that he could actively participate in shaping local culture by organizing concerts in Dublin. In the mid-1970s, while he was a student in Trinity he had volunteered to help organize campus entertainment. Other key ents entrepreneurs included Elvera Butler in Cork, Ollie Jennings in Galway, and two of Graham's Trinity college colleagues, Ian Wilson and Kieran Owens. Dave Kavanagh and Billy McGrath graduated from UCD student's union positions to the local entertainment industry; so did Charlie McNally, the president of UCD's student union in 1976–1977. Later, McNally promoted rock concerts in Dublin, often in collaboration with Paul Tipping, who had been the Trinity College Ents Officer in 1977–1978.

This group of ents entrepreneurs was particularly significant during the 1976–1981 period. Their student union roles coincided with the arrival of a new generation of bands labelled punk or new wave. It was a major cultural change for Ireland to welcome a significant number of new overseas bands who were succeeding in the sales charts. Fortunately for them, the ents entrepreneurs found some very significant Irish-born, London-based, allies to help them to bring these new bands to Ireland (M. Murphy 2014).

Paul Charles was one of the earliest music-business figures in England to appreciate the new punk and new wave bands from a musical, cultural and business point of view (M. Murphy 2017). Born in Magherafelt, County Derry, he had tuned into Ireland's small counter-cultural music scene early on and had managed one of the country's few notable progressive rock bands, Fruupp. Decamping to London, he had become a booking agent and arranged tours for Buzzcocks and other new bands. He began getting requests for the new bands from ents officers on both sides of the border in Ireland. When those bands expressed anxiety about travelling to Ireland, he explained:

> ... the students' gigging circuit in Ireland is great, it's the place where people from both sides [of the religious divide] come together to listen to music – you're totally safe'. (Charles 2016)

In the end, some of the bands agreed to tour in Ireland but with one condition. They insisted that Charles travel with them to prove that it *was* safe. He succeeded in bringing a new generation of bands to Ireland that influenced Ireland's young musicians, and he later credited the ents officers for making it possible to build a circuit of venues on both sides of the border. He recalled:

> ... it was a reliable circuit because it was the student's unions. Because it was connected with the different universities and colleges the money was safe. The organisation was safe in terms of you weren't going to get knocked back or anything. Because if you are going over to Ireland at that level and you lose one of your shows, your tour is immediately losing money. You really needed a reliable group of people. The social secretaries and the student's unions were all 100 per cent on the case. They were 100 per cent all great promoters. They were fans of music. And they all had that energy and enthusiasm, and they would go out and convert an audience to come and listen to these new bands we were booking. (Charles 2016)

Local acts as well as visiting bands benefited from the ents officers' dedication to bringing rock music to an Irish audience. Both The Boomtown Rats and U2 were helped in their local development by the ents entrepreneurs. In collaboration with Bob Geldof, and with UCD's student union resources, McGrath in 1976 organized the 'Falling Asunder' tour, featuring The Boomtown Rats, which reached its climax in Dublin's National Stadium. Soon after this, he promoted shows by Irish acts around the country and helped to solidify the circuit for live local rock music. He also managed Irish bands including Stagalee and The Atrix. The ents entrepreneurs often graduated into media production beyond the music scene. It is notable that McGrath, in addition to being a television and video producer, was also a stand-up comedian. He later became a key figure in developing Irish stand-up comedy into the multi-million-euro business that it has become.

In 1976 McGrath was succeeded as ents officer at UCD by Dave Kavanagh, who also played a key role in U2's early development and in fact became U2's Irish booking agent. For up-and-coming Irish rock acts, having an Irish-based booking agent with local knowledge was a serious boost. He didn't just book shows for U2; if the situation demanded, he also promoted those gigs. In 2014, Kavanagh recalled his role:

> I promoted the National Stadium gig in the spring of 1980 ... I said, 'We'll try the National Stadium. It's a big statement, it pitches the band on a certain level, and we'll invite all the record companies...' (Kavanagh 2014: 187)

McGrath with The Boomtown Rats, and Kavanagh with U2, proved that local rock bands could headline Dublin's major rock venues, such as they were, before they had international record deals. In terms of perception, this was a game-changer for both bands. It placed them in the company of successful visiting bands, and shortly after their gig U2 were offered, and signed, a long-term record deal with Island Records in London.

In addition to raising U2's live profile, the ents entrepreneurs were also responsible for U2's first appearance on an album. Charlie McNally, UCD student union president in 1976–1977, set up the Kick record label in 1979. Its debut release, *Just for Kicks*, was a compilation of emerging unsigned Dublin bands including U2. That said, the album worked better on paper than it did on vinyl and the label folded soon afterwards. But it was an example of local pop cultural entrepreneurs investing some resources in the local rock scene. That really mattered at a time when it wasn't always possible for young bands to find studios, sound engineers and producers, at rates they could afford.

Ian Wilson enabled bands like The Clash to perform in Trinity, where he was the Student Union President in 1977. He had also been a vital force as an ents officer. Soon afterwards, he played a crucial role in the development of Irish rock during the 1980s, when he selected and paid a large number of emerging Irish bands to record sessions for RTÉ's Dave Fanning's radio show (Gubbins and Ó Briain 2020). But, very significantly for the development of rock in Ireland, the new wave of ents entrepreneurs wasn't confined to Dublin. In Cork, Elvera Butler ran the Kampus venue with success and innovation (M. Murphy 2018). She was a dedicated supporter of local talent, and the venue had a sizeable impact on the Cork music community. Local acts were given prestigious opening slots with well-known international bands, and were also given free admission to the venue's gigs and were paid to do odd jobs at the venue. Butler took this social engagement a step further by recording four of those local bands and setting up a record label to promote them. The label, Reekus, became a vital conduit for Irish bands to record and be promoted. Well-regarded acts, including Microdisney, The Blades, Big Self, and Aslan, recorded for Reekus, and while Aslan soon signed with EMI, their story indicates how valuable the small number of local labels were for incubating domestic talent.

Aslan's home reputation never diminished despite a lack of overseas success. Between the summer of 1986 and the winter of 1988, they achieved ten Top 20 singles. Six of them made the Top 10. This level of success was close to U2's *Joshua Tree*-era commercial peak when seven of their singles reached the Irish Top 10, and generally number 1, during 1987 to 1989. But it is worth remembering that the Irish charts and airwaves at the time contained Dublin rock acts who succeeded globally as well as those who didn't.

Another ents entrepreneur, Ollie Jennings, progressed from promoting gigs in Galway to guiding local acts to domestic and overseas success. If the opinions of Dublin's cadre of rock columnists counted for anything, The Saw Doctors were Ireland's most unlikely pop stars. Yet, under Jennings's stewardship, the band not only became a formidable live attraction but also chart favourites. Their rural appeal never overshadowed their song-writing prowess and live diligence. 'I Useta Love Her', went to number 1 in the singles chart and stayed in the best-seller list for most of the year. It was one of nine hits The Saw Doctors enjoyed between the summer of 1990 and the winter of 1992.

While they were at university, the ents entrepreneurs of 1976–1984 existed on small budgets and under severe constraints. On-campus gigs were often frowned upon by the college authorities, who placed increasingly stringent restrictions on them. Yet the ents officers' efforts collectively made Ireland a far more gig-friendly country, and this encouraged more people to see live music by new bands. In an important sense they changed Irish culture, but they certainly didn't find the job easy. Elvera Butler was elected Ents Officer in University College Cork in 1976. Interestingly, her rival for the position, Eoghan O'Neill, also enjoyed a successful music industry career. He became a member of Moving Hearts. But Butler's career as a promoter didn't get off to the best start. Her first major undertaking, a concert in City Hall by Fairport Convention, was cancelled at the last minute. As the local newspaper reported (*Evening Echo* 1977), the English folk-rockers phoned Butler the night before the concert to cancel due to the 'reluctance' of one member of the band to travel to Ireland. Without a way to alert the music fans, Butler spent the evening at the venue handing out cash refunds to disappointed ticketholders. Thankfully, her next concert in City Hall (with The Stranglers) proved hugely successful, although the band's travelling entourage were intimidating to the young female promoter (M. Murphy 2018). New wave music had arrived in Ireland's major cities, thanks to the new wave of ents entrepreneurs who became a crucial bridge between the global music industry and the local scene. Ultimately, the scene provided the foundation for MCD concerts to grow into a multi-dimensional global powerhouse in live music.

Live Music and Ideology

While they were working as student entrepreneurs at their universities and colleges, the ents officers straddled the contract-driven music industry and the DIY scene. For savvy career-minded individuals it made sense to form alliances with the major promoters locally. Live Nation's John Reid, described in 2015 by one English newspaper (Blackhurst 2015) as 'the most powerful figure in Europe's booming live music industry', served as ents officer in Trinity in 1982–1983. Following this, he worked with the growing MCD firm, and as a tour manager and business manager to acts including Silent Running, Aslan, and Cactus World News. He emigrated to London and enjoyed a lengthy music-industry career with labels as well as live music promoters. While working in London and knowing that the Trinity Ball had one of the biggest talent budgets in Ireland at the time, he arranged for one of the acts he was working with to play there. The performance by Public Enemy in 1988 is often recalled as one of the key moments in Ireland's live music history.

The ents entrepreneurs of 1976–1981 made a lasting, and arguably, transformational, impression on the live music industry. Clearly, they existed in a place where the local scene and the global music industry met. Yet, for some young people in Ireland, including university entertainment's officers, the presentation of live music was part of an ideological worldview.

Not everyone in the local music scene was focused on global reach and business expansion. Some even experimented with alternatives to the centralized global music industry. The Hope Collective (M. Murphy 2016) sprang from Niall McGuirk's grassroots, punk rock, photocopied-fanzine ethos in the mid-1980s. He recalled in an interview (McGuirk 2011):

> … for me music was never just about entertainment. It was a way of maybe effecting change … around that time the miners were on strike [in England], so it was quite a political time. A lot of bands were political anyway. That would have been the kind of stuff I was interested in knowing about.

McGuirk pursued his interest in music, politics and social causes by producing and distributing his own fanzines and he later branched out into concert promotion. With a team of fellow volunteers, he operated the Hope

Collective (late 1980s to end of the 1990s) and promoted concerts by bands including Fugazi, Babes in Toyland, Bis, No Means No, Quicksand, NOFX, Chumbawamba, and Green Day. While McGuirk was writing some of his first fanzine articles, in 1984 another young Dubliner, Michael McCaughan, was booking the entertainment for Trinity College Dublin. He recalled his student union organization:

> ... music was about more than just getting out of your head and having a good time; it had a message, meaning, relevance and revolutionary potential ... [Concert promotion in Trinity] was very much a co-operative effort ... it was run by volunteers ... it was their love of music that kept them going. (McCaughan 2009)

To him, the centralized global music industry provided resources to some acts. But more importantly, it denied them to other acts:

> ... bands were marginalised because they had no publicity machine. They had no machine behind them ... those bands like The Golden Horde, The Pleasure Cell and Those Handsome Devils, who were extraordinary bands, never got the exposure they deserved ... because they didn't belong to record companies ... (ibid.)

The Ents Entrepreneurs: 1984–1985

As seen earlier, McCaughan wasn't the first music-loving student elected to arrange entertainment for an Irish university or college. But the time of his 1984 election represents a moment in the history of university gigs before they became, for the most part, dependent on the country's major live music promoters, MCD and Aiken. McCaughan's concerts took place during an era when the ents officers were still dealing directly with London-based music agents and were *personally* deciding what music would be hosted on campus. In later years, the major Dublin corporate concert promoters typically established those contacts and made those decisions.

The vast majority of Ireland's entertainment officers are elected for a one-year term. In McCaughan's time, the ents entrepreneurs were close in nature to the local DIY music scene, yet they were capable of staging large-scale and generally well-run concerts. In the later 1970s, the UCD weekend gig was the biggest regular rock event in the country, while during the 1980s the annual Trinity Ball entertained up to 7,000 people (Flynn 1987).

When McCaughan, sporting a mohawk haircut and with an election manifesto in both English and Irish, was elected Ents Officer for Trinity College, he drew up ambitious plans for providing a variety of entertainment. His aim was to stage a wide range of events so that 'every student could experience the music they loved' (McCaughan 2009). There was a problem, however. And it was a major one. He recalled being informed that the student union was in deficit and very limited funds were available for the provision of entertainment. If there is a downside to having a new entertainments officer every year, it is that they enter an uncharted realm. Their initial budget is determined by forces beyond their control. Despite this, McCaughan quickly adjusted to the new constraints and gathered whatever resources he could. Like most ents officers, his first task was to assemble a group of student volunteers to work with.

McCaughan and his team worked on a low budget and with DIY principles. Despite this, a number of the bands that they provided with opportunities graduated from that small scene and engaged with the centralized global music industry. Even before the college term started and students returned to the campus, McCaughan ran a series of lunch-time concerts aimed at tourists. These twice-daily sessions featured Liam Ó Maoinlaí and Fiachna Ó Braonáin from the recently formed Hothouse Flowers. During his year in office, McCaughan provided paid performance opportunities to unsigned local acts including Cry Before Dawn and Luka Bloom, who, like Hothouse Flowers, later signed with major international labels. He recalled one unsigned singer arriving unannounced in his office:

> ... this waif-like teenager came in and politely but firmly asked me could she play a lunchtime gig. There was a label coming over from London that wanted to see her perform. And, I suppose, her attitude immediately impressed me. There weren't many women coming in like that, to push their own music, because it was a very macho/male world obviously ... I immediately said yes, because the lunchtime gig was something I had control over. (McCaughan 2009)

The singer, Sinéad O'Connor, was subsequently signed by the label who had wanted to see her perform.

By providing local acts with concerts at Trinity, McCaughan was increasing their possibilities of being noticed by the global industry. The way that his DIY scene interacted with the professional global industry could often be comical, however. He arranged the key Dublin date for The Pogues' first headlining tour of Ireland and later recalled the initial telephone negotiations with the band's manager, Frank Murray:

> I was telling him how much I loved the band, how important they were, how they were pushing the envelope of Irish culture, how

> I thought they could be huge. I was an enthusiastic fan really. He quickly stopped me. He only wanted to know one thing: 'how much will you pay us?' (ibid.)

One of the volunteers who helped McCaughan with gigs at Trinity wasn't even a student there. Colm Walsh designed posters for campus gigs and later managed the band, The Intoxicating Rhythm Section (IRS). U2's manager, Paul McGuinness, invited Walsh for a business meeting when the band began to develop a local reputation:

> So we had this meeting and Paul McGuinness came in and said very properly: 'Lads, first thing you're going to have to do is sack the drummer' ... [I responded] 'We can't sack the fucking drummer, the drummer is my best friend. I hang out in his house almost every night. Where am I going to go at night?' You know, which just shows the shocking naivety of our attitude. (Walsh 2010)

In this instance there was a disconnect between the profit-driven music industry and the more casual approach of the local music scene. But even when the scene and the industry have different values, the scene can provide significant support to artists who are on major labels, or who will later sign to them. The Pogues were already signed to Stiff Records when McCaughan promoted their concerts. As mentioned earlier, Hothouse Flowers, Cry Before Dawn, Luka Bloom and Sinéad O'Connor all signed to major global firms after playing at McCaughan's concerts. Other acts he promoted either signed with independent labels in Britain or remained unsigned. They included Five Go Down to the Sea, The Stars of Heaven, The Pleasure Cell, The Virgin Prunes, Those Handsome Devils, and The Golden Horde. This support of local acts happened at a time when music venues in Dublin were limited.

For ents officers like Michael McCaughan there was an almost ideological dedication to investing energy in the local scene and bypassing the actual industry where possible. He reflected on his approach:

> My aim was to make music approachable, accessible to everyone. Rock music wasn't about big business, it was about community, giving people opportunities. Although the Hope Collective didn't exist at the time, what I was trying to do was based on really similar values. (McCaughan 2009)

With that in mind, it is worth exploring how the not-for-profit Hope Collective operated, but also how it benefited from ents officers who invested time and energy in the local DIY scene.

The Hope Collective

The ents entrepreneurs may have had limited resources, but some of those resources were very useful and were accessible to people and causes outside of the university. During McCaughan's time as ents officer, he made the Trinity meeting rooms available to local community groups and he also made student union music equipment available to outside groups, including the local anti-apartheid movement and the Nicaragua Solidarity campaign, for fundraising activities. The Hope Collective that McCaughan spoke of had far fewer resources. But they did answer one question: 'What do you need to become a concert promoter and bring bands like Green Day, Chumbawamba, and Fugazi, to Ireland?' Most people would assume you need a venue, money to pay bands, probably some music-industry experience and maybe even an office. The Hope Collective had none of these. This was DIY run on a shoestring budget. It was also collective activity with imagination, creativity, passion and organization.

The collective's founder, Niall McGuirk, tells a funny story. He recalled a frantic phone conversation he received from Courtney Love (McGuirk 2010). She wanted her band, Hole, to play in Dublin and was trying to persuade him to arrange a concert for the band. The call took place in a payphone just off Dublin's busy O'Connell Street. Outside the public phone box impatient people were anxious for him to finish his call swiftly, while Love described her band, her aims and her desire to perform in Ireland. Generally, bands phoned McGuirk at home, where the phone was located in his parent's living room. When he was not at home, his only option was to make gig arrangements from busy public phone boxes. The Hope Collective didn't have access to venues, they didn't have an office, and they didn't have much money. In fact, they took what entrepreneurship textbooks would call 'a lean start-up' to the extreme.

In business terms, the Hope Collective's only assets were access to the McGuirk family phone and a desire to bring bands to Ireland. Despite this, it operated for over a decade from the late 1980s to the end of the 1990s. While some punk groups had agitated for the barrier between artists and audience to be broken down, the Hope Collective actively worked to break down the barrier between the *promoter* and the audience. The members of the collective, despite undertaking all the organization of their concerts, paid into the shows. They were, like everyone else at the gig, paying guests.

To the Hope Collective, the bands, promoters, and members of the public were all equally valued members of a community. As promoters, they wanted their activities to be transparent. Personal connections mattered and attempts were made to greet people as they arrived at gigs and to thank them as they left. McGuirk recalled:

> ... we went through a phase where we'd give out popcorn and sweets and stuff just to make it seem like: 'listen, you aren't just consumers at the gig – we're not promoters, we're all just people together'. (McGuirk 2010)

For another of the collective's members, Miriam Laird, it was important for attendees to know that Hope was a collective, not-for-profit concern and that profits either went to named charities or funded more gigs:

> We wanted people to be aware where the money was going, and that there wasn't a profit being made by us. It didn't go to our pocket. So, we always made it very clear where the money was going. (Laird 2011)

This openness and inclusiveness meant that membership of the collective evolved. The audience was literally invited to participate. The fanzine writer, Anto Dillon, learned about the Hope Collective via freesheets and fanzines in Dublin record shops. He went to some of the gigs, interviewed collective members for his own fanzine, *Loserdom*, and was invited to come to the collective's weekly meetings and to participate.

> I became involved that way ... We used to have cups of tea and vegan biscuits ... at the time I was only learning about stuff. I became a vegetarian shortly after. I used to hear about stuff like this [at the meetings] ... about John Pilger and political stuff, Noam Chomsky. (Dillon 2012)

In many ways, the Hope philosophy was grounded in the underground practices of fanzines and cassette tape-trading. This was a world where music fans actively found ways to tell other music fans about their favourite music. For the Hope Collective, however, it wasn't enough to write about bands they loved in their self-published fanzines, or to put those bands on home-made compilation tapes. They wanted to bring those bands to Ireland so people there could see them play.

In one sense, the roots of the Hope Collective can be traced back to a simple act. Hugo Fitzgerald, a member of the Dublin band Kill Devil Hill, wrote to The Membranes in Blackpool. 'Why don't you ever play in Ireland?' he wrote. 'Why don't you arrange a gig for us there?' came the response (Fitzgerald 2014). He did just that. He booked the local Communist Party headquarters and arranged other shows for the visiting band. It was that straightforward. His Kill Devil Hill bandmate, Niall McGuirk, took the idea further. With an evolving group of volunteers, he arranged over 170 gigs in Dublin for visiting bands.

The Hope Collective did not lack tenacity or imagination when it came to finding venues for their gigs. But they didn't make life easy for themselves. Where possible they tried to avoid having their gigs in pubs, since that often meant excluding younger music fans. Because the collective did not have a venue of its own, it made a series of unlikely alliances with a range of venues run by veterans of the Irish music scene, a biker gang, the semi-State bus company, the Communist Party, local colleges and universities, as well as both the Church of Ireland and the Catholic Church. That said, in the 1980s and into the 1990s, the Dublin venues that embraced rock music were often not of the highest quality. Billie Joe from Green Day recalled the gig the band played for the Hope Collective:

> It was in this tiny room above a bar, which even by the standards of the places we'd been playing in the States was a bit of a dive. Anyway, we were about to go on when somebody, the promoter I guess, told us: 'no one's allowed to pogo or jump around 'cause if they do the floor's going to collapse ... It's the first and last time I've told a crowd to 'go fuckin' crazy ... but can you do it standing still please...' (Clarke 2009: 35)

The Hope Collective organized gigs exclusively by bands from the DIY scene. They had a strict policy against promoting bands signed with large global firms. McGuirk recalled: 'We had nothing against bands on major labels, but they had lots of people working for them, so why should we help them?' (McGuirk 2010). Because it wasn't governed by a profit motive, the collective arranged some gigs as fundraisers for a variety of causes, including the Rape Crisis Centre, the Stop Animal Experiments fund, the M.E. Association, the Vegetarian Society of Ireland, and the Irish Society for the Prevention of Cruelty to Children. They arranged concerts for acts from Northern Ireland, Wales, Scotland, England, the Netherlands, Spain, Germany, Norway, the US and Canada.

The Hope Collective were not the first people to bring DIY punk bands to Ireland. Some independently-promoted punk gigs had taken place in Dublin just prior to the Hope Collective activity. A series of these was organized by the members of the band, Three Ring Psychosis, whose members were from the Dún Laoghaire and Glenageary suburbs near Dublin. One of the members, Tommy Trousers, described his introduction to zines and tape trading via Deko, a member of the band, Paranoid Visions:

> There was a whole network of people. You'd buy records by mail order; you'd buy fanzines by mail order. And you'd start writing to people, and inevitably meet other people who did fanzines as well and you'd start trading tapes. Tape trading was a big thing. (Trousers 2011)

While trading home-recorded cassette tapes was technically illegal and the mainstream music industry was actively opposed to it, many of the tape traders were also buying large quantities of records legitimately. The mainstream record industry viewed them as 'pirates', yet the tape traders were often helping those labels' balance sheets.

One of the Hope Collective's standout gigs demonstrated the type of behind-the-scenes solidarity that can happen in music scenes. In November 1989, Fugazi from Washington, DC, played a gig in Dublin with the collective. Two local bands, The Slowest Clock and Not Our World, were also on the bill and the evening was a great success; the concert made a healthy profit of £1,400. After the show McGuirk (2002: 21) presented this sum to Fugazi's Ian McKaye. The American singer refused to take the full amount, saying: 'How about we take £550, and you use the rest to do other things?' In the commercial mainstream music industry where profits are the objective, this type of generosity is almost unimaginable. The collective used the money to set up a fund which enabled them to arrange concerts they suspected wouldn't break even.

In May 1992, the collective staged their most ambitious event, although the staging of the concert wasn't exactly straightforward. Fugazi were touring Europe again and the Hope Collective felt confident that a properly promoted show could fill the city's premier mid-sized rock venue, the St Francis Xavier Hall. This time, they clearly benefited from an alliance with early 1990s Trinity ents officers Edwina Forkin and Colm O'Dwyer. McGuirk recalled, 'We had no idea how to book the venue' so it was secured by the Trinity ents officers who signed a contract for the rental, via its owners, the Catholic Jesuit order. The mischievous and musical anarchist collective, Chumbawamba, travelled from England and were added to the bill. The Trinity ents staff paid for this. The Jesuit hall-owners were probably unimpressed when one of the band's members, Alice Nutter, donned a nun's outfit for the performance.

Controversially, the printed concert tickets included information about birth control and AIDS. The Jesuits objected and decided to withdraw permission for the concert. This could have been a disaster for the collective, but the Trinity ents staff stepped in and served the Jesuits with legal documents enforcing the original signed contract for the concert (Forkin 2011; O'Dwyer

2011). The show went on. Some 1,600 people attended, and all proceeds went to the Act Up AIDS campaign. It was an extraordinary achievement for a small group of amateur promoters, although it came at a time when there was a growing interest in 'alternative' music in Europe and North America.

Information can be passed from one scene to another via artefacts. McGuirk wrote a book about the collective and self-published it (McGuirk 2002). One schoolboy, Dylan Haskins, bought a copy in a record shop in Bray, County Wicklow, on his way home from school. He remembered:

> ... that was probably where I first read about a 'gig collective' and stuff like that ... I took the book home with me and I read it and a lot of it just resonated – like this is: 'wow I can do the gigs myself'. I had kind of been at gigs in Kilcoole [a town in County Wicklow with a small DIY music scene] already. But this was seeing differently – it was a step-by-step guide to how somebody did it and their starting points and how it grew. And literally how I put on my first gig was doing exactly what Niall had written about. (Haskins 2010)

In addition to organizing local gigs with other motivated young people, Haskins set up a record label, Hideaway, which enjoyed critical and commercial success with acts including Heathers. He networked with like-minded music activists all over Europe and in North America and arranged lengthy tours for artists. Later, he produced his own artefact, *Roll Up Your Sleeves* (2008), a documentary that celebrated his scene but also showed how similar scenes could be set up.

When 'alternative rock' found huge mainstream success in the US in 1991 with the release of *Nevermind* by Nirvana, it is important to appreciate that many of the new US million-selling acts had enjoyed tours in Europe prior to being signed by the US major labels. In a very real sense, the type of tours that people like the Hope Collective hosted provided very significant opportunities for those bands. Green Day are a great example of this, and they have subsequently enjoyed a huge level of commercial success with the major label system. Seven of their albums were certified for sales of at least one million copies each in the United States. Their highest selling album, *Dookie*, released in 1994, had certified sales of over 10 million. Yet the DIY groundwork that the band undertook – in particular their first European tour when they played the Hope gig – remained for their manager a litmus test to decide how serious any band is. He cited Green Day's early DIY activity as a 'textbook' example of how to build a long-term career:

> ... they got in a station-wagon and played 1,000 shows. Got themselves to Europe on their own and spent three months touring Europe ... I say to new bands: 'if you are waiting for someone to help you – just go home and get jobs'. (Rennie 2013)

Some people would describe the Hope Collective's motivation as idealistic, counter-cultural or anti-capitalist. Many of the local bands that they provided with opportunities never enjoyed mainstream commercial success. Yet, for members of the small Dublin music scene bands including The Bloody Jellies, The Lawnmowers, The Umbrellas, Jam Jar Jail, Pet Lamb, Ciunas, Tension, Sloth, In Motion, Mexican Pets, Keltic Konviction, Black Belt Jones, Joan of Arse, Redneck Manifesto, and Arnheim are not just obscure names on a list. They provided highly enjoyable, vibrant entertainment at a time when local DIY music was uncommon. Despite this, the activities of the Hope Collective should not be seen in complete isolation from the centralized mainstream music industry. There has always been considerable traffic from the DIY scene to the big labels. Many of the Hope Collective acts later signed to major labels: Green Day to Warner, Quicksand to Polydor, Richie Egan (Jape) to V2, Babes in Toyland to Warner, Chubawamba to Universal, Therapy? to A&M, and Whipping Boy to Sony.

Generosity and Co-operation in the Music Scene

The Hope Collective example indicates how the flow of support and resources between the DIY community and the for-profit music industry is not one-way traffic. The collective certainly helped bands with long-term ambitions to succeed in the commercial music industry. At the same time, it benefited from the mainstream commercial music industry. Members of the collective recalled one very unsuccessful gig they promoted. They met with the venue's proprietor, Smiley Bolger, a veteran of the Dublin music scene, at the end of the evening, to pay him the agreed rental fee. Generously he declined the payment, knowing that the collective had lost money on the gig (McGuirk 2010).

The Hope Collective's activities were admirable and, by all accounts, great fun. But plenty of co-operation and altruism happens in the for-profit music industry, too. As documented earlier, in their early stages, U2 enjoyed meetings, introductions to crucial music industry contacts, and free advice from members of the Irish music scene and music industry. But as they gained experience and developed their own contacts, they were open to sharing those resources with other members of the Irish music scene. The former ents entrepreneur Kieran Owens, who managed The Virgin Prunes, Cactus World News, Katell Keineg, and The Fountainhead, recalled how this benefited him:

> But one of the crucial things ... was the importance of sharing information. Principle [U2's management firm] were always very good ... if you were away or at a conference or you needed some support you could always phone somebody in Principle Management. Anne Louise Kelly ... was always brilliant and Paul [McGuinness], I mean full credit to him, it was coming from them ... there was nothing that you couldn't ask for in terms of advice that wasn't given. (Owens 2012)

Cynics may suggest that business-to-business favours often represent relationship building or the anticipation of favours being returned sometime in the future. Yet it is clear that principled, friendly altruism happens both in the music scene and in the for-profit music industry. It is vital to appreciate those human values when examining the industry. In addition, the assumed chasm between the scene and the industry may not be clear-cut in practice. There is an interesting coda to the DIY music manager Colm Walsh's story about his business meeting with Paul McGuinness from U2's organization. It shows how the profit-driven industry can still be a place where solidarity, community and loyalty mean something. It would be a mistake to think that all activities in the scene are altruistic and all activities in the industry are cut-throat.

When the seasoned manager of U2 heard that Walsh was going to ignore his advice to sack his band's drummer, and was instead staying loyal to his friend, McGuinness told Walsh a story (Walsh 2010). In U2's early days, an experienced A&R person from London had seen the band and urged them to fire *their* drummer, Larry Mullen, if they wanted to succeed. The band had refused. U2's subsequent commercial success with Mullen as their drummer proves that they made the right decision. Clearly, even for career-minded acts, it is worthwhile, at times, to push back against the industry experts and to stay loyal to your friends. We study enterprise and business through the prism of competition. But that might be the wrong frame through which to understand them. If we looked at commerce in a different way we would find more examples of co-operation and basic decency. The enterprise of music invites both careerists and idealists and they co-exist and overlap in interesting ways. The industry and the scene have something in common – they are both driven by people: even the biggest decisions in the music industry are governed by human factors.

8 Enya: '...not created by the record industry'

The achievements of Enya, and her Dublin-based collaborators, are particularly remarkable because they have never been replicated anywhere in the global music industry. In a business where, quite naturally, a successful act inspires imitators, no Enya-esque act has come anywhere close to the Donegal composer's commercial success.

The singer has maintained a mystique by limiting her public appearances, and she has never undertaken any significant touring. Yet, over time, she has continued to sell large quantities of her music. Because of this mystique, it is possible that some of Enya's fans, and detractors, were disappointed by a series of interviews that the singer/composer gave in 2015–2016. These challenged the myth of Enya as a reclusive fairy-tale princess, detached from reality. The biggest surprise in the interviews was just how *normal* she came across. In an interview with the business magazine, *Forbes* (Ness 2016), she was clearly up to date with, and had opinions on, such ordinary things as current television shows. She also had a sense of humour as well as a keen self-awareness, and a knowledge of the commercial decisions that affected her. Her knowledge of business and enterprise is particularly interesting because Enya is not only Ireland's highest-selling female artist of all time, but she has enjoyed a long, stable and fruitful creative and business environment.

By any industry measures her album sales are staggering. By July 1994 her first album, *Watermark* (1988), had sold over two million copies in the US (Duffy 1994: 119). *Watermark*'s total global sales exceed 6.5 million. In a business where an artist's reputation can be tainted when a debut album's sales are not matched by the follow-up, Enya had continued to grow her fan-base. *Shepherd Moons* (1991) had sold more than seven million copies globally by the summer of 1994. Three million copies were sold in the US where it had spent 138 weeks in the Top 200 chart. The album had sold more than a million copies in the UK alone, and over a quarter of a million each in Spain, Canada and Germany. Korea, Japan, Taiwan, Australia and the Netherlands recorded figures of over 100,000 each.

Enya's back catalogue has continued to deliver large sales, while her new releases comfortably sell in the millions. *The Memory of Trees* (1996) sold more than three million in the US. A greatest hits compilation, *Paint the Sky with Stars* (1998), sold more than four million, whilst *A Day Without Rain* (2001) sold more than seven million copies in the US. There, Enya has outsold Janet Jackson, Nirvana, Red Hot Chili Peppers, Rush, Green Day, The Who, and even Prince.

One of the most intriguing comments on her achievements came from Howie Klein, the President of her US record label, Reprise. It was possibly a strategic remark designed to spur sales and to differentiate the singer from her competitors at the top of the charts: 'Enya is one of those artists who was not created by the record industry; she's an artist in the purest sense of the word' (Flick 2000: 96). Enya may not have been 'created by the record industry', but she is a clear example of how the local Irish industry of music can deliver acts to the global industry. However, she certainly didn't conform to the industry's standard operating principles. Her ability to sell large quantities of albums, without resorting to the type of media tactics that turn artists into celebrities, is worth noting, particularly at a time when questions are being raised about the price of celebrity and the expectations of social media engagement.

'…feet firmly planted on the ground…'

Far from myth or mystique-building, Enya's early local Irish media coverage conveyed a sense of normality. In one of Enya's first mentions in newspapers from her native County Donegal, the journalist wrote: 'She is still the same unspoiled, good-humoured, friendly young girl I have known for many years – and one who had her feet firmly planted on the ground' (McGarrigle 1988: 18).

Even the national newspapers represented her as ordinary. This was a composer who enjoyed the 'quiet life, watching television … she loves the American soaps *Dallas* and *Dynasty* as well as reading novels' (Hayes 1988: 51). Enya's television tastes may have been mainstream, but her first solo music release had positioned her at music's cutting edge in Britain. Her inclusion on the *Taste Travel* cassette release in 1984 placed her in a series that included New Order, Tuxedomoon, John Foxx, Ludus, Cabaret Voltaire, Einstürzende Neubauten, and Virginia Astley. They represented the creative music underground, and Fachtna O'Kelly, who had guided The Boomtown Rats to the top of the UK charts, was credited on the packaging for introducing the Donegal musician to a wider audience. Individual Irish music industry figures were important in drawing attention to emerging Irish acts. To London music industry insiders, Enya was an artist with the cachet of 'underground cool' in 1984.

Enya's lack of pretence was a refreshing change from other 1980s 'pop stars' whose public personae were designed to capture attention and headlines. It is tempting to conclude that her own lack of a headline-grabbing personality allowed her music to be appraised on its own merits, at least initially. That is certainly the argument she made in an Irish interview in 2015:

> Because the focus was on the music, firstly, I didn't know that I had to become famous to sell it. There's no rulebook, so I felt like if I was younger, maybe I would have done things differently. But I was 27, I was really excited about the music – and therefore, I asked questions about the interviews and the promotion that I was doing. I'd say, 'What does this entail? Does it focus on the music? Or is it going to make me more famous?' And sometimes, when it was more focused on me, I actually would refuse, because I didn't feel the necessity. I wasn't looking for the fame; it was more the success that I enjoyed. (L. Murphy 2015)

Elsewhere, she explained how her initial success prompted her to decide how she wanted to be represented:

> I had a choice. I didn't have to front the music on the stage – I was just able to stay with the music. It wasn't important to me to do any interviews that would make me more famous. I just wanted to be in the studio. It wasn't like I had a plan of keeping myself shrouded in mystery. (Telling 2015: 109)

The early press coverage about how ordinary Enya was as a person may have provided the opportunity to project ideas onto her sound. One *Irish Press* journalist described how listening to Enya's music, in a dimly lit studio in Dublin, lent:

> an even more ghostly quality, summoning up visions of mists over mountains, of voices reaching out from a submerged civilisation, a touch of the supernatural. (Hayes 1988: 51)

Process and Credit

This music, described by journalists as 'ghostly', 'supernatural', full of 'visions of mists' and voices from 'a submerged civilisation', was the product of a collaborative process in a relatively nondescript Dublin suburban home. Contrary to the supposed mystique of the music, the *process* was openly acknowledged and even explained by Enya and her collaborators, Nicky and Roma Ryan. There was no attempt to obscure the recording process. In an interview in *New*

Hi-Fi magazine in 1990, reprinted on Enya's website, Nicky Ryan (Barkham 1990) detailed the meticulous recording process in the Ryan family home where he'd ask Enya to sing a section or syllable '60 or a hundred times'. It is an approach that Enya herself has frequently spoken about in interviews:

> Nicky would tell me to sing a note, or a sound like an 'Ah' or a 'Blonk' 16 or up to 80 times over, which sounds really silly but gives a lovely effect when layered together. (Hayes 1988: 51)

> I worked with producer Nicky Ryan, who first had this idea of using a voice like a musical instrument. (Telling 2015: 109)

There is another layer to Enya's narrative: the faith that the husband-and-wife Ryan team had in her. One account described the three-party process: 'the melody [composed by Enya] comes first. Nicky will create an arrangement, and Roma will write lyrics' (Kipnis and Legrand 2005: 56). The support of the Ryans was evidently a motivating factor in Enya's decision to pursue a professional career in making music in the first place. From 1988 on she was quoted about how much their hospitality and support meant: 'This was significant' (McGarrigle 1988: 18). Her early success was described in the Irish media as:

> a justification of the faith which her managers, Nicky and Roma Ryan, had in her talent when they persuaded her to stay in Dublin with them to work on her own style after the break-up with Clannad … Otherwise she would have returned to her native Gweedore and looked for a job, probably teaching piano to local children. (Flaherty 1987: 8)

In fact, the reason Enya was able to state 'I had a choice' about her presentation, despite being signed to the major label, Warner, stemmed from the distinctive supportive network that she enjoyed with the Ryans. She was quoted: 'We [the Ryans and Enya] are the people that make the decisions and it means we've been able to accept success in a very stable way' (McAnailly Burke 1989: 16) That is not to undermine the singer/composer's own force of personality or input. She has articulated her position in the process:

> My heart and soul go into everything I do. I'm very independent and strong-minded … I'm stubborn and aggressive when I work. I can be difficult to get along with, and make life difficult for other people! I always think I'm right … I just don't like to be pushed around. (McAnailly Burke 1989: 15)

Nicky Ryan, Sound Technician

The innovation and technical skills of sound technicians like Nicky Ryan meant that the 1970s Irish ballad and folk scene often sounded much better than it looked. The venues may have been dishevelled and dowdy, but the sound was often pristine. Fachtna O'Kelly, one of the prominent figures in that Irish music scene, recalled Ryan's live sound engineer techniques with Planxty's progressive folk music. Audience members would begin to clap along, sometimes, but not always, in time with the music:

> now of course you think that the sound guy is going to push up the sound louder to drown out the clapping, but when you do that people clap even louder. So, Nicky, with the brilliance that he had, would pull the sound right back down so you could barely hear it. People would have to stop clapping along, otherwise they couldn't hear it. Then he'd move it back up again so everyone could hear the band properly. (O'Kelly 2020)

Some of the curators of Irish rock, folk and the avant-garde wanted the music to be taken seriously and to be heard clearly. O'Kelly, who was a scholar of many forms of music, viewed Ryan as:

> the best sound engineer I ever heard in that sense, you know, he was a creator. He wasn't just taking and presenting. He made more of it. (ibid.)

During the 1970s and 1980s, Ryan built up considerable experience in Ireland. By the time he met Enya, via her family's group, Clannad, he was a seasoned live sound engineer with a track record of making Irish traditional music acts come across well in clubs, halls, and even fields. He had been responsible for the sound at some of the country's key music festivals including Ballisodare, Lisdoonvarna, and Riverstown. As well as working on live performances with the 1970s wave of progressive new acts who combined traditional airs with a modern verve and energy, Ryan also produced significant studio albums by Clannad, De Danann, Jackie Daly and Séamus Creagh, Christy Moore, Donal Lunny and Jimmy Faulkner, Seán Cannon, and Scullion.

Although Ryan had a wide and extensive range of experience in both live and studio sound, he was best known for his work with Clannad, the group formed by some older members of Enya's family from Donegal. Local newspapers at the time recorded that it was a visit by Ryan and the then *Irish Press* journalist O'Kelly (*Donegal Democrat* 1979) that persuaded the group to become full-time professional musicians in the first place. Originally, O'Kelly had managed the group, and when he departed to focus on his new act, The Boomtown Rats, Ryan became both their sound-technician and manager. According to numerous media reports, Ryan parted company with Clannad when he decided to focus on music which he felt was more experimental and adventurous. Enya, who had toured with her family members for two years, left at the same time, and moved to Dublin.

Ryan has recalled in interviews some of his early efforts to understand and manipulate recorded sound. Luke Turner (2015) wrote how, as a child, Ryan listened studiously to the sound a piano made when he stamped on the loud pedal. To him it was similar to a sound on a Beatles record: 'like the end of *A Day In The Life*, resonance going on forever'. He began experimenting with tape recorders, often capturing the sound of everyday objects like doors closing. He used a four-track Ferrograph tape recorder which enabled him to layer sounds on top of each other, a technique that helped to provide one of the crucial elements in his innovative way of recording Enya. He even won a contest to visit the Beatles in the studio, although he couldn't afford the trip to London to experience and enjoy his prize.

Shortly after the release of *Watermark*, Ryan provided *New Hi-Fi* magazine with an interview that gave insight into his experience and methods. While he was touring and recording with the various Irish groups, he was often pointing them in the direction of sonic possibilities.

> The sound and the ideas were things that were building up inside me over the years. As I was listening to past groups that I'd worked with – I'd think, 'Oh, if only they'd do that. It would be so much better'. But they weren't open-minded enough to do it, so I just decided to keep it to myself. Just swallow hard and keep it for another day. Enya was the other day. (Barkham 1990)

Ryan was an innovator, obsessed with sound and its possibilities. As a teacher in a Dublin school for deaf children, he had developed an innovative method to help the students *feel* sound.

> In order to dance, the children needed to feel as much bass in the floor and in their chests as possible – particularly in their chests because as soon as they can feel that, they know what the rhythm is doing. I designed a speaker while I was there, to try and introduce as much bass as I could into the sprung floor of the girls' dancing room. What I came up with was a speaker design based on the lower end of a pipe organ. It was an upright speaker consisting of a 14-inch square box, about six feet tall, and about six inches from the

> floor – with a 12-inch speaker facing upwards, and a three-inch port below that. (ibid.)

From there, Ryan soon moved on to undertake live sound work with local acts, including Philip Donnelly's band Portrait. Donnelly was a singular figure on the Dublin music scene and emigrated to the US where he played guitar with esteemed acts including John Prine. Soon Ryan was the sound engineer for Planxty, featuring Christy Moore. Ryan recalled: 'With Planxty it was quite a challenge to try and amplify the acoustic instruments and make them sound good – and that became my forte' (ibid.).

He moved from Planxty to Clannad and, as mentioned earlier, he was not only responsible for engineering their live sound, he also managed the group. His meticulousness was reported in Irish newspapers at the time (MacRuairi 1978). He recorded the Clannad concerts and after the show he would listen back to the recordings with the band, looking for ways to improve the performance and the audience's experience.

The Deal with Enya

Both the technical aspects and the enterprise of music have been generally dominated by men. In Catherine Strong and Sarah Raine's (2021) survey of recent studies on gender in the music industry they forcefully argued that what 'emerged is a picture of overwhelming and entrenched inequality' (2021: 1). While this gender inequality still exists in many industries, it is sobering to acknowledge Helen Reddington's conclusion that rock music has been 'the slowest of all recent cultural phenomena to incorporate the female creative producer' (2012: 2). In Ireland, local female acts are underrepresented on the country's key radio stations. As one analysis documented (Coogan Byrne 2020), in the twelve months from June 2019 only 10 per cent of the most played acts on radio stations, including RTÉ and Today FM, were female. The lack of women isn't just about numbers and statistics. The academic, Marion Leonard (2016: 3), highlighted how 'the gendered character of the music industry and rock music generally both reflects and serves to constitute the gendered character of wider social and cultural realities and structures'. In light of this, it is notable how the historical record shows that globally successful female artists from Ireland have been aware of, and actively involved in, their sound production, enterprise and presentation. This indicates that the historical exclusion of women from the industry obscures the actual workings of that industry in practice. It is interesting to note the recollections of two Irish women who were active in the field. They explained in 1997:

> Roma Ryan: All the emphasis was on work and there was no separation from it in our lives. Weekends didn't exist. We all just worked through them.
>
> Enya: We had quite fierce fights in the early days. Then at some stage we decided to stop arguing, simply record every single idea we had, listen to them all, then decide. (Gritten 1997)

When Enya and the Ryans began to assemble the results of their arduous recording sessions, they felt that their approach could suit film and television soundtracks. A tape of some of the home-made recordings was delivered into the hands of the film director, David Puttnam (Hayes 1988). Impressed, he commissioned the team to make their first commercial recording, a soundtrack for his film, *The Frog Prince* (1984). Nicky calculated that, for the price of renting time in a top-quality recording studio, he could design and commission his own home studio. With the help of Sean Meehan, a BBC electronics engineer, he had the studio built in the family home. Enya and the two Ryans recorded the soundtrack for *The Frog Prince*, although much of their recording was remixed by another producer. They were soon commissioned to provide the soundtrack for a BBC series, *The Celts*, which was a prestigious accolade. It was reported at the time (McEntee 1987) that the producers had considered Phil Coulter, The Chieftains, and Vangelis before deciding that the young unsigned Donegal singer would be the sound of the history series. The BBC released the music as an album, *Enya*, in 1987. It sold moderately well, but more importantly it established Enya and the Ryans as a team capable of making soundtracks for television and film. At the time, BBC album releases were distributed in Britain by Warner, and this brought Enya to the attention of the head of the company, Rob Dickins.

Dickins was only 23 when, in 1974, he was appointed head of Warner's publishing division in the UK shortly after he had received a degree in politics, sociology and Russian (Masson 2003). Nine years later, he was in charge of the firm's record company. As the head of Warner Bros. in the UK, Dickins was entitled to sign the acts that he wanted, and he set his sights on Enya. Yet, when details of the deal were revealed subsequently in interviews, it is clear that the Irish team had a strong sense of what they were unwilling to concede to the major label. Dickins was quoted: 'One thing that Nicky Ryan said to me when we did the deal was, "we don't want pressure to do singles"' (Duffy 1994: 119). That was a valuable concession to win from a major label, where singles are often the prime promotional tool. Enya may have been new to record deals, but team Enya had a firm idea of what they wanted in a record deal with a major firm. Enya was later quoted:

> I said that I needed three years between each album. You wouldn't get that kind of contract today. I was very excited about being signed for a solo album, but I still also thought, 'I can't do an album a year, if that's what they expect'. (L. Murphy 2015)

From the outset, Enya's team had the support of the label head, and the ability to concentrate on albums rather than hit singles. It is also notable that Dickins adopted an approach to acquiring Irish talent that was contrary to that of his industry rivals. When the natural tendency is to follow trends and to sign acts who sound like currently successful ones, he was quoted:

> Other companies were signing up bands in the style of U2 and here we were signing this ethereal Irish singer. But I was the boss, so I got my way. (Gritten 1997)

That said, getting things his own way, in Enya's case, didn't imply that he, or his label lieutenants, had any input in the creative process. The singer pointed out:

> ... only when we're at a stage when we can think about a release date do we invite Rob over to hear it. He's the only one allowed to come and listen. (Gritten 1997)

While all media quotes from label executives should be viewed as self-promotional exercises, it is worth noting how Dickins didn't recall predicting the level of commercial success that Enya attained:

> Sometimes you sign an act to make money, and sometimes you sign an act to make music. This was clearly the latter. I would have been a genius if I knew this was going to sell millions of records. I just wanted to be involved with this music. (Duffy 1994: 119)

This may have just been a very savvy way of saying that Enya's large sales took the industry by surprise, or that Dickins was the type of executive who took chances on unorthodox artists. But it also reveals an important point about the relationship between Ireland's local music scene and the global music industry at this time. The key decision makers in London were willing to let a small Irish enterprise deliver music to them with little or no input from the experienced corporate headquarters.

'...fame and success'

Just because Enya's record contract apparently didn't compel her and the Ryans to write hit singles to please the label, it didn't mean that they couldn't write one if they felt like it. At the completion of the recording for the debut album for Warner, they decided to try something different. Anyone accusing Enya of reclusiveness or aloofness clearly hasn't read her 1988–1989 diaries which were published both in *Hot Press* and the *Irish Independent*. There she recalls the recording of 'Orinoco Flow', when Roma Ryan flew to London to supply lyrics for a relatively spontaneous (in Enya/Ryan terms) composition.

One interesting feature of the song is how, in addition to the exotic places listed, the words include a testament of faith in Rob Dickins as well as an apparent reference to one of the album's studio technicians. Having been personally signed by Dickens, Enya was well-positioned to stand her ground artistically. Having a hit single solidified that position, and 'Orinoco Flow' was a hit, a major one. In October 1988, U2 reached the number 1 position in the British charts with their single, 'Desire'. It lasted a week at the top before Whitney Houston replaced it for two weeks. She was replaced at the top by Enya with 'Orinoco Flow', a song that sounded curiously out of place in the charts where acid house music was bursting from the clubs and onto the airwaves. Enya stayed number 1 for three weeks; on her debut *Top of the Pops* appearance, she shared the bill with D Mob and their anthem, 'We Call it Acieed'. She wasn't following trends; she was making her own. At the time, she was quoted:

> Nobody expected this, nobody ... least of all me ... Three weeks ago we were talking about what we were going to do to keep the album going, increasing the level of promotion and deciding that we were going to try to get it on the road in some way. (Byrne 1988: 16)

Enya's distinctive, nurturing, mutually supportive working relationship with the Ryans allowed a sense of freedom that is uncommon in the music industry, where celebrity, headlines and metrics often grease the wheels towards stardom and sales. The Irish media coverage included one particularly telling conclusion:

> 'I get to work with people who have always encouraged me,' she says, shrugging. 'They have brought it to where it is; they have believed in me, and as a singer and a musician, you really do need people around you that believe in you from day one, instead of going, "Now you wrote that – can you write something like this?" They just kept saying "Go for it!"' ... (L. Murphy 2015)

Inevitably, a power imbalance exists between the smaller Irish music industry and the better resourced British industry. This leads to situations where the borders between them are unclear. In the mid-1990s, the Irish acts signed by labels in London continued to bring success to the UK music industry. Tellingly, *Billboard* magazine concluded that Enya:

> has helped reconfirm the ability of the UK to nurture new multiplatinum, international artists at a time when Britain's status as a pop A&R source has been in doubt. (Duffy 1994: 119)

Despite this claiming of Enya for the UK music industry, it is clear that she is very much a success story of how the local Irish music industry can nurture talent. In fact, her success had several encouraging distinguishing features. Now Ireland was delivering an Irish act – with an Irish producer, manager and lyricist – to the global marketplace. Enya and her team had managed to prove that it was possible for an act to achieve long-term multiplatinum sales without the standard process of relentless touring and promotion. While she did a considerable amount of promotion and press internationally, her Irish-based enterprise never ceded control to the standard music industry promotional process.

In fact, the stability of Enya and her team in Dublin, with its three-member tolerance of input and argument, gave her a degree of artistic control that is rare in the global music industry. This creative freedom is worth considering seriously when the music industry has been the site of intense pressure on performers, young and old, with a particularly intense type of pressure often being applied to female performers. It is hardly surprising that myths have been projected onto Enya. That has frequently been the price paid by unconventional women in the music industry and beyond. The great mystery of Enya is why the globalized music industry has never replicated her success. She and her team have been surprisingly open in documenting the creative and business path they have undertaken, yet no subsequent act has adopted a similar business model with equivalent commercial success. The moral of the story may be that a solid organizational base, even in a small market, can provide a long-term platform for a successful and sustained career. Enya's legacy may be something rare in the music industry: *success without compromise*. She summed up her perspective:

> The fame and success are two different things. I didn't feel I needed to be more famous to sell the music, I just did what felt right. It might have been different if I were younger. A lot of people enjoy fame, each one to their own. I was studying classical music, I had a

> background in Irish traditional music, I just didn't know how it was all going to come together, but there it all happened for me, in my late 20s. I just thought that this is great. (Turner 2015)

In her case, it was the ability of the members of the local scene to act creatively and co-operatively that brought her global attention. Nicky Ryan described how the three members of the Enya team were able to work together without any interference from the global music industry: 'We also have the Irish Sea between us, which is kind of handy' (Turner 2015). Previously, Ireland's music acts had so often felt isolated from the global music industry. Now they viewed that distance as an advantage.

9 The Corrs: '...genetically engineer the perfect pop group'

It is a great story. A Dublin schoolteacher pens a book about a band forming. It is a huge success and gets made into a film. In 1991, a band is formed *specifically* to audition for the film. At the Dublin audition they are seen by a local freelancer with no music management experience. He decides to manage them. The book was *The Commitments* (1989) and the band were The Corrs. But it is important to understand that the initial enterprise and ingenuity behind *The Commitments* was pure Dublin DIY. Unable to interest any publisher in his novel (White 2001: 30–31), Roddy Doyle started his own publishing company with his friend John Sutton and a £5,000 bank loan. It sold a thousand copies, and when Doyle sent the positive reviews to publishers, he finally secured a deal and an advance of £1,200 from a London-based company.

On the other hand, at first glance, the success of The Corrs seems to have little to do with any DIY activity on the Irish music scene. Unlike some local acts, The Corrs never 'paid their dues' with endless gigging in small Irish venues. In fact, they had only played a handful of gigs when the US ambassador, Jean Kennedy Smith, saw them in a Dublin club. She invited them to perform at a prestigious private gig in Boston. While they were in the US, they were seen by the established record producer, David Foster, who had worked with acts including The Tubes, Celine Dion, and Chicago.

The idea of the band being *seen* is worth noting. The Corrs, whose good looks were frequently commented on by the media, comprised three sisters and a brother. One article gushed:

> If scientists wanted to genetically engineer the perfect pop group, they could hardly have done a better job ... to fulfil the geneticists' wildest dreams, combining looks, talent, stamina, enthusiasm, and oodles of Irish charm in one dynamic best-selling package. (Kelly 2000: 36)

According to David Foster, he was initially so impressed by their appearance that he made time to listen to their music. They 'looked so stunning that I had to take them into the studio immediately to hear what their music was about' (Bessman 1995: 11). He could *see* and *hear* the market potential. After all, as the media enthused: 'Who could resist them? Three sweet Irish colleens who look like supermodels, a big brother who could conceivably succeed Pierce Brosnan in the James Bond role' (Kelly 2000: 37). The Corrs were signed by Atlantic Records in New York, released their debut album in 1995 and sold millions of albums globally.

But there is far more to The Corrs' story than the tale of the three 'supermodel' 'colleens' and their big brother, discovered by the US ambassador and a North American industry gatekeeper. It is a story that highlights how the Irish music scene worked during the 1990s. Talent was available, both musical and managerial, but it needed a specific prompt, an opportunity to respond to. In the case of The Corrs, it was the local filming of *The Commitments*, rather than the existing live music circuit, that gave them their initial impetus. Yet, along with their Irish manager, they were identifiably involved in many of the key activities that led to their global success. It may be a global success story, but it is also a story of Irish enterprise, including the enterprise of the band members.

The group members were frequently quoted on the personal respect they had for their manager, yet by all accounts it was a partnership of equals. This makes The Corrs' career interesting in the context of an industry that places an emphasis on how artists, particularly young women, appear. It continues to be an industry where women are a minority, in the key, and lucrative, areas (Smith et al. 2023). Between 2012 and 2022, an average of 86.8 per cent of the Billboard Top 100 songs annually were credited to male writers, while only 12.8 per cent were written by women. It was even worse when it came to studio production. There, the ratio of men to women is a staggering 131.5 to 1.. So, it is worthwhile to examine a case where there is ample evidence that the group members were highly aware, knowledgeable, and involved in their own key career decisions.

The Start

It is possible to construct a narrative from The Corrs' initial activity and their media coverage. The Dublin musician John Hughes had been in one of the many Dublin bands that got a record deal in the 1980s but never sold many albums. Like The Corrs, his group, Minor Detail, were a band of siblings, and included his brother, Willie. The band had signed directly with a US branch of the Polydor firm, and their song 'Canvas of Life' even made the Top 100 singles chart there in 1983. At a time when Spandau Ballet, The Police, Ultravox, and Eurythmics were in the US charts, Minor Detail's sophisticated synthesizer pop was not out of place. Even though they were signed in the US, their debut album was produced by the local Irish producer, Bill Whelan, in his pre-*Riverdance* days.

Clearly, by the time he met The Corrs, Hughes knew a bit about how the global industry worked, although he hadn't found a way to make a living from it. His family background was in local enterprise; they owned a well-known clothing shop in Dublin's Capel Street, but Hughes had not yet found his niche. After stints in a few local bands that never achieved success, in the early 1990s he was putting together another project, the Hughes Vision, when he was offered some work on a film being made locally. One of the casting directors, Irish-born Ros Hubbard, was a life-long friend, and she invited Hughes to help with co-ordinating the film's music.

At the time Hughes was writing songs with a young keyboard player, Jim, who asked if he could perform at the open audition for musicians. Hughes agreed, and Jim enlisted his sisters, who performed 'Knock on Wood', although they weren't selected to appear in the film as a band. This was hardly surprising as they had never played together in public before then. It wasn't a wasted day though; Ros Hubbard had a track-record of identifying young people who looked good on film, and she liked the young musicians. Two of them got a few days' work as extras, Jim got a small part as a musician, and his youngest sister, Andrea, aged 15, was even given a few speaking lines, memorably: 'go and shite' (*The Commitments* 1991).

Hughes was later quoted on his recollections of the film audition:

> When they finished, Ros Hubbard, *the* woman in this whole story, suddenly said to the band, 'I'm going to say something and John Hughes is going to kill me, you're going to let him manage you'. (Sullivan 1998: 12–13)

Hubbard had stated: 'I'm 25 years in the business and I know stars when I see them and they're stars'. She had previously run a Dublin-based modelling agency. Later, she was credited (McCarthy 2016) with recognizing the pre-fame looks and talent of actors including Saoirse Ronan, Jonathon Rhys Myers, and Kate Winslet. Hughes was later quoted: 'I never intended to become a manager – I just failed at everything else' (Collins 2011). What is truly remarkable is that like Fachtna O'Kelly with The Boomtown Rats, Paul McGuinness with U2, Nicky Ryan with Enya, and Moya Doherty with *Riverdance*, Hughes was another Irish manager with no previous chart success in Britain or the US, who took an Irish act to large-scale global success. Ireland was producing new band managers who competed successfully with well-connected, long-established US and UK artist-management firms.

Having decided to manage the group, Hughes travelled to meet them in their family home. The Corrs came from Dundalk, a town almost midway between Dublin and Belfast, whose entertainment environment had been shaped by District Justice Goff in the 1930s and 1940s. The group's parents had been in a local band, Sound Affair, who performed cover versions of songs by The Carpenters, Simon and Garfunkel, The Eagles, and ABBA. Their father, Gerry, was quoted: 'There wasn't an Abba song out that we didn't know' (O'Hanlon 1996: 36). The younger Corrs recalled being encouraged in their music activity while growing up with parents who played crowd-pleasing pop music. Andrea was quoted: 'They were musicians themselves and it is really all they would have ever wanted us to do. They completely supported it' (Carr 1996). The children had been taught piano and keyboard by their father and had received lessons locally in traditional Irish instruments. When Hughes met them, two of them were still in school and there was no sense of an 'instant success' story following their stint in *The Commitments*.

One of The Corrs' earliest opportunities, and apparently their debut television appearance, came courtesy of Bill Whelan. Hughes and Whelan had stayed in contact after he had produced the Minor Detail album; he proved to be a valuable industry contact and invited the young group to appear on *An Eye on the Music* (1991) with the noted US songwriter Jimmy Webb.

It is notable that The Corrs didn't undertake their first Irish tour until the spring of 1994, almost three years later, and it was a low-key affair. Despite the absence of any significant radio airplay, they secured two notable television appearances, on RTÉ's *Pat Kenny Show* and ITV's *Kelly* programme. The former reportedly proclaimed them as 'the next Cranberries' and they were described as a 'unique blend of their own style of contemporary traditional/rock music' (Foley 1994), as cryptic as that was. Their lack of live work was part of a deliberate strategy, according to Andrea Corr:

> We didn't take the traditional route of going out to perform anywhere we could and hoping we got noticed. We concentrated on writing and recording and creating something we could take to a record company. (Sheehan 1996: 49)

By comparison, U2 in the late 1970s had used local gigs and local releases to raise their profile until they attracted the attention of overseas labels. While The Corrs were preparing material at home to attract major label attention, they had begun to define their sound. Stylistically, as their local newspaper noted, The Corrs' sound was 'modern traditional Irish music with a difference'

(*Dundalk Democrat* 1993: 5). According to some of the brief press mentions they received at the time (Carr 1994a), they hoped to visit New York during the summer to meet with record producers.

The Corrs' most notable Irish press coverage in 1984 quickly followed that US visit. The Eurovision-winning songwriter Shay Healy wrote that the band had performed in Boston for a select gathering in the city's John Fitzgerald Kennedy library, which commemorates the Irish American president. They took to the stage following a politician's speech, by which time, according to the report, 'the audience was fragmenting into groups that were talking and groups that were going to the bathroom' (Healy 1994: 70). A 'stranger to the band', Senator Ted Kennedy, brother of the late US president, took to the stage and informed the audience that The Corrs were 'guests of the ambassador who had flown in especially for the gig and they deserved proper attention'. They received a standing ovation and an encore. Sometimes having a diaspora helps Irish acts in unexpected ways.

The invitation for a little-known Irish group to perform in Boston has become an accepted part of The Corrs' success narrative. Ambassador Jean Kennedy Smith, a sister of JFK, had been persuaded to see the band perform in Whelan's club in Dublin by Bill Whelan, and duly impressed, she invited them to play at a private World Cup party in Boston (O'Sullivan 1998). The invitation and the way the visit raised The Corrs' profile are particularly relevant in the context of Hughes's later recollection (O'Sullivan 1998) that, at the time, most labels were uninterested in the band. In the group's authorized account of their career (Gaster 1999), two early gigs were arranged in Dublin to attract record company interest. The gigs had been well-attended by friends of the group, although the local record label personnel hadn't even bothered to show up. Six months later, the Whelan's gig attended by Bill Whelan and the US ambassador had also been snubbed by the local record label gatekeepers.

The Corrs in the US

Shortly after the Boston gig, the group signed a deal with two New York-based imprints of Atlantic records. Lava Records (founded by Jason Flom) was home to the middle of the road 'alternative' acts Matchbox Twenty and Kid Rock. The 143 label was founded in 1995 by the producer David Foster who had worked with Chicago, Kenny Loggins and Kenny Rogers. Foster became involved in producing The Corrs' debut, and the band decamped to Malibu for five months of recording.

In July 1995, when their debut album was finished, Atlantic introduced the band to the press. It was immediately clear that their looks were going to feature prominently in their promotion. As noted above, their producer David Foster described why he made the decision to listen to their songs: they 'looked so stunning' (Bessman 1995: 11). In a similar vein Atlantic's president, Val Azzoli, advocated a marketing campaign driven by a visual element 'because of their looks, and they're so charming and sincere – you just want to hug them all the time'. If Atlantic were clear on how to market the band – with TV appearances, one-on-one interviews, and plenty of organized visits to meet with industry decision-makers – they seemed less clear about where the band fit musically in the market. Azzoli was quoted: '[The Corrs are] important to Atlantic, because we don't really have an act of this type. They're a poppy kind of folk – a Wilson Phillips kind of act, which we've never had' (ibid.). Wilson Phillips, a trio of vocalists, had enjoyed two best-selling albums in the US at the start of the 1990s.

Foster explained where he saw The Corrs fitting in the US market:

> They'll fill a big slot that's available right now, that's a Wilson Phillips kind of slot – though that might look bad in print! Andrea has a Karen Carpenter softness – though it's impossible to compare anyone to Karen. The music has more of an edge than Wilson Phillips or The Carpenters, and there's also an element of Yes, because the music's complicated. (Bessman 1995: 11)

The Corrs themselves appeared to have a more defined perspective on their music than the experienced label executives. They were quoted more succinctly on their sound. To musician Sharon it was 'a mixture of Irish and modern', to vocalist Andrea: '[The] melody and harmony vocal aspect is very important'. As vague as this may have been, it sent a clearer signal to the market than imagining the sound of a Wilson Phillips-type band with an element of Yes' prog-rock lite and a soft Karen Carpenter vocal tone.

A notable aspect of this early positioning is that the band were given some credit for their own musical development and vision. This was an encouraging counterpoint to the notion of music executives manipulating young musicians. The album may have been recorded in Malibu, but the songs and sensibility were the product of the young Irish musicians. While Foster had co-written one song on the album, he had allowed the band to set the tone. Significantly, Jim Corr was credited with co-producing the album. Foster was quoted:

> I guided and nudged instead of rolling up my sleeves and getting messy ... There may have been a few times when I pushed a more Celtic vibe. (Bessman 1995: 11)

The Corrs enjoyed considerable freedom in deciding how they should sound. Andrea was later quoted: 'We had everything pre-written and pre-demoed before we went out there' (Carr 1996). In a compliment to the group's musical development in Ireland away from industry scrutiny, they recalled Foster saying: 'If we end up with an album that's totally different than your demos, then we failed' (Bessman 1995: 11). The home-studio the band used in Dundalk – as well as Jim Corr's experience as a musician with acts in Ireland including the cabaret singers Linda Martin and Red Hurley, traditional singer Dolores Keane and the high-rated synthesizer act, The Fountainhead – was clearly an asset appreciated by experienced US music executives.

If The Corrs' looks were striking, their timing appeared to be impeccable. On 20 January 1996, they entered the *Billboard* Top 200 at a time when female voices were rewarded with high sales in the market. Joan Osborne, Sophie B. Hawkins, Natalie Merchant, Sarah McLachlan and Gwen Stefani's No Doubt were all charting in the singles chart along with established female superstars like Madonna and Whitney Houston. Most intriguingly, Everything But The Girl were in the Top 5. Tracey Thorn, one of the most celebrated voices of Britain's post-punk independent scene, had been paired with Todd Terry for this remixed single. Even many of the male acts in the charts, like the Goo Goo Dolls, Deep Blue Something, and Collective Soul were playing a very palatable brand of rock. In the more profitable album chart, Enya's *The Memory of Trees* was in the Top 20. US music shoppers weren't only buying large quantities of albums by women, pop acts and melodic rockers; they were buying Irish, too.

Forgiven, Not Forgotten entered the album charts at number 168. But not everything in the Atlantic Records' plan panned out. Instead of moving up, the album quickly disappeared from the charts entirely and was no longer one of the 200 best-selling albums in the US. It briefly revisited the charts in March and April, for a week each, before disappearing completely again. The Corrs' debut had only managed a total of four weeks in the charts. By the standards of a major label who had invested visibly and heavily in a new group, this was a severe setback. Yet initially it had appeared that everything was in place for The Corrs to 'break America'. The first single, 'Runaway', had received a healthy measure of airplay, and made the singles charts, peaking at number 68. Atlantic publicly demonstrated its belief in the band with paid advertisements nationally, and the band followed up their extensive promotional duties with some of the highest profile gigs a young group could want. They filmed expensive music videos with high-production values in LA. They even performed in front of large audiences, opening for Celine Dion, Michael Bolton, and The Rolling Stones. In fact, it is difficult to imagine what Atlantic could have done differently to establish the band in the US market. But the disappointing result of this campaign was unexpected. While sales were not miniscule, they averaged about 8,000 units a week (Sexton 1998) from its release until the follow-up appeared in April 1997. *Forgiven, Not Forgotten* had failed to break into the US in a significant way. If The Corrs wanted success, they would have to look elsewhere.

Hughes was later quoted: 'Getting a record deal is like being picked for the team – you haven't played a game, never mind won the cup' (Gaster 1999: 32). Clearly, signing with a major international label was not an absolute guarantee of success. The following year when interviewed about The Corrs' relative lack of US success, Atlantic's Ron Shapiro also used a sports analogy. Breaking into the US was a 'ball-game with a different set of rules' (Taylor 2000: 101). Evidently the US market operated differently from other national markets. But it is significant that The Corrs had emerged into the US marketplace at a time when acts from Britain were struggling to find any great success there; Irish acts were frequently conflated with British acts. Clearly, when Britain is struggling to export its music product to the US this has implications for Ireland's musicians who frequently depend on record deals from London-based firms. As *Billboard* highlighted (Newman and Flick 2000), in 1985 almost one-third of the 100 best-selling albums in the US were by acts from the UK. In 1999, only one of the top 100 was from the UK. That is a drop from one in three to one in a hundred.

The Corrs in Ireland

But all was not lost; in Ireland the deal with Atlantic, the promotional campaign, and all of the marketing elements (including expensive videos, photo shoots, and the album recording) provided The Corrs with media attention and the tools to tackle their home market. While they lacked a home audience grown by extensive touring in Ireland, the story from the States and the enthusiasm of the Dublin staffers of Atlantic's Irish subsidiary evidently made a difference.

Inevitably, an Irish group with a female front-person was going to be compared with The Cranberries. The *Irish Independent* critic found The Corrs 'teeth-rottingly saccharine pop' and 'cloyingly inoffensive', so it was little consolation that he felt 'they don't turn the stomach as much as the Cranberries' (Byrne 1995: 26). On a more positive note, albeit with less truth, it was observed elsewhere that 'like the Cranberries before them, The Corrs have been hitting the high spots in the United States before making any impact at home in Ireland' (Dwane 1995: 16). But unlike The Cranberries, Irish music-buyers didn't wait for actual success in the States before embracing The Corrs.

The single 'Runaway' was released in Ireland in advance of the album and was poised just outside the Top 10 when the album *Forgiven, Not Forgotten* hit the market in time for the bumper Christmas selling period. The album charted higher than the single, which peaked at number 10. This set a consistent pattern for the group; their albums were better sellers than their singles. In fact, only one of their singles, 'Breathless' (2000), reached the Top 5. This ran contrary to the industry notion that pop acts sell singles and rock bands sell albums. In Ireland, The Corrs were being treated by the market like a serious rock act.

The album continued selling as Corrs stories appeared in the Irish media. A high-profile prestigious gig, supporting Celine Dion in Dublin, was accompanied by appearances in the US TV show *Beverley Hills, 90210* and US promotional activities. The Corrs enjoyed a swift rise to become one of the country's biggest local sellers, but in the absence of a major US breakthrough, they would need overseas success elsewhere to recoup Atlantic's investment.

The Corrs in Australia

The industry story of The Corrs' Australian success highlights their visual appeal, musical training, ability to make friends and to improvise during unexpected situations. In July 1996, the managing director of their label in Australia recalled his introduction to the band:

> [Atlantic] sent a preview promo [video] reel down for our conference last year, one band stood out for us all – and that was The Corrs. The melodies hit me as something special, and their appearance was so striking that I started to believe in them. (Baker 1996: 66)

Inspired by this audio-visual presentation the label released the album, but just like in the US, it failed to attract large sales. Early press reports in Ireland put Australian sales by May 1996 at just 7,000 units (Haugh 1996: 2). Despite this, the group were flown there for a week of press and promotion and, unexpectedly, the backing track for their appearance on the *Midday* TV show malfunctioned. For some acts this would be a disaster, especially if they were dependent on the pre-recorded studio sound. The label staff were impressed when The Corrs 'did the performance acoustic and fully live without a blink'. The Corrs were trained and competent musicians with the ability to improvise. The TTFM radio station was similarly impressed by the band's ability to perform live; to them it indicated the group's 'potential for career longevity' and the station gave them significant airplay.

The airplay contributed to the debut single, 'Runaway', becoming a chart hit. At the time, and coinciding with the band's first tour in the country, Australian critics were predicting the follow-up would be a hit too, partly thanks to a 'superb video' (Sheehan 1996) produced by Atlantic in LA. The industry predictions for the group were based not on any US success, but on continuing strong sales in Ireland where the debut album had exceeded 90,000 units. In Australia, being Irish, and having the promotional materials generated by a US label, was a distinct advantage. In fact, to some in Australia, The Corrs were evidence of the continuing strength of Irish popular culture, making it a 'Third Force' (Sheehan 1996) in global music alongside the US and the UK. The Corrs were represented as normal Irish youngsters, and this was a consistent aspect of their self-representation: playful, bright, energetic, positive and normal – the sort of uncontroversial individuals that Australian audiences could relate to. Andrea was quoted: 'We're very down-to-earth people. We like going to the pub the same as everybody else' (Sheehan 1996). When the journalist predicted Australian success for the group: 'I hope you're right. It would be great if it does well so far from home.'

Not all critics were so supportive; one review of the debut tour labelled the band's cover of 'We Are Family' as 'a big mistake' (Blake 1996: 29). Overall, 'at times the group sounded like an Irish Wilson Phillips. Pure pop. A little too sweet.' While the journalist enthused about all of the group's traditional Irish elements, she lamented the band's rock leanings: 'filthy guitar solos almost destroyed the delicate harmonies'. The band's live presentation differed from their studio recordings, so inevitably some preferred the original. But it was clear that The Corrs' melding of Irish traditional music with pop and rock was palatable to the mass Australian audience. The band's personal drive was also in evidence; during the tour they combined in-store performances along with their concert duties. When they began the tour, their debut album was number 4 nationally; by September, it was number 1. When the media covered their next Australian tour, they were able to highlight that not only had The Corrs sold far more tickets for this tour, but that their debut album had sold half a million copies there and had spawned four hit singles (Elder 1997). As one observant journalist noted (Bradley 1997), a third of all Corrs albums sold globally had been bought in Australia. Thankfully for The Corrs, US market success was not a necessary precursor for an Irish act breaking elsewhere.

The Corrs in the UK

While the band had enjoyed some moderate early success in the UK, where *Forgiven, Not Forgotten* had gone gold, it did not reach the same level of success in the Irish or Australian markets. 'Runaway' had peaked at number 48 in the UK, so they were a known quantity, but not an iconic one. When the follow-up album, *Talk on Corners* (1998) failed to find a mass audience, The Corrs were in serious danger of being seen to fail in both the US and the UK.

According to The Corrs' approved insider account (Gaster 1999: 118), Hughes and the band's London-based booking agent, John Giddens, decided that, without significant radio play, they had to find an alternative means of reaching the mass market. Giddens suggested renting the Royal Albert Hall and persuading the BBC to televise a live St Patrick's Day concert, promoting the recently released album. The BBC agreed. Once again, mass-market visual culture was deployed. This was not without risk, however. As one critic observed, the hall was 'a solemn venue that rarely comes alive when played by pop and rock groups' (Cartwright 1998: 39), although in this case he felt it worked. He wrote how 'both albums suffer from overly slick production, [however] live The Corrs are something else'. In fact, they had succeeded in transforming the 'expansive and illustrious space into the world's largest Irish pub'. It was, according to a later report, the gig that enabled The Corrs to 'tip the balance in the UK' (Sullivan 1998). By early December, *Talk on Corners* had sold 1.4 million copies there. By the end of the year, it had sold more copies than any other album that year. It became the fourth highest-selling album of the decade (Freeman 1999).

The St Patrick's Day BBC tie-in should be seen in a wider context. It was just one of the elements in a campaign where The Corrs benefited from astutely combining their music with current technology and trends. Just like Enya, the band found a key ally in Rob Dickins, who had recently been promoted and was now the head of their label in the UK. He knew how to establish Irish acts in Britain and had been instrumental in the early marketing of Enya (as noted earlier, he was the executive that she had mentioned in her song, 'Orinoco Flow'). He felt The Corrs 'needed a little shift to the left, not in terms of their music or their substance, but in terms of their credibility' (Sexton 1998: 10). That shift occurred when he listened to some of the mixes that Atlantic's New York headquarters had commissioned but didn't feel were worth releasing. One of these, the Fleetwood Mac song, 'Dreams', had been remixed by Todd Terry who had previously brought US success to Everything But The Girl.

Dickins released the track, and it reached the Top 5 in the UK. In terms of the shift in The Corrs' sound, he recalled: 'It needed to be more modern for the UK market. We were just taking what they did and making it more accessible' (Sexton 1998: 10). He arranged remixes of other Corrs songs and committed £100,000 to a marketing campaign on British TV and radio. By October 1998, their second album, including the 'Dreams' remix, had sold a million copies in the UK and had been number 1 on three different occasions (Sexton 1998).

Fortuitously for The Corrs, 1998 was also the year the major record firms began to appreciate the appeal of another new technology – DVD (Andrews 1998). The combination of appealing visuals, with a far higher sound quality than VHS video tapes had provided, was seen as a potential boon for labels. It was significant that Warner launched its DVD product with four artists: Madonna, Eric Clapton, Fleetwood Mac, and The Corrs. The group's sound may have been devised and developed in Ireland, but the marketing tools, including videos and DVDs that were provided by the US and UK labels, stimulated high sales in in a number of countries. When a Corrs single, 'Breathless', finally reached number 1 in the UK in 2000, they had already become chart-toppers elsewhere. 'Breathless' was their fifth song to top the charts in Spain.

In 2000, The Corrs' global appeal was so strong that they were selected by the music industry trade body, the International Federation of the Phonographic Industry (IFPI), as their artist 'spokesmen'. It was a clear acknowledgment of the group's international stature and reputation. They were selected at a time when the industry was dealing with its protracted battle against illegal music downloading. The Corrs were the public face of the campaign. Sharon Corr was quoted in the campaign's promotional materials:

> You don't buy a book and not pay for it; you don't buy your groceries and not pay for them. Things in this world are not for free, and that's for a reason – so we can all make a living. (Masson and Sexton 2000: 10)

The Corrs were now established as global ambassadors for the global pop industry.

Conclusion

In Blue (2000) was another number 1 album in the UK charts for The Corrs. When it was knocked off the top spot, it wasn't bad news for the Irish music industry as it was replaced by another Irish act, Ronan Keating, formerly of Westlife (Betts 2004: 522). It was the first time that one Irish act had replaced another at the top of the UK album charts. Irish acts were no longer just appearing in the charts. They were dominating them.

The Corrs were prompted to form in the first place by a particularly Irish overlap of literature, film, and popular music. Their case illustrates key points about the 1990s global music industry. Acts from the UK were struggling to make inroads in the US; the UK labels were no longer seen as a major source of talent for the US market. This had implications for Irish artists as they continued to be signed by London-based offices of the multinational firms.

The Corrs and Hughes can be viewed as an Irish taskforce within the global industry. While funded and resourced by Atlantic's central command in New York, on the ground they were left to their own devices. They certainly enjoyed the benefits of expensive videos, photo shoots, tour support, producers, and recording studios courtesy of Atlantic, although typically in the music industry all such costs are owed by the artist to the label and must be recouped before the act gets paid. Yet it was their own vision, their tenacity, and their ability to campaign vigorously on their own behalf that contributed to their eventual large-scale success. It is worth noting that even artists signed by major labels require a sense of enterprise and the do-it-yourself work ethic. It is also notable that 'not breaking' the US does not mean the end of a career for an act, even one signed to a US label. Other territories can contribute meaningfully to sustaining the career of artists, Irish or otherwise.

10 *Riverdance*: Creating Profitable Local Culture

The packaging and commercialization of live Irish dancing productions is an extremely lucrative combination of Irish culture and enterprise. The sociologists Hilary Tovey and Perry Share (2003: 542) were aware of the local origins of the live dance phenomenon when they posed the question, 'Could Hollywood have invented *Riverdance*?' It is a fair question and a pertinent reminder that the production wasn't incubated in Beverley Hills, 90210, but in Dublin 4. To Tovey and Share, this was evidence of the ways that 'local cultural entrepreneurs', even in a small market and with limited resources, can use that local knowledge 'which is less available to the culture business at the centre of the global system'. Local cultural workers, they argued:

> know their territory, they are competent in its cultural practices and sensitive to its meanings, and this derives primarily from their involvement in the local forms of life. (2003: 542)

Naturally, individuals working *within* an assertive global culture industry will try to gain knowledge of any culture that could be profitable, so we should not take local knowledge as a permanent source of competitive advantage. But Tovey and Share's conclusion invites the question of how *Riverdance* was incubated, developed, and taken to the market.

In July 1993, a freelance television producer in Dublin was offered a project by the national broadcaster, RTÉ. Her initial reaction was to decline the opportunity: she was the mother of two young children and had decided to take time away from work to focus on her family. She discussed the project with her husband and then decided to accept, under the condition that she could make the job work for her creatively. It was, after all, just a few months of work. That was how Moya Doherty recalled initially approaching the task of directing the 1994 Eurovision Song Contest (Smyth 1996a: 23) to be hosted in Dublin. The part of her concept that captured the attention of the global audience was a short music-based showcase while the judges' votes were collated – it was called *Riverdance*. It contributed to the perception, and even evolution, of Irish culture, but it is an example of not only Irish music but also of Irish cultural *enterprise*. More importantly, this was cultural enterprise generated not by the centralized music industry but by local entrepreneurs in Ireland who retained full ownership of their product. In doing so, Doherty and a small team of innovators and initial investors generated not only an internationally successful entertainment product, but also a new industry. They transformed Irish dancing from an amateur (although highly competitive) activity into a large global industry.

Doherty was an interesting choice as producer; she had been well-reviewed as a young actress (Hickey 1975) and had credentials in front of the camera. She was a co-host of RTÉ's pioneering breakfast programming in 1984, although she later was quoted: 'I couldn't take the attention ... I was really uncomfortable in that place' (Donohoe 2013: 86). However, Doherty was eminently capable of turning a narrative into a compelling mass-market spectacle: 'I love other people's stories, and telling those stories' (Donohoe 2013: 86). She had recently produced a documentary for RTÉ on child abuse, *The Silent Scream* (1993), that was part of Ireland's cultural conversation and reappraisal of its core values. Her husband, John McColgan, was also an experienced television executive. He had a considerable track record not just in Ireland, but in Britain too, where he had been a producer for TV-AM. Together they were experienced in many aspects of television production, both live and recorded.

There were two major stages in the production of *Riverdance* and, although they overlap, as businesses they should be understood separately. First, there was the RTÉ-commissioned public broadcast element on the Eurovision show; and second, there was the commercial stage presentation. Both required different skill sets. To Doherty, 'one of the really good things about *Riverdance* ... it grew out of public service broadcasting, out of a desire to do something positive' (Smyth 1996a: 35). While the initial Eurovision budget was substantial, it was still relatively modest in comparison with the funds Sony, Universal or Disney could commit to major new products. Given the sums generated by the project, it is significant that Doherty, McColgan and the composer Bill Whelan managed to assemble a team capable of taking the production to the global market based solely on local enterprise and investment. Much of the talent, onstage and behind the scenes, was local also, although it is notable that *Riverdance* initially depended on principal dancers from overseas.

The Product

Music is a vital element of *Riverdance*, and when Doherty accepted RTÉ's offer of producing the Eurovision broadcast, she wrote a memo outlining her vision. It focused on the five-minute segment when votes were being tabulated. It specifically rejected the nostalgic and clichéd nature of many Irish representations: 'This would not be a "back to our roots" routine, rather the opposite' (Smyth 1996a: 24). She outlined her vision:

> Essentially it would be a five-minute commissioned work from a contemporary Irish composer. A percussive piece which would give us an opportunity to showcase top Irish musicians, dancers, performers and singers ... (Smyth 1996a: 23)

At its core was a 'vibrant, sexy, contemporary Irish tap dance routine' featuring two named dancers, Michael Flatley and Jean Butler (Smyth 1996a: 23). The chosen composer, Bill Whelan, not only played a vital role in the production's artistic sensibility, he was also instrumental (through his network) in its early business foundation. Whelan was no stranger to television. A 1991 RTÉ production he undertook demonstrated his pluralist approach to Irish culture. To him, Irish music belonged to the world, and interacted with other cultures in a mutually beneficial exchange. He was quoted on his perspective when promoting his television series, *An Eye On The Music* (1991):

> I feel very strongly that splitting music into different camps is very unhealthy. If you have an interplay you are giving people a wide musical exposure – you're avoiding ghettoization. (Black 1991: 31)

The 10-week series aired on Sunday evenings and was a high watermark for the national broadcaster. It was adventurous musical television of the highest quality and featured both eclectic and popular artists. The RTÉ Concert Orchestra accompanied artists from diverse locations and multiple genres. Hothouse Flowers made music with Guo Yue, the Japanese flautist; Ultravox's Midge Ure performed with The Chieftains; and Andrew Strong – fresh from his exposure in *The Commitments* film – was one of the many local acts included. Engine Alley, Luka Bloom, Paul Brady, Don Baker, and The Dubliners were also featured, while The Corrs made their television debut on Whelan's show. Overseas guests included Lloyd Cole, Prefab Sprout's Paddy McAloon, Beverley Craven, Tanita Tikaram, and US songwriter Jimmy Webb. Few contemporary music shows *anywhere* could boast of a line-up that accommodated Elmer Bernstein as well as The Sex Pistols' manager, Malcom McLaren. It was a standard of music television that any major international broadcaster would have been proud of.

Whelan didn't view global popular culture as a threat to Ireland's native music. On the contrary, he believed that Ireland's growing global assimilation was stimulating local culture. He was quoted: 'It's no coincidence that there's been a huge resurgence of interest in traditional music as we find ourselves drawn more into a world culture' (Black 1991: 31). *Riverdance* was located at this intersection of traditional music and world culture and Whelan's personal career provides some insight into how he acquired the skills and experience required for such an undertaking.

By 1994, Whelan was an established figure in the Irish music scene, occupying a distinct position that straddled pop, traditional and orchestral music. The only son of two musicians, he learned piano while growing up in Limerick. He had even built a home studio there as a schoolboy. He had also taken part in public concerts as a teenager, including Jesuit fundraisers for Catholic overseas missionaries. During one event, he was featured with three friends in a show that included a singing priest, a quiz, and a champion Irish dancer (*Limerick Leader* 1963). In another, Whelan was included along with dancers from a local dancing school (*Limerick Leader* 1970). While the clergy were still active in organizing local variety entertainment in 1970s Limerick, the city also experienced a touch of Hollywood glamour thanks to the success of the local actor Richard Harris. This provided Whelan with a key early opportunity to display his talent. In 1970, he contributed music for the film score of *Bloomfield*, starring Harris and Romy Schneider. The small size of Ireland's music scene often provided its key participants with a range of music experience. In larger markets producers generally specialize in one area: Ireland's producers got a wider education.

Despite the opportunities that he secured in Limerick, Whelan later recalled the credibility gap he encountered between Ireland and the major music centres. His early Irish recordings were made at a time when 'You had a great problem trying to connect with people [in the overseas industry] and making them regard Ireland as a serious place to come from' (Stewart 1989). He did, however, encounter success when he performed with Planxty, who were at the vanguard of the movement that was making elements of traditional music vibrant and popular with young audiences.

Whelan was also learning the sonic aesthetics of international pop: two of his Johnny Logan productions – 'What's Another Year' (1980) and 'Hold Me Now' (1987) – won the Eurovision Song Contest. He had even produced a track on U2's *War* (1983) album. Just as significantly, he had, in collaboration with Donal Lunny and Planxty, composed the music used during the Eurovision in 1981. He continued Seán Ó Riada's tactic of combining Irish traditional music with classical orchestration in his version of the *Ó Riada Suite* which was performed publicly in 1987. He followed this with equally ambitious orchestral compositions for civic celebrations, including *The Seville Suite* (1992) which was commissioned by the Department of the Taoiseach, and

Mayo 5000 (1993). During this period, he was also composing specifically for Irish theatre productions featuring dance.

Locally, Whelan was establishing a track record for combining identifiably Irish music with other national traditions within the small, and tightly networked, local music scene. But he was also working with some of the people who were essential to the *Riverdance* story. The *Mayo 5000* celebration performance had been produced by Moya Doherty's husband, John McColgan, and included dancing from a Birmingham student, Jean Butler, and a Chicago construction entrepreneur with Irish roots, Michael Flatley.

When Moya Doherty began to develop her vision of what eventually became *Riverdance*, she met Whelan in Dublin to further the project. By December 1993, a fully developed artistic draft had been completed. Whelan had previously worked with the ANÚNA choir on the *Mayo 5000* project, and he incorporated their voices into *Riverdance*. Once the music was composed, the two featured dancers, Butler and Flatley, were flown in for three weeks of rehearsal with local dancers before the live broadcast (Smyth 1996a: 30).

Whelan's previous Eurovision break-time music had been released by Warner's in Ireland, probably on the strength of Planxty's name. This time, however, none of the major labels were interested in releasing the *Riverdance* single. For the major multinational music firms this was an oversight that ranks close to missing out on signing U2. For a small investment in a local project, they could probably have secured a portion of rights to the *Riverdance* music. As we will demonstrate, the multinationals' failure to identify talent with major commercial potential ultimately benefited Paul McGuinness, U2's manager. It is worth keeping in mind that it wasn't just EMI, Warner's, Sony, and RCA who misjudged *Riverdance*'s revenue stream; by their own admission, even its originators were taken by surprise.

Taking the Product to Market

Having failed to interest any of the major global music firms, Whelan and the managing director of his music publishing company, Barbara Galavan, persuaded the insurance company Church & General to fund the recording of the single (Smyth 1996a: 35). The publishing company, Celtic Heartbeat, had been recently set up after its principals – Galavan, Paul McGuinness, and Dave Kavanagh (Clannad's manager) – had identified a niche in the global market for an identifiably Irish music product. During an interview with Jim Rogers in 2014, Galavan recalled the foundation of the Celtic Heartbeat label, originally a joint venture with Warner in the US:

> At that stage they [Warner] had Clannad and a number of other Irish acts, so they were becoming more and more aware of that wave of interest in Celtic music, so what we tried to do was to sign Irish-oriented acts coming out of the traditional Irish music genre and launch them onto the international stage. (Galavan 2014)

While the major multinational firms were uninterested in the *Riverdance* theme music, it found a home on U2's label, Son Records, and it was released just before the 1994 Eurovision Song Contest. When the televised performance captured the public's attention, the single went to number 1 in the Irish charts on 5 May and stayed there throughout the summer and into September. In Britain it reached the Top 10. The single rejected by the London-based firms became a successful Irish-owned export to Britain. However, another *Riverdance* product was even more successful.

A video of the Eurovision performance was quickly made available to raise money for famine relief in Rwanda. Immediately it became the fastest-selling video in Irish history and generated £300,000 (Smyth 1996a: 38). Re-emphasizing that *Riverdance* was not originally developed as a commercial product, Doherty recalled that at the start of the project, 'I had no real experience of the hard commercial world, so I wasn't thinking of its financial potential' (Smyth 1996a: 35). This recollection does not take away from the fact that Doherty, McColgan and Whelan were well-placed to quickly assemble a team in Dublin to provide them with all they required to take *Riverdance* to the global market.

Developing the Business Product

Following the popular reaction to the performance at the Eurovision, RTÉ suggested a one-hour Christmas special, but again Doherty initially balked. She wanted to figure out the direction *Riverdance* should take. The broadcaster and U2's manager each gave the team £10,000 (Smyth 1996a: 38) in development funds to explore where the production could go, and Doherty and the team decided on a two-hour theatrical show. Doherty and Flatley then undertook a search for suitable dancers, while Whelan lined up some of his previous collaborators and set about composing the music for a more fully developed show (Smyth 1996a: 41).

The show's ensemble grew to incorporate several performers Whelan had previously worked with. Among them were the Spanish flamenco dancer Maria Pagés, the Hungarian musician Nikola Parov, the Irish choir ANÚNA, as well as prominent Irish musicians including Davy Spillane. While *Riverdance* is frequently viewed as a dance production, it is important to remember how prominent the music was; to emphasize this the musicians were onstage rather than in the orchestra pit.

Many of the other key behind-the-scenes roles were filled by local personnel based in Ireland. The prominent artist, Robert Ballagh, was commissioned to design the set and his artwork appeared on some of the merchandise. Around this time, he also received the prestigious commission of designing Ireland's new bank currency. One commentator pointed out how the new bank notes included 'scenic backdrops that could be straight out of *Riverdance*' (Hartigan 1997). Popular culture was now intimately entwined with key aspects of national culture.

To make *Riverdance* into a touring production, however, required more than creativity; investors were needed to fund auditions, rehearsals, fees, and design. Doherty and McColgan invested personally in the production, and in addition to RTÉ and Paul McGuinness (Smyth 1996b), so did two other Irish music entrepreneurs, Maurice Cassidy and Tommy Higgins. Smaller sums were advanced by the owner of the Point Theatre, Harry Crosbie, and by Allied Irish Bank. Doherty later recalled: 'I wouldn't even bet on a horse, I'm so cautious' (Smyth 1996a: 45). Although few investments in Irish cultural history have been more profitable, the investments came with no guarantees. In terms of turnaround as well as turnover this was new territory for a live Irish theatrical production.

Riverdance opened in Dublin's Point Theatre in February 1995. The entire run sold out, but some sophisticated and canny activities helped to achieve this. According to the official account (Smyth 1996a: 46), Doherty had persuaded her former RTÉ colleague Gay Byrne to suggest on-air that *Riverdance* tickets would make an ideal Christmas gift. In addition, two of the investors (Cassidy and Higgins) had significant experience in the sales and promotion of concert tickets and they deployed a successful tactic. Although the show had been booked for a six-week run, only tickets for a small number of dates were initially released for sale. When these tickets were purchased, *Riverdance* could legitimately claim the shows were 'sold out'. The remaining shows were then put on sale with the cachet of an in-demand production.

The production quickly transferred to London (Smyth 1996b) where, again, it was a financial success with every seat for every performance sold. While ticket sales brought in as much money weekly as they had in Dublin, the increased rent and advertising costs meant the margins were tight. The London production needed sales of at least 90 per cent for each show to break even. It achieved this, although profits were smaller overall than they had been in Dublin. In July 1995, *Riverdance* returned to Dublin for six weeks. Since the sets were already built, and the company was already rehearsed (Smyth 1996b), a 'respectable profit' was enjoyed.

In fact, demand was still strong, so *Riverdance* returned to London in October of the same year. This time, however, things didn't go smoothly. In a highly publicized dispute over earnings and 'artistic control' the show's high-profile dancer, Michael Flatley, was fired. The production continued with headlines, but without him.

Creating a Duopoly

Flatley retained his fan-base, his ability to generate headlines, and his self-belief. He quickly started his own touring show, *Lord of the Dance*. While this outcome was unexpected and traumatic at the time, it meant that Doherty, Whelan, McColgan and Flatley hadn't just created a successful commercial vehicle featuring Irish dancing, they had created an industry.

The similarities between *Riverdance* and Flatley's production are obvious. Both were live shows driven by Irish dancing. But the key presentational differences indicate how *versions* of Irish culture are marketed to global audiences. Perhaps the most notable difference had its roots in that pre-*Riverdance* difference of opinion between Doherty and Flatley. In his desired version of the performance, the dance would climax with Jean Butler in his arms or sitting on his knee. Doherty objected, feeling that 'the sexual chemistry has to be distant' (Smyth 1996a: 33). The *Riverdance* account states that while the show 'tapped into the [Irish dancing] genre's subliminal sexuality, its presentation was still coy' (ibid.).

There was very little coyness about Flatley's show. The promotional materials for *Lord of the Dance* boasted how he had personally 'brought a sexual element to a formerly chaste and modest dance form' (Temin 1997). His productions and his self-representation revel in flamboyant showmanship. One US critic claimed that *Lord of the Dance* existed at 'the intersection of schlock, sex and spectacle' (Cooper 1997: 31). She argued that 'to have an ensemble of women suddenly strip to black halters and pantyhose smacks more of lap dance than step dance' (ibid.).

Other cultural critics in major US newspapers also found fault with Flatley's hyper-sexualized version of Irish culture. 'Lord of the Flashdance' (Hulbert 1997) read one headline, while the *Boston Globe*'s critic described how 'the women eventually strip down to skimpy two-piece outfits. Erin Go Bra' (Temin 1997). The same critic argued that *Lord of the Dance* is 'an extravaganza that's more a homage to leather apparel and hair volumizers than to artistic heritage' (Temin 1997).

Many of the critiques of *Lord of the Dance* highlighted how women were being presented. Jennifer Dunning in a *New York Times* feature that praised certain aspects of the show but found others problematic, wrote:

> The shining colleens of sentimental memory probably no longer exist in Ireland. But mops of teased hair, layers of obvious makeup and sleazy mini-dresses give the dancing women, led by Bernadette Flynn and Gillian Norris, the look of junior sales clerks without a future. (Dunning 1997)

This reminds us that these theatrical presentations, whether authentically 'Irish' or not, provided opportunities for both *Riverdance* and later Flatley to redefine how Irish culture was seen.

The combined enterprise of *Riverdance* and Michael Flatley clearly illustrated that culture is not permanent. Its borders are never fixed. Individuals and groups can borrow from aspects of culture, recontextualize them, wield and even manipulate them for various purposes. In the case of the commercialization of Irish dancing in the 1990s, this new version of Irish culture was not being imposed on Ireland by some remote outside force. These productions were realized by people from *within* the culture; Doherty in Ireland, Flatley in the epicentre of the Irish dancing world in the US. They were entrepreneurs with the skills and the ability to bring a version of Irish culture to the global marketplace. Whether that was palatable, desirable, or representative of agreed Irish culture was irrelevant. What is significant is that the modern media skills needed for mass-market penetration were now available to the Irish themselves.

Bringing the Product into Homes

Before online streaming became mainstream, sales of video cassettes were a lucrative revenue stream for both the music and film industries. Home video sales were also highly profitable for *Riverdance* and Flatley. Doherty and McColgan were experienced television producers, so it was hardly surprising when *Riverdance* released a high-quality video of the live show. What was surprising was the level of success. A British firm, VCI, previously best known for its *Thomas the Tank Engine* children's videos, was engaged to distribute the product. The firm's director of marketing, Carole Gaskell, was quoted:

> We thought that we would only target the tape to the Irish and that only people who saw the show would buy it. To be honest, we were quite surprised to see sales spread beyond those groups, mainly by word-of-mouth. (Fitzpatrick 1996: 110)

In the US the *Riverdance* video was rush-released by Columbia Tri-Star in March 1996 to coincide with the show's New York debut, and sales were reported to be 61,000 units at a $24.95 retail price per unit. That said, with low tape duplication costs, once the initial production investment was recouped, tapes generated more revenue per unit than CDs. Later, Columbia Tri-Star relaunched the video and both *Riverdance* and *Lord of the Dance* achieved the type of sales enjoyed only by the biggest Hollywood blockbusters.

By the time Flatley's video (also priced at $24.95) was released in the US in February 1997, trade magazines were anticipating high sales and noted that *Riverdance* 'broke the ground for this kind of response' (Fitzpatrick 1996). By then, *Lord of the Dance* had reportedly already sold a million copies overseas on video. *Riverdance* had sold twice that number and reported trade figures were 1.5 million copies in Ireland and the UK alone (Bambarger 1996: 116). In the UK, according to its distributor VCI, it had achieved a commercial distinction. It was the highest-selling non-Disney title in UK history as well as the highest-selling music video.

This earlier overseas commercial success prompted a major sales campaign for *Lord of the Dance* in the US. *Billboard* magazine reported that a $500,000 advertising campaign was undertaken to promote the video (Fitzpatrick 1996), in addition to a television campaign – featuring a documentary-style infomercial – in the country's biggest markets. The influential network, PBS, was scheduled to broadcast the video soon after its release. The campaign worked, and when *Lord of the Dance* was made available *Time* magazine noted that *Riverdance* and *Lord of the Dance* were the second- and third highest-selling videos in the US (Bellafante and Dam 1997). Only the marketing might of Disney with their rereleased version of *Bambi* (1946) could prevent the Irish from topping the US and UK charts.

Amateur Steps: Flatley's Development

In light of these two approaches to presenting Irish culture, it is worth examining Flatley's early career and enterprise. His (2006) co-written autobiography provides recollections of his early dancing performances, as well as the business of the Irish dance productions that he was involved in. The latter reflections provide valuable insight into the enterprise of Irish dancing. While he was an accomplished and highly decorated Irish dancer, it is notable that, until *Riverdance*, dancing was not his profession. He supported himself via a series of jobs and even ran his own construction business in Chicago until it failed.

Flatley's story echoes the experiences of many other Irish emigrant families of the era, as we noted earlier. Ireland was the only Western European country whose population declined between 1900 and 1950 (Share et al. 2007: 151), and unusually its women had both a higher death rate and a higher emigration rate than in other countries (ibid.). As a result, employment and marriage prospects were low. Flatley's mother, from County Carlow, was one of the many women who emigrated from Ireland in the post-WWII years. She left in 1947, the same year that the dancer's father left County Sligo (Flatley 2006: 15). They met in Detroit and married in 1956 before moving to Chicago. The young Irish people, whom the Church had tried to keep separate in Ireland with the restrictions on 'non-locals' attending dances in the 1930s, were meeting and marrying in the US in the 1940s and 1950s. They were also raising their American-born children with aspects of Irish culture. Flatley recalled the records of The Clancy Brothers and Irish folk tunes in the family home, a Christian Brothers' education, and Irish dancing lessons from an early age.

The visits of musicians from Ireland were a feature of life for some Irish Americans, and for the Flatleys they proved to be important, linking the family with the Irish music scene as well as the professional industry of Irish culture. The traditional musician, Séamus Tansey, recalled being invited to the Flatley home following a gig in Chicago in 1972. There he saw, and was apparently impressed by, the dancing of the teenage Flatley (Flatley 2006: 36). An even more vital moment for the young Flatley was a mid-1970s visit by The Bothy Band to Chicago, when he met the group's founder and flautist Matt Molloy (Flatley 2006: 71). When Molloy joined The Chieftains in 1979, he recommended Flatley to the group as a dancer to accompany them during some of their live shows. This exposed Flatley not just to the Irish American audience, but also put him in direct contact with the professional business of Irish music and performance.

Flatley recalls touring with Comhaltas Ceoltóirí Éireann in the US in 1981–1982 (2006: 58–59), but it was an invitation for him to perform with The Chieftains on their US tour in 1981 that connected him most directly with the business of Irish music culture. Already a serial winner of amateur Irish dancing championships both in the US and Ireland, he hadn't found a way to make Irish dancing pay beyond giving occasional paid dancing lessons. The Chieftains also invited him to perform with them in London's Royal Albert Hall, the venue where, in 1975, they had realized they could become full-time professional musicians (Glatt 1997: 102–105). It is worth noting that the move from amateur to professional occurred relatively late in life for both The Chieftains and Flatley, particularly when pop music's new entrants were typically marketed to the youth market.

When Flatley was invited to perform at the *Mayo 5000* celebrations in 1993 (Flatley 2006: 85), he was approached by Moya Doherty about future possible collaborations. Doherty and her husband had, by this stage, enjoyed impressive success both in Ireland and abroad. Their combined resumés included hands-on experience in live television and theatrical performance; they understood what looked good on television and how to stage it. As they proved with *Riverdance*, they also had the business acumen to raise funding for domestic Irish cultural productions.

Professional Steps: The Flatley Business

The very public split between Flatley and the *Riverdance* team, and the subsequent legal battles, revealed key financial details about commercial Irish dancing. This is the sort of commercial information that is not usually available and it provides a very useful insight into the commercial realities of cultural production.

Flatley claimed he received £500,000 as part of the initial settlement (Flatley 2006: 146) when he was removed from *Riverdance*. Knowing he was out of *Riverdance*, but determined to pursue dancing as a profession, Flatley decided he could headline his own touring production. But to underwrite the show he needed outside investment, and he approached Bill Tennant at Universal's VVL subsidiary, who paid £800,000 in advance for the show's video rights (Flatley 2006: 144–46). Whilst Flatley's music was composed by another Irishman (Ronan Hardiman), for his business management Flatley, perhaps naturally, being American born, gravitated towards London and Hollywood managers. He joined forces with the experienced music manager John Reid, who managed Elton John, although the relationship did not last.

In Flatley's narrative, the split with Reid was caused by sales of the *Lord of the Dance* video (2006: 186). Ironically, it wasn't the failure of the video that prompted the termination, but its success. It went to number 1 in Britain but 'no one had even bothered to tell me' (ibid.). The London concert promoter Harvey Goldsmith attempted to broker a reconciliation between Flatley and Reid (2006: 188) but it was too late to save the business relationship. Breaking the contractual relationship with his English manager inevitably involved a court case to decide if Reid was legally entitled to either a share of Flatley's future revenue or to income he claimed he was owed by the dancer. The stakes of these disputes can be gauged by the substantial legal costs. Flatley claims he advanced £350,000 to lawyers to press his claim (2006: 229) while he also recalls Reid's statement at the conclusion of the trial of a 'substantial payment received' from Flatley (2006: 230).

Flatley then engaged an American, Bill Tennant, as his manager (2006: 200). Tennant was an experienced Hollywood veteran (Bart 1993), and a former vice-president at Columbia Pictures. He had made the deals for iconic films including *Butch Cassidy and the Sundance Kid* (1969), *Easy Rider* (1969), and *Rosemary's Baby* (1968). By the early 1990s, Tennant had revitalized the VVL home video business. He was therefore intimately familiar with how to develop and promote videos, a lucrative source of revenue for both *Riverdance* and Flatley.

Despite this, after a short time and a feeling that Tennant 'was underestimating me' (Flatley 2006: 212), Flatley engineered a termination from his manager, although this time avoiding any public court cases. If Tennant had indeed underestimated the commercial possibilities of Flatley's vision, it was because, for a cultural product that had grown out of the 'public service' RTÉ in Ireland (Smyth 1996a: 35), it was unprecedented. *Lord of the Dance* was generating £1 million a week (Flatley 2006: 189) even before debuting in the US. Flatley's account cited contemporary newspaper reports (2006: 190) that his show grossed £5.3 million in Britain with 210,000 seats sold, while advance sales for the debut Australian tour grossed £13 million with 250,000 seats sold in advance.

Lord of the Dance proved that a competitor to *Riverdance* could gross large sums in the US. There, high-profile media appearances, including the national Larry King and Jay Leno shows (Flatley 2006: 189) and, crucially, appearing at the Oscar ceremonies (2006: 203), raised Flatley's profile. Yet not all the reviews were positive. While comments including 'schlock elevates personality over talent, the commercial over the cultural' (Cooper 1997: 31) must have stung Flatley, they did not stop large numbers of tickets being bought for his performances. In fact, they served to reinforce his reputation as a 'self-made' man. He appeared on the 1997 *Forbes* list of '25 Highest-Earning Entertainers' and made frequent references to his worth and wealth, while his autobiography contains details of his material achievements and acquisitions to support his extravagant claims.

The building of both the *Riverdance* and Flatley brands proved that people in Ireland, and people of the Irish diaspora, could not only develop some of the world's highest grossing cultural products, but they could also own them. This was far removed from the long-standing media representations of poor Ireland in need of handouts, or the coy, innocent performance styles of some Irish acts. Perhaps the ultimate compliment to *Riverdance* and its celebration and commercialization of Irish culture came in an early review from the *Times of London*. A critic exclaimed:

> The show's producers have achieved something remarkable: global hybridisation. Now, how about applying a similar exercise to the British Isles and exploring the connections between Irish, English and Scottish dance? (Meisner 1995: 36)

Ireland's success could provide a formula for celebrating the cultural links between Britain and Ireland. Could London have paid Dublin a greater compliment? The Irish, ever the storytellers, now had the media experience to tell and monetize stories in their own way.

Consequences of the Creation and the Split

Doherty and Flatley found distinctive ways to present a live theatrical performance driven by Irish dancing. *Riverdance* was quickly 'cloned' by Doherty so that multiple troupes could tour simultaneously. At any given moment, up to three *Riverdance* groups could tour in different territories. While *Riverdance* sold more tickets, Flatley secured higher ticket prices to his shows. One was an ensemble production, the other a superstar-driven vehicle.

The fact that Irish dancing was now being discussed as sexy and sensual, even newsworthy, was a dramatic change unpredicted in the 1980s. Irish dance, once an area of self-expression and national identity, had now become a *spectacle* in the truest sense of the word. One of the most important aspects of *Riverdance* and Flatley's productions is that they were hybrid Irish culture: a marriage of music and visuals. In this context, it is worth noting that some of Flatley's early performances with The Chieftains came when the band had already married Irish music with appealing visuals. In 1984, one US journalist had written that 'soundtracks bring out the best in The Chieftains' (Himes 1984: 27) and he had argued that soundtracks had even been responsible for the group's commercial breakthrough in the US. According to a Paddy Moloney quote, part of the reason for Flatley's inclusion on their US tour had been 'to recreate one dance scene from the film' *The Year of the French* (1982). By the mid-1990s, with Irish dance spectaculars and pop music, entrepreneurs of Irish culture were no longer recreating notions of culture: they were creating them anew. They were now capable of combining music and creative performance to attract global audiences to Irish culture. The split between Flatley and *Riverdance* allowed the dancer to inject large doses of Hollywood glamour and glitz into Irish dancing. Yet it was cultural entrepreneurs in Ireland who had come up with the concept for *Riverdance* in the first place and had delivered it to the mass international entertainment market. In a very important sense, this was Ireland telling its own stories to the global audience.

11 Boyzone: 'Search is on for an Irish Take That'

To some observers, Boyzone could be viewed as a get-rich scheme hatched by a music industry Svengali. One Boyzone narrative is that they were assembled by the Dublin-based manager, Louis Walsh, in his pursuit of a version of Take That. But that account fails to acknowledge the enterprise, vision and industry of a few young Dubliners who got the project off the ground in the first place. It is worth retracing the early steps in the group's development to appreciate the contribution made by various individuals to its success.

Thanks to Walsh, Boyzone became household names. Thanks to Boyzone, Walsh became the Irish music industry's most recognizable 'behind-the-scenes' figure, and he surfed the wave created by the 1990s convergence of television and pop music. Reality television, with all of its inherent contradictions, brought a new era of pop music acts to the mass market before they had even released any product. A by-product of that process, the talent show 'judges' being made into public figures, raised Walsh's profile considerably.

If growing up in Dublin's new wave music scene had been great preparation for Bono to deal with the internet age, Walsh used his time in the Irish showband/cabaret scene to develop the skill set and acumen that made him prosper in the 1990s media terrain. When acts are developed and exposed via slickly produced, emotion-filled television 'talent' shows, how the audience *feels* about the act really matters. The contest is not to find the best, but the best *liked*. The media landscape enabled the new wave of pop talent shows. Whilst phone companies were the paid facilitators of these talent shows, newspapers were the unpaid facilitators.

The X-Factor show's popularity was staggering and even the broadsheet newspapers celebrated its economic success. In 2010, the *Guardian* reported that phone votes for the show totalled over 15 million (Plunkett 2010). That said, the *Telegraph* placed the show in its historical context. Its high viewership of 13.4 million was over three million viewers fewer than the *Opportunity Knocks* talent show in the 1970s. But the earlier show had failed to take advantage of its popularity. *Opportunity Knocks* celebrated commercial pop; *The X-Factor* celebrated the commercialization of pop. The newspapers documented some of the *The X-Factor* financial figures (Hensher 2010). The 2009 season had generated £75 million in advertising revenue: an ad space, lasting 30 seconds during the final, cost £250,000. The 2009 final alone had generated £8 million in phone votes, so it is understandable why one telecommunications firm, TalkTalk, signed a £20 million sponsorship deal with the show's producers. One dairy firm had even signed a £5 million co-branding venture.

Although it was a British programme, *The X-Factor* was incredibly significant for Irish pop. Ireland literally had a seat at the commercial juggernaut's top table, with Louis Walsh missing only a single series between 2004 and 2017. As the show's brand was built, so was Walsh's celebrity status. Irish acts were also included in the show from the very first series. The local press coverage of the Irish entrants illustrated aspects of *The X-Factor* business model. *The Irish Times* (McDonagh 2004) reported on the activities undertaken to mobilize votes for the Sligo singer, Tabby Callaghan.

Perhaps the article was slightly tongue-in-cheek, but it still highlighted the serious campaigning. The speeches at a local wedding were 'interrupted after an urgent message came through' that *The X-Factor* voting lines were open. The priest at Sligo cathedral 'finished off his sermon with an exhortation that they should vote for Tabby' while the Sligo County Council voted on a motion 'congratulating 23-year-old Tabby on his success and urging the public to vote for him'. It was passed unanimously. The local 'Friends of Tabby' campaigners, with 'military precision', were delivering 3,500 votes for him via text within 90 minutes of the phone lines opening in London each week. A local journalist identified the kernel of *The X-Factor*'s commercial success:

> People are as proud of Tabby as they are of Westlife but it is different because everyone feels they have a stake in this – their vote is keeping him in. (McDonagh 2004)

For television shows like *The X-Factor*, every vote did indeed count. Each call generated revenue for the show's owners.

It was hardly a surprise that talent shows were benefitting from the tribal instinct to cheer on the locals. They had been a feature of Irish social life for decades. In the 1970s, Irish communities came together to organize shows they *actually* had a 'stake in', notably *Tops of the Town*. There were few illusions that appearing on the show would lead to stardom. But this had changed by the 1990s. Now Irish communities came together to watch local acts on global television shows, and they paid global phone companies for the privilege of voting for those local favourites. The way that Irish people now connected with local entertainment had evolved, and the stakes – the prospect of global pop stardom – were much higher. Instead of paying an entrance fee to a local hall, the price of their 'stake' was now paid to a global telecommunications provider. They were also in direct competition with other communities, geographically, and fan-based, who were also paying to vote for their favourites. As the mainstream global music industry struggled to develop and market new artists, *The X-Factor* and Syco, the label formed to exploit its success, were leading the way. By 2010, according to reports (Hensher 2010), the firm was responsible for 70 per cent of Sony UK's music's profits.

Walsh benefited from Boyzone, Westlife and *The X-Factor* and he was the epicentre of global pop in a particularly profitable period. While Ireland had enjoyed rock success previously, most notably with U2, this was a position in global youth-pop that Ireland had never held before.

Network and Management Skills

Before his eventual success and high profile, Louis Walsh was a hard-grafting, persistent journeyman figure on the Irish music scene (Jackson 2001). He had grown up in rural Mayo, with parents who enjoyed Jim Reeves records. As a youngster, he ran the fan club for a local Mayo showband, The Royal Blues, and was later offered a job with the Tommy Hayden agency in Dublin. At a time when the showband business was downsizing into the cabaret circuit, he booked bands, including Lyttle People and Time Machine, who brought a dash of pop, and even light rock, into Irish cabaret.

In the 1980s, continuing the decentralized business model of the showband era from the late 1950s, local promoters and venue operators in Irish towns enjoyed the advantage of their powerful position. Without any alternative, Walsh and other agents were forced to do business with them. The local venue owners knew their markets, so profits for the Dublin-based booking agents like Walsh were not high. That said, Walsh enjoyed some commercial success with Johnny Logan and Linda Martin, both of whom won the Eurovision Song Contest, although this was during the 1980s when Walsh recalled 'the Eurovision certainly lost its appeal … you weren't guaranteed a hit [single] out of it' (Jackson 2001). He then booked rock bands onto the Irish circuit for a standard 10 per cent fee, although he recalled that he had frequently struggled to get paid his commission. When he began the Boyzone project, he had been bringing dance popstars from England (such as Sonya and Sinitta) for personal appearances. The journalist Joe Jackson (2001) recalled that Walsh was low on funds when he began managing Boyzone. He shared his management commission with John Reynolds because the latter had invested £10,000 in the project. It is a reminder that Walsh wasn't one of the better-off members of the Irish music scene at the time. Yet that didn't prevent him from achieving global pop success with multiple artists. His intangible resources – his network, his local insight, music knowledge, obvious hard work, and determination – compensated for this lack of finance. All he needed was a successful act.

The Group

Walsh put his media skills to use and found helpful allies in the Irish newspapers to promote his group, before they had performed – or had even been formed. The *Evening Herald* journalist Katie Hannon was particularly supportive, and quickly became part of his publicity campaign. On 1 November 1993, with the headline, 'Search is on for an Irish Take That', she wrote that Walsh was seeking young recruits with 'perfect pecs and varied vocals' (Hannon 1993a: 10). According to the story, thanks to a 'fortuitous encounter' Walsh already had two parts of his yet-to-be-assembled pop group: 'It's one of those happy coincidence stories that will gladden the hearts of *Smash Hits* readers in years to come' (ibid.). According to this story, Walsh had noticed two young men, Mark Walton and Shane Lynch, dancing in Dublin's POD nightclub. Even better, 'both work out regularly and have done some modelling' and 'they can sing and both have taken piano lessons' (ibid.). The two young men featured in the next stage of the media campaign: the well-publicized search for members of a new Irish boy band. Two weeks later the paper devoted two-thirds of a page, and a large photo, to the story with the headlines: 'They're all set to get the girls swooning' and 'Take That Irish-style'. Hannon (1993b: 3) wrote: 'We will shortly have a home-grown version of the teen sensations who have been taking the pop world by storm'.

The article retold the story of how Lynch and Walton 'were "discovered" by Louis while grooving to the latest sounds at the ultra-hip POD nightclub'. Since the newspaper had announced Walsh's plan two weeks earlier, he had 'been inundated with phone calls'. He had even managed to get them interviewed on Pat Kenny's prominent national radio show, and 'several major record companies' had expressed interest. BBC and Channel 4 television were 'clamouring to feature the final product'. It was scarcely believable, but it was printable, and that is what mattered. Just as *The X-Factor* would do later, the newspaper got its readers to have a stake in the new group. Readers were invited to suggest names for the group: the winner was promised some Wrangler clothes.

But a different version of the 'discovery' by Walsh is told in one of the official Boyzone books. In this account, the original band members were very active in their initial 'discovery' process. Shane Lynch was quoted on his recollection of seeing a *Smash Hits* TV show when he was 17:

> I was watchin' various bands and I thought 'I could do that, that's what I want to do'. I was 17, a mechanic at the time, didn't know if I could sing. I was in a choir once! I got the name of Louis Walsh, called him up, asked to meet him, sat down and talked to him and said 'The next time Ireland has a pop group, are you interested in managing it?' He said 'Yeah, great, wonderful, let's do it!' (Fallon 1997: n.p.)

Journalists at the *Evening Herald* (1993) continued to treat the assembly of the group as a news story. On 18 November, the *Evening Herald* reported that Walsh had originally planned to put 12 hopefuls through their paces, but 'such has been the reaction to news of the band, Louis now believes he will have to spread the auditions over two days' (1993: 19). The project was a success before it had even started.

The paper promised that its readers would be the first to know the line-up when it was finalized. By playing such a fundamental role in promoting the project, *Evening Herald* journalists would have envisioned future headlines: 'I was there for the birth of a band!'. On 8 December 1994, 13 months after the first mention of the project, the paper ran that headline. Hannon's access to the group gave her a first-person perspective on their formation. She had even attended the Boyzone auditions which, despite her encouraging articles at the time, she later described as 'not for the faint-hearted'.

> Although the urban-myth that hundreds thronged the place has taken root, the truth is the gathering was closer to the 30 or 40 mark.
>
> As for the standard: It was painfully embarrassing. They were all so beautifully turned out, but so many were astonishingly ... well ... bad. (Hannon 1994)

It was certainly an urban myth, often accepted as a fact, but it was one that Hannon had helped to construct.

Promotion

Shane Lynch later wrote that the auditions weren't quite as important to the group's formation as the 'urban myth' has claimed: 'I knew the lads from various things – Mikey through college, Stephen through dancing, Ronan and Stephen had been mates' (Fallon 1997: n.p.). The 'open auditions' had just been another clever element in promoting the group. But when Walsh had his team of young stars-in-the-making, his publicity efforts increased. He also formed a management partnership for the group, now named Boyzone, with John Reynolds, a nightclub owner and the nephew of an Irish Taoiseach.

By May 1994, when the group was officially launched at Reynolds's POD nightclub, the national newspapers were celebrating the band. 'Boyzone are no mere Chippendales' (Dillon 1994) and 'Boyz show their stuff at the POD' (Phelan 1994) read the headlines, while Walsh was positioned as the canny, controlling Svengali, even selecting the group's songs. He promoted his vision for the group:

> No drugs – absolutely not, and I'd prefer if they didn't drink or smoke either. Girlfriends are alright, as long as they stay out of sight. (Phelan 1994: 38)

The following month, June 1994, as the press publicized Boyzone's debut public gig (Welch 1994), they also claimed that the band would be opening for the current teen-sensations East 17 on their European tour. To add to the perception that Ireland had now produced a slick, competitive professional group, it was reported that £52,000 had already been invested in Boyzone. But even if this was true, to get to the international market Boyzone needed to find a record company that would fund them.

The *Evening Herald* journalist Eamon Carr was intimately familiar with starting a band from Dublin with global ambitions. It might have been two decades earlier, but his Horslips experience had proven that the local scene could be tackled with a combination of sophisticated promotion and marketing. What is notable is that he documented Boyzone not as an artistic expression but as a business start-up: 'the men in the moneyzone' ran the headline; 'they could become our first genuine pop export' was the possible economic outcome (Carr 1994b: 15). He helpfully broke down that Boyzone balance sheet, a potential 'how-to' for any budding Svengali in a small music market:

Auditions: £1,000
Stylist/Photography: £8,000
Recording: £22,000
Video/Choreography: £16,000
Design/Promotion/Printing: £5,000
Total Expenditure: £52,000

Irish acts attempting to make an impression on the global music industry could draw on local stylists to make them look appealing to that market. In this case, the stylist, Sonya Lennon, was publicly acknowledged by Walsh and his team. Carr was able to follow up this business story the next year when Boyzone headlined the famed Royal Albert Hall in London.

> In purely business terms, the Boyzone success story has been a text book case of market identification, meticulous planning and maximised promotion opportunities. (Carr 1995: 21)

The Record Deal (Global Label: Irish Branch)

Walsh and Reynolds had launched the band at a fortuitous time. PolyGram Ireland was being steered by Paul Keogh and he was ready and willing to invest in local acts. Reynolds was quoted, 'We had to get him [Keogh] involved; we know he's good and he's into marketing' (Carr 1994b).

Keogh was new to the music industry when he was appointed head of PolyGram in Ireland. To some, he was a surprising choice. One financial reporter (Quinlan 2017) later wrote: 'Keogh readily concedes that, unlike other music company bosses, he knew little about music'. Keogh asserted that his mandate was to make a profit: 'I ran a *business*' [emphasis added]. He had extensive experience in the fast-moving consumer-goods industry. His background was in the drinks industry, where he had worked in marketing for Guinness. Despite its association with its iconic brand, the UK firm at the time was a diversified company and Keogh had established his reputation as product manager for the Carlsberg, Steiger, and Furstenburg brands and for the non-alcohol Kaliber beer. He had also worked on the Budweiser campaign when the beer was launched in Ireland. He was later quoted on one of his tactics (Quinlan 2017). According to his recollection, Budweiser had a bad reputation in the key student target market, where it was perceived as a poor-quality, low-alcohol product. To counter this perception, he arranged for a Budweiser truck to be parked in the grounds of Trinity College Dublin during the annual summer ball. The truck was deliberately left unlocked and unattended so that students could liberally help themselves to quantities of the beer. If they woke up with hangovers, Budweiser's image as being lightweight would be shattered. Apparently, the plan worked. In any event, Budweiser became Ireland's best-selling lager.

If Keogh was able to give away free beer to students, he was also able to sell large quantities of albums. During the 1980s' music industry boom, many consumers repurchased their vinyl collections on the new, more expensive, and profitable medium of CD. Keogh was working on a Budweiser promotion – the Irish Derby horse race sponsored by the brand – when he met Maurice Oberstein, a horse-owner and the president of PolyGram records in the UK.

Oberstein was looking for someone to lead PolyGram's Irish operation and he hired Keogh.

The activities of the major labels in Ireland were not just confined to sales and marketing. They were also very influential in shaping the country's culture of music enterprise. Inevitably, they were active in pressuring the government to treat their concerns seriously. The International Federation of the Phonographic Industry (IFPI) was an established media and lobby presence, and Keogh was the head of the organization in Ireland in both 1989 and 1995. Naturally, the global major firms were an influential force in the body and as the head of the local branch of a multinational firm, Keogh had no illusions about what his role was:

> We are answerable to our shareholders, we have to mix being adventurous with keeping a clear business head and stay in our position in the top four record companies worldwide. (Keogh 1993: 23)

At the same time, Keogh and the major international firms could find common cause with Irish acts; combined, they made a more formidable lobbying force. The industry felt that it had plenty to gain from lobbying the Irish government. Even as U2 were enjoying major success, the national newspapers carried headlines including 'We're poor record buyers' (Sheridan 1988), 'Ireland holds dismal record' (Sheridan 1989) and 'Music tax no hit with industry' (O'Brien 1989). These reported Keogh's argument that Ireland's market for music was being hampered by government policy. In 1988, the papers reported that New Zealand, whose population was similar in size to Ireland's, had a music market that was twice as big (Sheridan 1988); Ireland's small market was attributed to the slow adoption of the new, more expensive, CD format. Ireland, according to Keogh, had the 'lowest per capita spending in Europe' on music. The average annual spending on music per capita was £13 in the US, £14 in France and the UK. In Ireland it was £3.99. To Keogh: 'The reason for the lagging behind is the consumer perception of the high price of albums and discs' (Sheridan 1989: 15).

Industry representatives blamed the Irish government for the high prices of albums locally, and they were furious that music products faced a 40 per cent import tax and a 25 per cent sales tax. Aware that close to 50 per cent of Ireland's population was under 25, Keogh represented the buying and listening to music as a public good. He argued that buying and listening to music benefited society:

> We are penalising them with this high level of taxation. Wouldn't it be better to have them buying records instead of some less desirable

> items and to have them listening to recorded music instead of hanging around on the streets? (O'Brien 1989: 8)

In 1993, just as Walsh and Boyzone were looking for a record company to partner with, Keogh (1993) was publicly identifying what he perceived as obstacles to profitability for PolyGram in Ireland. The Irish market was still hesitant about adopting CDs; CDs only made up 40 per cent of the recorded music sales. Vinyl represented a paltry 5 per cent of the market. Most Irish consumers bought the cheapest type of sound media, cassette tapes, which accounted for more than half of the value of total music sales. Disturbingly for the centralized music industry, one-third of tapes sales in Ireland were blank tapes used for home-recording. While we showed earlier how home-made tape collections were a vital aspect of the punk and DIY scenes, naturally, the industry powerbrokers viewed home-taping on blank cassettes as a major threat to their profits. Irish consumers, 300,000 of whom were unemployed, were assembling their own music collections on home-recorded music cassettes from radio, records and CDs.

Naturally, in the small Irish music industry, Walsh and Keogh came into contact. Keogh was later quoted by Quinlan (2017) in a piece for the *Irish Independent*:

> Louis [Walsh] came in to me one day with John Reynolds saying 'I have a brilliant idea, the Irish version of Take That'. I told him 'I've heard worse from you Louis'.

Although he felt Walsh was exaggerating when he claimed that both EMI and Sony wanted to sign Boyzone, Keogh was interested enough to commit PolyGram funds to sign and develop the act. That said, he was quoted as claiming that he 'panicked a little' (ibid.) when he saw the band's early television appearance on *The Late Late Show* in November 1993.

Despite the highly public amateurish performance on TV, the Irish newspapers continued to boost the boy band, and by December 1994 Hannon was able to boast, justifiably, and with pride, that she 'was there for the birth of a band!'. Now they were using 'Madonna's choreographer' and Take That's former producer, Ian Levine. The recording session with Levine sent a signal, albeit an expensive one, that Boyzone were (or deserved to be) in the same league as Take That.

Although they were signed to the major label PolyGram, Boyzone were able to enjoy several benefits of the local music scene. These included cost-effective yet high-quality promotional tools. Thanks to the availability of high-quality local studios and producers, they were able to record in Dublin at budget rates. The single, 'Father and Son' – produced at the STS studios by Paul Barrett, who was known for his work with U2 – reportedly cost a mere £600 (Foley 2002). It went to number 1 in Ireland.

Boy bands require a market-specific contemporary mix of sound and visuals, and in 1994 Ireland was able to deliver locally produced high-quality videos for a reasonable price. Bill Hughes (from Athy, County Kildare) directed the band's early videos and communicated the band's teen appeal in a way that had been so laughably lacking in the early *Late Late Show* appearance. As Carr (1994b) documented, Hughes had 'undercut' his normal fee to help the emerging venture.

Another one of Walsh's cost-effective marketing schemes for the band involved having them stand outside the Dublin Point venue when visiting boy bands played at the venue. As the concertgoers streamed out, the band would introduce themselves and hand out photographs of themselves to their target market. But by December 1994, instead of meeting Take That fans as they streamed out of the city-centre venue (Westlife 2009: 86), they were meeting their own audience who screamed at them during in-store appearances.

Boyzone continued to be supported by the Irish branch of PolyGram. In addition to Keogh, managers at the label (including Ailish Toohey) organized, scheduled and planned opportunities for them. As Eamon Carr reported in 1998, they quickly became 'the most successful chart-topping band Ireland has ever produced' (Carr 1998). As boy bands became more lucrative, naturally others were signed. Some of the local methods of promotion were clearly designed to feed the hype. One anonymous industry worker told us about one tactic. When in-store appearances were organized, the band's fan club members were alerted. With the knowledge that most of the band's fans had already bought their current single, Irish record label workers simply handed cash to the fans. They used the money to queue to buy copies of the single and to get to meet the band. The shops got sales, the record label fed the 'buzz' for the band, and the fans got some time with their idols. Everyone was a winner. Apart from people who want a straightforward and accurate pop sales chart, that is. Clearly this tactic meant that new and independent artists who could not afford such tricks were excluded from the chart.

Boyzone's commercial success eclipsed the previous achievements of Ireland's acts on the British charts. The Boomtown Rats had enjoyed two UK chart-toppers; U2 had managed three. The Rats and U2 were seen by some as *rock* groups; it had been a quarter of a century since an Irish *pop* star, Gilbert O'Sullivan, had achieved two UK number 1 singles in the early 1970s. By 1998, Boyzone had four; the following year they had six. Amazingly, the group's first 16 singles released in Britain reached the Top 3 of the sales charts.

Albums are more lucrative than singles, and here Boyzone's achievements were even more remarkable. Their first four albums reached number 1 in Britain. *Billboard* (Pride 1999) reported on the success of the fourth of these, *By Request*, in 1999. Boyzone sold 280,000 units in the first week of its release. Even more impressively, the Irish group sold more than the rest of the Top 20 *combined*. Ireland was finally at the pinnacle of the fast-moving consumer pop world.

Ireland's Pop Position: Epicentre or Periphery?

Many members of boy bands have struggled to sustain an audience as they grow older. Yet, between 2000 and 2009, Ronan Keating had graduated from Boyzone and had brought four solo albums to number 1 in Britain, thereby proving that Irish pop stars could outlast their boy bands. Ireland, to use the cliché, was punching above its weight in pop, and PolyGram Ireland's local signing had been one of the multinational's most profitable signings.

But Boyzone's commercial ascent was not as straightforward as it might appear. Within the PolyGram company, the key decision-making flow from Dublin to London was not smooth. In fact, Keogh, as the head of PolyGram's Irish operation, didn't initially find the London headquarters supportive of his local act. As Carr (1995) reported, Keogh's parent company had originally rejected his group, despite his enthusiasm and investment in them. Some of his Boyzone activities were undertaken '*in defiance of his peers in London*' (emphasis added). He was quoted: 'We had a typical Irish scenario. Signed to an Irish company but can't break them internationally' (Carr 1995: 21). In a later piece (Kerr 1999: 48) he was quoted as saying that 'Most people thought it [Boyzone] wasn't going to happen, including my own [London-based] record company'.

Years later Keogh recalled that he had spent £250,000 on Boyzone (Quinlan 2017). If true, and there is no reason to question it, PolyGram enjoyed a massive return on its investment. But some of this investment was made on initially breaking the group in Britain *without* the authorization of the company's office there. This investment was prompted by Walsh securing a major opportunity. To Keogh and PolyGram Ireland 'we were running out of time because Louis had got them on the *Smash Hits* tour' of the UK (Quinlan 2017). That type of high-profile opportunity can sway radio stations to play singles. Keogh was quoted: 'so we serviced the UK market from here [Ireland] which was a first ... we had to learn how to flog [records to] the English market'. In other words, the Irish branch paid for promotion in the British headquarters' own territory. It was only once Boyzone took off and were established that 'an embarrassed

British PolyGram' eventually began committing their own resources to the group (Carr 1995).

One Irish newspaper reported on a phone call that Keogh received from Mo Oberstein, who as head of PolyGram in the UK had first hired Keogh to run the Irish operation. By this stage, Oberstein had left the firm and he gave his protégé a warning:

> Keogh, you've got to get out. You're not meant to sign successful acts in Ireland. You're showing up all the guys who are paid huge money in England to find the next boy band. (Kerr 1999: 48)

Keogh was quoted: 'I've always tried to challenge the system' (Kerr 1999: 48). Yet that system was apparently still in place. That system dictated that the music industry remained centralized, and Ireland was still at its periphery, even when it was delivering successful acts like Boyzone to the global marketplace.

12 Westlife: 'He's got to be kidding me'

Naturally, the success of Boyzone inspired other Irish boy bands who went in search of record deals and stardom. One English A&R man, scouting for talent, recalled in his 2004 autobiography a phone call from a manager in Dublin telling him that he:

> should come to Ireland immediately because he had put together a fantastic boy band ... they were six Irish lads with the best voices he'd ever heard.

Naturally the English executive asked what they looked like: 'Amazing, just amazing', he was told. He flew to Dublin.

> ... my first thought was, 'He's got to be kidding me'. I thought some of them were really ugly ... two of them at least had great voices ... But I felt, in visual terms, the group would never work.
>
> 'I'm not signing the band,' I told him flatly, 'I just can't market them, they look all wrong. Why don't you just keep [two] and get some other better-looking members.'
>
> 'No [said the manager], I'm afraid I'm not going to do that, I'm going to stick with them.'
>
> I told him if he changed his mind to call me.

Two months later the manager phoned him again, declaring:

> 'I've done it; I've changed the line-up – come and see. I've got rid of four of them and I've brought in some new members'. (Cowell 2004: 103)

The English executive returned to Dublin, was impressed, and signed the band.
    The band manager was Louis Walsh, the A&R man was Simon Cowell, and the band was Westlife. Previously, Cowell had enjoyed some success with Five, a boy band designed to be a male version of the Spice Girls. He also had prior

experience with an Irish act who had a hit in Britain, 'Them Girls Them Girls', by Zig and Zag. The irreverent popular television puppets, while musically not Ireland's pop high point, had made it to the British Top 5 in December 1994. Cowell was somewhat of a maverick in the music industry and delighted in taking acts without credibility into the pop landscape. He succeeded with two thirty-something actors, Robson and Jerome, as well as The Power Rangers.

There is absolutely no question of how formidable a team Walsh, Cowell and Westlife were. Like clockwork, Cowell released an album on his Syco label every year by the group just in time for the key Christmas market. Astonishingly, they maintained this pattern for 12 years. The albums generally went to number 1 in the British charts.

Cowell's autobiography reinforces the myth of him as a modern pop culture pantomime villain; the hard-nosed, yet continually right music man. Even the title, *I Don't Mean to be Rude, But...* (2004), plays up to his public image. Yet his personal narrative provides insight into the Irish entertainers who worked with him during his public career at the modern overlap between television and music. Cowell's music industry account of Westlife as a group that Walsh 'had put together' (2004: 103) masks the hard work that the band had done themselves *before* they came to his attention.

While Boyzone had limitations that prevented even greater success (notably in the US market), with Westlife Walsh found himself at the front lines of market-engineered pop. With Boyzone, he had first-hand experience of taking a group of Irish lads to large global sales. Naturally, he wanted to enhance his reputation and enjoy even higher sales with his next product, so it is tempting to view Westlife as designer-pop built and engineered by an industry insider. However, that narrative side-lines the enterprise of the actual band members. Even before they encountered Walsh, the group members had shown considerable enterprise. This was not the tale of Walsh handpicking and assembling a group of adolescents and introducing them to each other. While it is unlikely that a 'boy band' based in and managed from County Sligo could have successfully taken themselves to global market success, they did acquire the skills there to prepare themselves for that eventuality. There was a considerable amount of do-it-yourself activity in the early development of Westlife.

The group's official biography, *Our Story* (2009), represents the three founding members of Westlife – Shane Filan, Kian Egan and Mark Feehily – acquiring those music and organizational skills in their native Sligo. It places this activity in the context of their family backgrounds. Supportive family members provided resources, and the group's first paying customers were from the local community.

Shane Filan was one of seven children born to parents who were both entrepreneurs. They ran a café and lived above it. Filan's mother is described as the manager, while his father was the chef. While there was 'no real background of singing or music' (2009: 3) in his family, the young Filan was encouraged to sing at family gatherings and later appeared in his school musicals. His future band mate, Kian Egan, was also one of seven children, and as a schoolboy had performed in public poetry recitals. An older brother gave him early piano lessons while his older sister staged variety shows at the local community hall. After his father bought him a guitar, and inspired by Green Day and Metallica, Egan briefly joined some local rock bands and performed at school events. The third member of the Sligo group, Mark Feehily, grew up outside of the town where his grandfather, a prominent local entrepreneur, owned a pub. Feehily recalled listening to his father's record collection, and being exposed to US TV music channels, thanks to a home-installed satellite dish. Like Filan, he appeared in local school musicals, including *Annie Get Your Gun* and *Oliver Twist*, as well as variety shows.

Young performers need places to perform in and Sligo was well-served, thanks to an early 1980s initiative to deliver a venue to the town. The 340-seat Hawk's Well Theatre, which had opened in 1982, was funded by the local council, the tourist board, and the Arts Council of Ireland. It hosted both local and visiting productions. Feehily later recalled how the 'Hawk's Well Theatre plays a big part in my story and that of Westlife' (2009: 24). It was at the theatre that he attended his first musical, *Grease*, staged by Mary McDonagh, a local producer, director and choreographer. McDonagh had cast both Egan and Filan in the musical, something the latter described as 'the first big break I got' (2009: 4).

After seeing Boyzone on TV, the Sligo youngsters decided to form their own boy band, Six As One, with three other locals. When Mary McDonagh's *Grease* returned for more performances, she included the band, who performed Backstreet Boys' covers during a break in the performance, to a favourable response. She then arranged for them to perform a headlining show at the venue, and they delivered a full set of boy-band covers. Soon, several of the six began to write their own songs and in November 1997, having changed their name to IOYOU, they released a single, 'Together Girl Forever'.

While it often appears that boy bands are a product of the centralized music industry, it is worth noting just how much IOYOU achieved in the local scene. Sligo is a small town on Ireland's northwest coast, but it had an accessible theatre and an impresario who gave the group their first performance opportunity with the *Grease* show, followed by their own headlining shows. It also had a local newspaper that enthusiastically reported on the new group.

Headlines like 'Huge demand for Boys band tickets' (*Sligo Champion* 1997a), 'The boys are back in town' (*Sligo Champion* 1997b), 'I O You delight large crowd' (*Sligo Champion* 1997c) and 'I O YOU single launch on Friday' (*Sligo Champion* 1997d) helped to raise their profile. They even made the front page with charity Christmas carol singing (*Sligo Champion* 1997e).

Sligo boasted recording studios good enough to produce a single, as well as a record shop to sell it. The record shop released the single, on CD and cassette, on their own label, Sound Records. The town's non-music businesses were also supportive; the local menswear shop provided stage clothes, while the local hairdresser groomed the band. The local shopping centre even hosted a show as part of the 'Sligo Shopping Spree'. In December 1997, the band made their debut national television appearance in a brief feelgood piece about them singing to children at a local hospital. They also played their first gig outside of their hometown in neighbouring Castlerea. In January 1998, the group performed at half-time during a Sligo Rovers football match.

Convinced of their commercial potential, McDonagh offered the band a management contract, but Filan's mother had another idea (Filan 2014: 30–33). She had been born in the same village as Louis Walsh although they hadn't met, and she persistently phoned his office for weeks. When she finally made contact with Walsh, she convinced him to meet her son. Two of the group met with Walsh in Dublin. He had seen them in their television appearance, and with only three days' notice, he offered them the opening slot on The Backstreet Boys' two Dublin concerts. In the late 1990s boy-band world, The Backstreet Boys were as big as you could get, so the concerts provided IOYOU with the chance to appear in front of their potential home audience.

Suitably impressed with their performance, Walsh decided to manage the group, but he demanded changes. What was good enough for a local Sligo boy band didn't meet with his ideas of what future world stars looked like. Walsh wanted personnel changes. The band members remembered the difficulty of telling their friend Derek that he was no longer in the group (Westlife 2009: 56–59). When the next group member was axed, Walsh personally made a phone call to inform him (2009: 62–63). He also arranged the auditions for their replacements.

There is no question that the combination of Walsh and Cowell steered Westlife to their eventual international success, and that success can help us understand how the music industry functions. Their debut single, 'Swear It Again' (1999), was written by the established pop songwriter Steve Mac, who was selected by Walsh (Westlife 2009: 61). Stylists and photographers were engaged by Cowell and Walsh – at least five of each according to the band – while the video for the song, which cost £150,000, was shelved when Cowell didn't like it (2009: 96). They knew that, for boy bands, image was (almost) everything, and the group featured as cover stars on key magazines including *Smash Hits* before they had released any music. The song was recorded in Sweden's Cheiron Studios, guaranteeing a sound similar to the other radio hits made there. It entered the charts at number 1. As we noted in the Introduction, drawing from Ola Johansson (2020), Cheiron was a major element in Sweden becoming a dominant force in global pop music production.

No Irish act had achieved the UK chart success that Westlife enjoyed in the period from April 1999 to November 2000. During those nineteen months, their first six singles went to number 1. With an irony that Cowell probably didn't appreciate, their seventh single was kept from the top spot by a novelty song from the television character Bob the Builder.

Business and Boy Bands, Social and Personal

From both of their accounts, the group and Cowell enjoyed a close relationship, albeit one where his opinion dominated. 'I have never ever, ever backed down … the minute you start to compromise on a band or an artist, you're finished' (Cowell 2004: 113). He wrote that 'working with Westlife is textbook A&R' and compared the dynamic between a record label executive and an artist to working in film, where:

> everybody has to know their place … Westlife's success is due to the fact that they have amazing voices, great charisma, and they put their trust in me and their manager. (2004: 114)

In the group's account, Kian Egan was quoted:

> Without him [Cowell], we wouldn't be Westlife and we wouldn't be where we are today in my opinion. In those early days, and I'm being very honest here, we were, 'What do you want us to do? Yes, sir, no, sir, three bags full, sir.' That sounds terrible, but actually we *liked* what he was suggesting [original emphasis]. (Westlife 2009: 100)

This account was written when Cowell had morphed from being an A&R man into being one of the most powerful players in the global music industry, via the television shows, *American Idol*, *The X-Factor*, *America's Got Talent*, and their counterparts on British television. His Syco record label had released records by acts including One Direction, Little Mix, Olly Murs, Alexandra Burke, and Leona Lewis. These television shows marked a new stage in the relationship between music and television. In a sense, the artist was the centre of attention, but in practice the artists were at the centre of a modern media triangle whose sides are television, tabloids, and audience. The 'judges' on these shows, and the televisual appeal of the artist narrative, is at the heart of these presentations. While previously it mattered how an artist looked, now it mattered how their *story* looked. Both Cowell and Walsh have enjoyed prominence in this new role where the executive or gatekeeper has become the star.

This prominence of the 'judges' overshadows the artist, who, after all, will be replaced in the next series, or even in the next week. The process mirrors the traditional short shelf life of boy bands for whom a younger, more 'relatable' group is always threatening. For Westlife, even a small public reduction in their market power felt like a setback. This is a potent reminder of the precarious nature of a pop star's life; the media (including artist autobiographies) are engaged in a constant process of representation.

The Boyzone/Westlife Irish boy-band phenomenon coincided with dramatic changes in the Irish economy. The published narratives from the Westlife camp provide a very clear illustration of how individuals and financial institutions interacted during the period known as the Celtic Tiger. Shane Filan writes about his recollection of early 2000s Ireland:

> The Irish economy was booming, everybody was talking about the Celtic Tiger, and I decided to buy five houses in Sligo and rent them out. (Filan 2014: 129)

An Irish bank was happy to lend the funds he wanted, and they only required a 10 per cent deposit. At the time Filan was worried about Westlife's future; Brian McFadden had just left the group. There is an irony in his description of the investment as a 'safety net' to counter his anxiety about the group's future. Yet it seemed like a shrewd move at the time, and within 18 months Filan's houses had increased in value by €500,000 (Filan 2014: 140). But buying ready-built houses meant that the builder enjoyed a significant mark-up. Why not cut out the builder by buying a site and arranging your own construction? That is what Filan did when he formed a partnership with his brother (2014: 141), and they bought a site in the neighbouring county for a million euros. It came complete with planning permission for 45 houses. Once again, the bank was happy to lend the funds, and quickly after that the brothers expanded their property portfolio by purchasing yet another site. This one cost over one million euros.

The Filans weren't the only Irish people snapping up property at the time in the hope of quick profits. Fintan O'Toole (2009: 9) described the outcome of the national spending splurge between the mid-1990s and the end of the 2000s: Irish households and firms had the highest level of debt in the European

Union. The Celtic Tiger economic era, starting in the mid-1990s, 'saw Ireland being touted as a role model for other economies' (Lucey et al. 2019: 1), but in the long run a dimmer view was taken by some commentators: 'the Irish model of development had come to seem more like a threat than a promise' (Lucey et al. 2019: 8).

Successful popstars bought mansions, and the media took delight in breathlessly reporting the details. Filan bought his 'dream home' in Carraroe, County Galway. Then another property developer purchased a nearby site. Distressingly for Filan, the developer planned to build a 15-storey hotel on the site. In a move 'to protect my home, my family and our privacy' (Filan 2014: 142), Filan decided to buy the site that separated the proposed hotel from his family home. Once again, the bank was happy to lend the funds. Filan offered €1 million for the land but ended up paying €2.5 million. Naturally, he needed money to develop his expanding property portfolio, and the bank continued to lend him the funds to do that.

At the same time, Westlife (now without McFadden) needed to release another album. Cowell, despite his newfound public profile as a television personality and celebrity talent judge, had time to reimagine the group: 'You've lost a member, lost a voice, so we need to change things around a bit. You're going to be the Rat Pack' (Filan 2014: 143). Cowell's vision was a more sophisticated singing group, distancing themselves from the whole idea of a boy band, and harking back to the Las Vegas crooners of Frank Sinatra and his contemporaries.

Life in Westlife was public by design, and favourable newspaper and magazine coverage played a vital role. They quickly graduated from *Smash Hits* and *Top of the Pops* magazines to the tabloids and then, when well-heeled and recognizable, to the British lifestyle celebrity magazines. As one of the group recalled in their autobiography: 'fortunately, *OK!* and *Hello* have always been kind to us' (Westlife 2009: 156). It would be a mistake to confuse this kindness for charity, however: the magazines were invested in celebrities whose colour photos could shift copies. In this symbiotic relationship, the magazines were often happy to support the lavish lifestyles they featured. Weddings were popular with readers: for the magazines it was worthwhile to part-fund and get exclusive photos from a Westlife wedding. The band's Nicky Byrne recalled:

> It was a very lucrative offer ... we could afford to throw the most fairytale wedding for all our family and friends. We hired the Chateau d'Esclimont, just an hour away from Paris, had a free bar the whole weekend and invited 400 guests, no expense spared, and

> that could not have happened without the input of the magazine.
> (Westlife 2009: 156)

The Irish newspapers reported that the magazine's wedding gift to the couple was £850,000. But it wasn't without controversy. The Irish newspapers were happy to critique the event. One paper claimed that the couple "have been criticised for holding the ceremony outside of Ireland" (McDermott 2003). Emma Connolly's (2003) headline, 'It's the wedding that style forgot', summed up such hostile attitudes. The double-edged sword of celebrity culture deals was evident in quotes attributed to the publicist co-ordinating the event. Holding the *Hello!*-exclusive ceremony in France was 'a ploy to try and have some peace and quiet amongst family and friends'. As unlikely as this seemed, the media event produced an even more unlikely outcome. One Irish journalist (O'Connor 2003) wrote that 'the Taoiseach [Irish prime minister] emerged from it badly wounded'.

The bride's father was indeed the then Irish Taoiseach, Bertie Ahern, and the newspaper reported that he had been booed by locals at the event which was policed by 'British bulldogs, threatening tattooed heavies' (O'Connor 2003) as well as by armed French police. According to this press report, one of them had 'kung-fu kicked an Irish journalist'.

Naturally two sides of the story emerged. Byrne wrote:

> the media said the security was a shambles, people were booing outside – this was all bullshit. But worst of all, as Georgina drove through to the wedding in a blacked-out car, one of the press shouted at her and called her a whore. (Westlife 2009: 157)

Whatever the details were, it was clear that the press didn't always feel that celebrities deserved respect. The media clearly had power and they could break reputations as easily as make them. McFadden's departure from the band highlighted this reputation-breaking ability. The Irish media coverage of his first solo performance reinforced the idea that the new pop stars were viewed as celebrities rather than music artists. A measure of their success was the presence of other celebrities at their public events. The first part of a lengthy *Evening Herald* article (Healy 2004) certainly wasn't focused on music: his first solo performance was reported a 'no-show by celebrities', McFadden 'without any support from his music industry colleagues'. Humiliatingly, readers were told that he 'didn't even attract D-list celebrities'. More than a hundred tickets had been given away in competitions, while the remainder of the attendees were 'self-confessed friends and family'.

The piece included a litany of alleged artistic, business, and personal failures. McFadden was 'full of hatred and bitter resentment' and his songs were 'self-pitying'. His new video had been withdrawn due to complaints from a Dublin school, and he had allegedly engaged in an 'illicit night with a lap dancer before his wedding'. Recently his wife had 'been spotted enjoying a late-night heart to heart with Robbie Williams'. Elton John was quoted:

> I nearly died when I listened to 'Irish Son' [McFadden's single]. I absolutely hated it. It's the worst lyric on a record I've ever heard. I had to take it off in case I committed suicide. It's just horrible. (Healy 2004: 3)

Without the Westlife brand and machine behind McFadden, the Irish media treated his concert not as his celebration but as a career obituary.

Meanwhile, with his expanding property portfolio, McFadden's former bandmate, Shane Filan, was enjoying the heights of Westlife. The bank continued to lend him money (Filan 2014: 150) so he borrowed another €10 million and began developing his County Leitrim site. He even invested in a helicopter with another businessman. But Cowell's idea of reinventing the band along the lines of Frank Sinatra wasn't as successful as their previous releases; they didn't even reach the number 1 spot in Ireland. That said, success is relative, and most pop groups would be delighted if any of their albums sold 600,000 copies, as *Let Me Be Frank* did in the UK. But when sales figures have become part of your narrative, any dip can be interpreted as sullying your status.

Filan's reputation as a successful pop-star-cum-businessman was about to become even more tarnished. After he had spent 'hundreds of thousands of pounds' on planning permissions for his properties, the bank decided to 'pull the plug' (Filan 2014: 215). They no longer felt he was worthy of credit. They had initially lent him the money without knowing for sure he could repay it. When he couldn't, they simply acquired the properties. Either way they won. That cold commercial logic is a reminder of the era within which Westlife existed, when the supposed income – their potential earnings – of future popstars became a feature of their press coverage. Wealth and pop success were intrinsically linked as Ireland grew into its Celtic Tiger image.

But for artists like Westlife who plied their trade during this time, celebrity status was not straightforward. They existed within a media culture where press coverage – like continued loans from banks, or continued investment by record labels – was *not* guaranteed. Indeed, for the media, a story about a pop star failing was just as attractive as the story of their rise. In the context of Westlife, it is also worth noting the differences between banks and record labels. When you borrow money from a bank and you buy something with it, you own it provided you repay the original loan. But when a record label invests in you, even when you repay all the money that they spent, they still own the rights to your recordings. In an era of rapid success and almost instant celebrity, record labels (like banks) play the long game.

13 U2, the Virgin Prunes and Graphic Art

Ireland doesn't just produce pop music; it also produces the visual representations of pop. The cover of The Virgin Prunes' (1982) single 'Pagan Love Song' is one of the most striking visuals in Irish pop. Guggi, one of the group's frontmen, stares out at the viewer, his face and upper torso smeared with colourful tribal make-up. The back-cover features another of the band's singers, Gavin Friday, grinning unsettlingly with his face soiled theatrically with black and white make-up. The message is clear: the contents of this package were not designed for the mass market. On the other hand, the cover of U2's *Joshua Tree* (1987) album is clearly aimed at that mass market. It is striking in its black, white and gold elegance, the cinematic letter-box proportions of the band photograph proclaim monumental permanence. This was rock for the ages. For both The Prunes and U2, different as they were, it is apparent that artwork was an integral element of their representation.

The two record sleeves share the same graphic designer, Steve Averill. To access the global market, Irish acts may have signed record deals with overseas companies, but they were able to work with skilled graphic designers in Ireland who helped them to stand out in that global market. At times the design of music products may feel far removed from corporate mainstream advertising, yet as music industry theorists have often noted, music scenes influence style, trends and fashion. In Dick Hebdige's seminal work, *Subculture: The Meaning of Style* (1979), he argued that the unique and rebellious styles and symbols of youth cultures may initially challenge the mainstream but 'they inevitably end by establishing new sets of conventions; by creating new commodities' (1988: 96). While this sounds as though the innovation of counterculture gets turned into crass commercial products, in a more positive sense, mainstream culture gets altered in some way by the culture from the margins. Theorists, including Buxton (2005: 435), have argued that the styles originating from music subcultures have been successful in 'formulating a design aesthetic in the wider sense'. To him, 'rock music plays a role in [mainstream] product design'; later, other industries use music's styles and designs to sell their products. Music packaging, unless achieved in small numbers through hand-crafted DIY processes, is, quite literally, industrial design. Ireland's popular music graphic designers – like our sound technicians and tour managers – have to compete with the best globally.

It is worth placing these creatives within their local historical context. Recently there has been a heightened appreciation of what visual art means in Ireland. The Irish cultural commentator Mick Heaney (2011) argued that 'Ireland's visual culture had long been eclipsed by accomplishments in other creative fields'. Despite this, he maintained that 'Ireland's visual imagination is alive and well, and catching up with our literary heritage' (ibid.). Heaney quoted Luke Gibbons, the cultural theorist, who argued that the respect for visual culture was evidence of Ireland's growing modernity: 'modernity is bound up with spectacle … even rock music and *Riverdance* are bound up with image and spectacle' (Heaney 2011). He also quoted the founder of Dublin's innovative exhibition space, The Science Gallery, as saying:

> By being too rigid in your definition of fine art, you miss interesting work, be it posters, album covers or new digital devices. (ibid.)

It is interesting that Irish cultural experts and cultural practitioners viewed pop music design as part of the country's cultural landscape. Industrial designs – in this case, record, CD and digital graphics – were (and continue to be) a powerful tool for stimulating interest in pop music.

As with other elements of its industrial development, Ireland had lagged behind other European countries in terms of investing in design skills for industry. Cyril Barrett (2010: 590) has documented the slow but eventual embrace of product and graphic designers in the country. In the early 1960s, the task of improving industrial design was assigned to Córas Tráchtála (Irish for Trade Board), which was set up by the Irish government to develop the country's exports. A group of Scandinavian industrial designers was commissioned to study ways to aid Ireland, and they delivered a report – *Design in Ireland* (Scandinavian Design Group 1962) – which recommended starting an institute of visual arts with a design department. Sadly, it wasn't adopted at the time, and it wasn't until the 1970s that the National College of Art belatedly included 'Design' in its name. In the 1960s, public figures who were aware of the need for high-quality industrial and craft design were voicing their distress. Some of Ireland's most vocal supporters of a more modern Irish economy warned against the familiar trap. If you protect local industries too much, they are unequipped to compete globally. But if you ignore them, they can wither. The head of the tourist agency, Bord Fáilte, was quoted on the state of Irish industrial art:

> The fine arts had occasionally been killed or weakened by too much kindness while the applied arts had been so often allowed to fend for themselves in the back rooms of night technical schools. (*Irish Press* 1966: 7)

Clearly, for a small country with an open economy there was value in having access to local designers who could compete globally. Steve Averill might be the best-known of Ireland's pop designers, but he is also a good example of how one individual can inhabit multiple roles in both the local music scene and the music industry. As a musician, club impresario, record-shop staff member, fanzine publisher, music journalist and band adviser, he contributed in numerous ways to the Irish music environment. He was a member of The Radiators from Space, The SM Corporation, Tell Tale Heart, and The Trouble Pilgrims. He even played with The Virgin Prunes in a famous concert where they supported The Clash. He had been instrumental in the innovative (but short-lived) Middle Earth club in Dublin and had worked in a Golden Discs record shop. He published the *Freep* and *Raw Power* fanzines, helped with the *Heat* zine, and reviewed albums for *Hot Press*. Despite his multiple roles, he is best-known as a graphic designer.

Averill had been obsessed with music and graphics from his early childhood. He recalled in an interview with co-author Murphy in 2018:

> I wanted to be what was then called a commercial artist, you didn't really have the term graphic designer [at the time in Ireland]. I wanted to produce work for a commercial arena as opposed to being a fine artist. When I had gone along to NCAD [National College of Art and Design] to see what was available, I was told more or less by the tutor that they only did fine art and sculpture, he was very condescending: they didn't do commercial art. (Averill 2018)

Averill was an avid consumer of US and British rock, particularly the more progressive and eclectic groups. It followed that his inspirations in terms of graphic design for music products were from the US and Britain. But there was one notable local designer that he admired. Jim Fitzpatrick's artwork and design had made Thin Lizzy's albums stand out on the shelves. Averill recalled: 'I knew his work prior to him being a sleeve designer, I knew him as a poster designer'. He was also an admirer of Charles O'Connor's graphic work for Horslips. Ireland hadn't produced many world-beating rock bands at this time, but Irish rock acts had some of the best-designed sleeves anywhere, and they were designed locally.

13 U2, the Virgin Prunes and Graphic Art

Averill's career took a rather unorthodox route. After a summer in London when he finished secondary school, he returned to Dublin and attempted to develop his design skills. The only course he could find that interested him was in the Dublin suburbs, at the Dún Laoghaire Technical School, a one-year basic course in design. From there he got a job with a Dublin printer. He remembered: 'I was told it was a career move but in fact it was absolutely not a career move, it was an awful job and an awful place to work' (Averill 2018).

But through his work at the printers, he met Phil Walsh, a director at a leading Dublin advertising agency. The main advertising agencies in Ireland were using words and images to sell products and ideas and it is notable how many of their staff were involved in the local music scene. Walsh was a well-known figure in this fast-developing advertising industry and for decades won awards for his creativity. He was acclaimed for his creative ads from the 1960s (*Irish Press* 1966) to the 1990s when he was recognized for his Harp Lager beer television commercial (*Irish Independent* 1992). Averill viewed Walsh, who worked at the Arks agency, as a mentor:

> Arks were probably the most creative advertising agency in Dublin. He took me on as a junior, even though I had no background or experience. I worked there and that's where I met Barry and Eamon and Charles and other people that were involved in music and design. (Averill 2018)

The Barry, Eamon and Charles in the agency were founding members of Horslips, so Averill was well-placed to watch their early music enterprise. They even involved him in some of their discussions about how to progress with their vision. When Charles O'Connor designed the Horslips debut album sleeve, it proved that the Irish music scene could foster high-level design creativity. This made an impression on Averill.

> The *Happy to Meet, Sorry to Part* album was a magnificent design based on the eight-sided concertina with the die cuts in it, a very expensive piece of design to do. That was an independent label, they were their own label, they were their own team. (Averill 2018)

Naturally, Averill was looking for ways to combine his own passion for both music and industrial art and, by chance, the advertising agency provided him with that opportunity. When a local choir recorded an album for charity, a colleague at the agency suggested that Averill could design it: 'It was very straightforward, but it was interesting for me to take on the role of designer and find the best way to communicate about music in a visual way'. Averill's next project was for himself; when he formed The Radiators from Space, he influenced not only the music, but the visual presentation.

Although the members of Horslips were now full-time musicians, they encouraged their former colleague. Horslips' drummer, Eamon Carr, recorded The Radiators for Midnite, his new label with Jackie Hayden. Furthermore, Carr brought the recording to the attention of Ted Carroll in London, who released The Radiators' records on his Chiswick label. Averill designed the band's striking record sleeves and posters, which to him was the first step in 'controlling my own look and feel for what I wanted to do' (Averill 2018).

Two of the most noted acts that quickly followed The Radiators onto the local music scene in 1977/1978 were DC Nien and U2; Averill designed artwork for both bands. In fact, his design work for U2 probably represents one of the longest partnerships in rock history between a graphic designer and an act. With very few exceptions, he has designed the album and single covers for the band over the last forty years. In addition, he has designed packaging for Irish acts including The Virgin Prunes, Hothouse Flowers, The Fountainhead, In Tua Nua, Cactus World News, Moving Hearts, Clannad, The Dubliners, and Mary Coughlan as well as traditional Irish music acts. He has also designed artwork for Elvis Costello, Depeche Mode, and The Mavericks, and collaborated with another graphic designer, Shaughn McGrath, on some of his work. But his long-term relationship with U2 doesn't imply complacency. The band are keenly aware of their constant need to make an impression on the global marketplace. Averill was quoted:

> U2 and I have a strong relationship, but they have said from the first album onwards that if we don't come up with the goods then they reserve the right to go elsewhere. And I know that on a couple of occasions – when they've been unsure – they've had other people work on ideas. The positive is that you can't fall back on your laurels and think you've definitely got their next album; you've got to come up with graphics that are world-beating. (Clayton-Lea 2014)

In the context of the availability of 'world-beating' graphics for Irish music acts, it is worth examining Averill's creative process.

Presenting Irish Pop: The Creative Design Process

The Virgin Prunes stood out in the Dublin post-punk music scene where they mixed visuals and performance art with a direct, threatening, confrontational style. There was a perhaps underappreciated humour to their activities, and although elements of their stage performance were spontaneous there was a meticulousness to their record sleeve designs. An art director, like a record producer, can facilitate the creativity of musicians, rather than imposing their own vision. Averill recalled the hands-on involvement of the band members Guggi and Gavin Friday:

> Gavin and Guggi were at the forefront of the visual ideas ... Guggi was also a visual artist and some of the imagery was based around covers that he'd drawn or painted. So I worked with him and I always tried to find a type of graphic style that worked with what he was trying to do. They were aware of who they were, what they were, and where they were going with it. It wasn't totally throwing things at the wall and seeing what sticks. They had a path that they wanted to pursue. (Averill 2018)

A hallmark of Averill's work is that his designs look like they belong to the music artist rather than to him. He worked to discover the act's own vision and then translate that into an appealing graphic presentation:

> I tried to understand the act, what they wanted to do, how they wanted to get it across and then I sat down and did very rough sketches of how I thought the direction might go. One thing I learned quite early on was I never stuck hard and fast to my original ideas. I might go in to do an album cover and say 'this is what we're going to aim for with the album cover'. But I would wait until we saw the shots, because often a shot that you didn't intend to take, or wasn't the main thought, suddenly when you saw it, you'd say 'wow, this is so much better than the first idea, let's go in that direction'. (ibid.)

Crucially, he was able to work with several local photographers – including Conor Horgan, Amelia Stein and Shane McCarthy – whom he trusted to deliver the high standard of images required: 'I was involved with working with the photographer, picking the photographer'.

> I'd pretty much always be at all the photo sessions. That was a point in the process where you could begin to shape the artwork; you could look at what was happening and say 'well maybe if we tried this...?' (ibid.)

Most design commissions for albums also included a request for photographs that could be used for press and promotion. So, it wasn't just albums and singles that were showcasing local graphic artists and photographers.

Naturally, Averill's professional reputation in the music industry was enhanced by the success of the U2 albums he designed. When the Dublin band Something Happens! wanted to use Averill to design their *Been There, Seen That, Done That* (1988) album, the Virgin label's art director in London, Catherine McRae, needed no convincing: 'I knew his work well, I know he could do a great job. I trusted him and I trusted the band' (McRae 2006). She had only one proviso:

> I just didn't want the artwork to look 'Irish'; their music had international appeal. The finished job looked fantastic. I was really pleased with it.

Not all projects commissioned by overseas major labels went so smoothly. International labels based in the US and Britain could direct how Irish culture was represented. Averill recalled:

> I did the first Emotional Fish (1990) album, and we had a particular image by a fantastic photographer called Harry Thuillier Jr. which we were going to use. Everyone in the band and their management had agreed this was a great image. And then, at the last minute, I was told that the marketing department [of the overseas label] had said 'no, no, no – you can't use that, you have to use an image of the band on the cover'. (Averill 2018)

This interaction is a reminder that music industry design occurs at the intersection of art and commerce. The practical realities of this often meant that the artist was on one side and the label on the other. For Averill, designing the artwork could be a lengthy process, although sleeves for singles were often produced quickly. At times the process could take months, and Averill would frequently hear early recordings of the songs and then begin to plan and present work to the act or the label. But sometimes significant changes were required, often at the last minute:

> Titles can really affect how you did the artwork. Before U2 released the *Pop* (1997) album, the title and the cover artwork were a different title and different image. We got told very late in the process that the album was going to be called *Pop*. So we had to rethink our approach to the cover very, very quickly. Probably within 48 hours or so we had to come up with new design. So we just looked at it, myself and my colleague, Shaughn McGrath, and thought about how somebody like a Roy Lichtenstein would approach pop art now if he had a computer; if he could do art on a computer rather than painting. (ibid.)

Later, it was the record label, rather than the band, who felt that an album name-change might be required:

> When it came to *How to Dismantle an Atomic Bomb* (2004), the record label said, 'look this is a very dangerous title, we don't like it'. But the band had the right to go with it. The label argued: 'if anything happens in the world within a few days, or a few weeks before the release, that relates to any type of a bomb attack, we'll have to change the title completely'. So we had to work out a back-up plan in case anything like that happened and we had to change everything at the last minute. (Averill 2012)

From his teenage years, Averill recognized how intimately connected music and its visuals are. His thoughts on this are relevant for music acts and labels in small markets:

> It amazes me that so few music acts have a close and long-standing relationship with graphic designers. Labels always try to control everything, but it seems risky for a band to depend on designers who don't understand the band's background, their aspirations, what they have to say. (ibid.)

Ireland has also produced other designers who deliver high-quality artwork to local acts. Notably, Niall McCormack's graphic work contributed to the visual appeal of releases by Jubilee Allstars, Pet Lamb, Ultra Montaines, The Great Western Squares, and Joan of Arse. Boz Mugabe designs eye-catching artwork for punk bands including Paranoid Visions. Other local designers combine high-end graphics or concepts with a DIY approach. Any Other City's release of Girl Band's (2012) *France 98* 12-inch EP came hand-wrapped and rubber-stamped in brown paper and string. Encouragingly, musicians were also taking a hands-on approach to ensure that their music packaging reflected them accurately. Lisa Hannigan's *See Sew* (2009) album depicted some of her own hand-stitched work. Damien Rice's, initially self-released album, *O* (2002) included some of his own illustrations. Even musicians who felt they lacked the necessary visual art skills to execute their own album artwork found helpful artisans close at hand locally. A striking example of Irish DIY design came when the producer and musician, Brian Crosby, compiled and produced a best-selling album to benefit Oxfam. He labelled the collective of musicians – including Glen Hansard, Gary Lightbody, Lisa Hannigan and Neil Hannon – as 'The Cake Sale'. The cover artwork for the 2006 self-titled album is one of the most striking in Irish pop music. It features an array of colourful letters formed out of decorated pieces of home-make cakes. In the album credits, the baking and design are credited to Crosby's mother.

Another notable high-quality series of designs emerged when U2 set up a record label, Mother, in 1984 to provide Irish bands with a music industry platform. Steve Averill was tasked with designing its identity. The early singles on the label included a die-cut sleeve while the label logo was reconfigured for each release to reflect the individual singles. This was Irish-made, boutique-style, music industry artwork, designed to attract the attention of global labels and a global audience. Globally competitive design skills were available to Irish bands even on their debut releases.

Conclusion

David Hesmondhalgh (2020) has clearly demonstrated the 'enormous power' of the major streaming services 'to influence the lives and careers of musicians, through adjustments to their [the streamers' payment] algorithms' (2020: 3610). The question of how much musicians should be paid when their music is streamed remains a controversial issue. Once again, this highlights how Irish musicians and songwriters are dependent on decisions made by commercial companies that serve their own interests and not the interests of Ireland's music community. One popular view is that streaming has led to a decline in the standards of popular music, and in how 'seriously' listeners take it. But Hesmondhalgh (2021) cautions that this can lead to oversimplification, a conclusion based on his examination of the criticism aimed at streaming services. He cites the striking research that highlights the passion and thought that some users devote to compiling playlists. Clearly, that is not 'passive' listening.

The success of the streaming services, however, highlights another consequence of the way the global music industry adjusts to change. Will we look back at the power of the major streaming services as another example of the music industry misjudging a situation? MTV built its business on music videos provided by the music industry, but once it had built its brand and established its reputation, changed to delivering reality television shows. In a similar way the music industry provided a way for platforms like Spotify to build their brand and consumer base with popular music and then deliver podcasts to the mass market.

The development of the internet and streaming services has certainly provided musicians and music workers with significant data on music use. The research of Baym et al. (2021) led to their conclusion that the music industries deploy the available datasets to 'shape business decisions, allocate resources, and aid in strategic planning'. On the other hand, artists and managers used the data (2021: 3428–29) 'to craft persuasive stories intended to motivate the future investments and commitments'. Spreading the news that an act is high in the Irish charts can clearly be part of telling the 'story' of the artist in the hope of persuading people to provide them with opportunities.

As we have shown in this book, historically the supportive creative enterprise behind every Irish global music success was different. It is certainly clear that acts from Ireland were aided in very significant ways before they signed with major labels. In fact, would these acts have achieved their eventual success without the supportive local scene? It is a speculative question, but without the local support in Ireland, life would have been a lot more difficult for those acts, and the world market may never have got to enjoy their music. But does the fact that Ireland successfully fostered high-selling music acts for decades mean that it is likely to continue doing that? In other words, does a series of very notable past successes indicate that Ireland will deliver more large-selling acts to the global music market? Very worryingly for Ireland, recent dramatic shifts in the business of music indicate that new acts from Ireland will find it increasingly difficult to achieve global success. This pessimistic view is based on some key recent developments in the commercial business of music. The pop music charts highlight one glaring danger sign.

The published charts for the best-selling singles in Ireland during 2021 make for interesting reading. They should, of course, be placed in the context of a global pandemic and reduced public socializing during the year. The COVID-19 pandemic caused consternation and distress for most music artists. It was also a serious blow to the major global music firms. But, on the other hand, the restricted socialization in Ireland, and in many other countries, resulted in an increase in music consumption at home. Premium audio streaming increased by 17 per cent in the year: overall growth in the 'singles sector' in Ireland was up 15.5 per cent (Griffiths 2022). This was good news for the major transnational music firms. However, the news for local acts was not so encouraging.

In 2021 only one Irish artist reached number 1 on the Irish singles charts: Meduza, featuring Dermot Kennedy. The song, 'Paradise', was an international collaboration; the Italian production team, Meduza, were credited as the primary artist. In other words, there wasn't a single number 1 on the local charts in 2021 that was solely Irish. Local acts were not just rare at the peak of the charts either. The Irish were also largely absent from *anywhere* on the weekly Top 10 bestsellers list. In fact, during the full year, Irish acts were only in the Top 10 for a collective 39 weeks; fewer than 8 per cent of the Top 10 songs on an average week were from Irish acts. As we identified in Chapter 3, critical commentators, including John O'Flynn (2004), Jim Rogers (2013) and Jim Carroll (2016), had been flagging this danger for a number of years. In light of this, it is unsurprising that not one of Ireland's ten biggest selling singles in 2021 was by a local act, and only *four* of the 50 highest sellers were Irish. All but one of those four songs featured Dermot Kennedy. With Kennedy, Ireland represented 8 per cent of the total Top 50 best sellers; without him, Ireland was down to just 2 per cent of the total.

One of the earliest academic analyses of the Irish music industry was Rob Strachan and Marion Leonard's 'A Musical Nation: Protection, Investment and Branding in the Irish Music Industry' (2004). This article acknowledged the global success of Irish rock and pop music; 2.3 per cent of global sales were by Irish acts, making Ireland the fifth highest-ranking country-of-origin for popular music. Yet, despite this *global* success, the authors identified serious flaws in the *domestic* music industry which, they argued, 'was clearly in need of development and support' (Strachan and Leonard 2004: 48). They illustrated how local and global music industries connect in an asymmetric way and they concluded that the industry was undermined by 'problems that have historically led to the global success of Irish artists being of principal benefit to companies based in other countries' (ibid.). This analysis invites the question: how did a country with such successful popular music exports, including U2, Enya, Sinéad O'Connor, The Corrs and The Cranberries not possess a well-developed domestic music industry? The authors partially answered this in their conclusion that Ireland could only be considered 'a truly industrially productive as well as creative musical nation' (ibid.) if the country secured music industry rights and revenue flowed from the core of the global industry back to Ireland.

Disturbingly, but perhaps predictably, given their conclusions, following Strachan and Leonard's study there was a steady decline in Ireland's market share in the key British market during the next decade. In the year 2000, Irish acts comprised over 6 per cent of Britain's total music market of both singles and albums. However, by 2008 Irish acts accounted for just 2.6 per cent of the album market and 1.8 per cent of the singles market (IFPI 2010). Ireland's declining domestic market share should be placed in the context of the situation elsewhere. Lee Marshall (2012) documented the recent trends in global music sales and concluded:

> there does seem to be an overall trend of local repertoire increasing its market share in the first decade of the century. It is, of course, an increased share of a smaller market, but the figures suggest that music fans have been *more loyal to local artists than global hits.* [emphasis added] (2012: 3)

Consistent with this trend towards domestic markets supporting local acts, the global industry's trade association, the International Federation for Phonographic Industries (IFPI) has frequently invoked the phrase 'investment in local repertoire'. For example:

> Investment in local repertoire remains the lifeblood of the international music industry. Album charts in individual markets demonstrate the continuing strength of local repertoire as a share of overall music sales. In many markets, local artists account for the vast majority of the top selling albums of 2013. (IFPI 2014)

And:

> Album charts in most markets show that investment in local repertoire is alive and well. In many countries, local repertoire accounts for the vast majority of the top selling albums of the year. (IFPI 2013)

Their 2013 statistics identified how local acts account for 85 per cent of the 20 best-selling albums in France and 70 per cent of the 10 best-selling albums in Germany. The market strength of domestic repertoire was also evident in 13 other non-English-speaking markets selected by the IFPI in the above surveys. If Ireland's domestic music industry was healthy, and indeed 'local repertoire was the lifeblood of the international music industry', it should be possible to find evidence that 'investment in local repertoire is alive and well' as the IFPI stated. In fact, the opposite is apparent, and the Irish market statistics indicate low support for domestic acts. The Irish situation continued to be in stark contrast with other European countries. In 2006, Ireland's domestic music consumption as a percentage of total music consumed ranked third *lowest* of the 21 European countries surveyed. On average, 44 per cent of the music purchased in each country was by local artists. Ireland, at 21 per cent, was less than half this figure; only Switzerland and Austria purchased fewer domestic recordings as a percentage of their total markets (IFPI 2006).

The domination of Ireland's sales charts by overseas acts highlights the increasing success of the centralized major music firms. It is easy to see the most profitable scenario for them: a small number of their acts are designated as priorities, and they succeed in as many countries as possible. When this happens, the best-selling lists will look very similar all over the world. Naturally, in some countries, there is a push-back against this globalization of hits. But that requires both resources and the desire to have your own country's songs heard. The published sales charts indicate that Ireland has failed in this respect. This can be clearly seen when the Irish best-sellers are compared with the UK best-sellers. Thirty-one of the 40 'biggest' singles of 2021 in Ireland were also in the UK's 40 biggest singles of the year (Griffiths 2022). With uniformity like this, it is no surprise that most of the songs that top the UK charts also top the Irish charts. In 2021, 13 songs topped the UK charts.

The majority of them (eight) also topped the Irish charts, while another two of them got to number 2 in Ireland.

Albums make greater profits than individual songs, so if the Irish feature strongly on the album charts, then the crisis situation of the singles charts doesn't matter so much. Sadly, the Irish best-selling album list also very closely resembles the UK list. Thirty-two of the UK's 40 biggest selling albums in 2021, that is, 80 per cent of the total, also made the Irish Top 40 best-sellers list (Official Charts 2022a, 2022b). Thirty-seven of the UK 40 biggest sellers made the Irish Top 50 best sellers. That is over 92 per cent in common. Despite this, for people who like to see local acts on the local best-seller charts, there is better local representation on the weekly album charts than on the singles charts. For example, in 2021 four albums by local acts reached the top: Dermot Kennedy, Imelda May, The Script, and Inhaler were number 1 for a combined total of 15 weeks. The previous year, in 2020, even more Irish acts topped the weekly charts: Dermot Kennedy again, as well as Hudson Taylor, Niall Horan, Gavin James, and The Coronas. In 2019, six Irish acts got to number 1 on their home charts: Dermot Kennedy, Hozier, Picture This, Westlife, Mick Flannery, and The Script. Yet, over the three years, Irish acts were number 1 for 43 of the total 156 weeks. But it is certainly an improvement on the singles charts, where, as we showed earlier, the Italian/Irish collaboration, Meduza, featuring Dermot Kennedy, was the only Irish number 1 in 2021.

Clearly it is very significant when an Irish act achieves the highly prized chart-topping position. However, sadly, that doesn't seem to indicate that they can compete in the charts over a meaningful length of time. According to the published charts, between 2019 and 2021, Inhaler, Imelda May, Hudson Taylor, The Coronas, Gavin James, and Mick Flannery disappeared *entirely* from the Top 50 within *five weeks* of reaching number 1. In the most extreme case, Gavin James debuted at the top of the chart, but did not have enough sales to even get him into the Top 50 the very next week. It is as if fans of these Irish acts buy the albums in the week of release, and then fans of overseas acts assume control of the charts immediately.

What explains this lack of local interest in Irish acts? Why are acts from Ireland less competitive? There is one possible reason: the quality is no longer high. But this is a position that we strongly disagree with. Recent high-quality output from Fontaines DC, Murder Capital, Pillow Queens, Kynsy, Soda Blonde, Kojaque, Luka Palm, Just Mustard, Lankum, Lisa O'Neill, Carrie Baxter, Trad Rave, Telefís, Obskur, Selló, and Tolü Makay, amongst *many* others, indicates that there is no lack of music talent. Instead, our lack of competitiveness stems from a local failure of enterprise as well as from the limited opportunities that international labels offer to Irish acts.

The way that the global music industry compiles the Irish charts also makes it difficult for local acts to compete on those charts. As the Official Charts Company (n.d.) makes clear, the Irish charts are based on sales of CDs and vinyl as well as digital sales. In addition, audio streams from commercial services are included, and since 2018 some video streaming services are part of the equation in the UK and presumably in Ireland too. When calculating the weekly chart, 100 digital streams from a paid streaming service are counted as one actual sale, but so too are every 600 streams from a free streaming service (Ditto Music 2018). This means that music listeners can have an impact on the charts without actually purchasing music or making any economic contribution to the artist. The Irish charts of 27 June 2022 included Kate Bush at number 1 with 'Running Up That Hill' (Official Charts 2022c), a single that had featured in a recent *Stranger Things* episode. Evidently, no Irish act was able to access such chart-changing global media opportunities at that time.

The chances of emerging Irish acts reaching the global stage are clearly lower when the local market does not support them. Without local sales success it is difficult to sustain a career or to raise your profile. Local acts are better supported in other countries, as the industry statistics indicate. In New Zealand, a relevant market for comparison with Ireland with a similar population size, nine local albums were in the Top 40 best seller list at the start of February 2022 (NZ Top 40 2022). That is three times as many as in Ireland where only three local albums were in the Top 40 (Official Charts 2022d). But the overall lack of support for emerging acts should be seen against the background of a global pattern that has negative consequences for Ireland. To Howie Klein, the former president of the major label, Reprise, 'never before in history have new tracks attained hit status while generating so little cultural impact' (Klein 2022). His point is that songs become hits but quickly exit the charts; they lack staying power. His conclusion is partially drawn from the work of Ted Gioia (2022) who posed the question: 'Is old music killing new music?' This article appears to answer the question with the disturbing statement that 'all the growth in the market is coming from old songs'. New songs seldom make a sustained impression because 'older songs make up over 70 per cent of the market'. In fact, the 200 most popular *current* songs on average represent less than 5 per cent of total music streams.

In this data analysis the 200 most popular *new* tracks, songs released in the last year and a half, represent, on average, less than 5 per cent of total music streams. In other words, over 95 per cent of the songs being streamed are older. Maybe though, it makes sense: with so many songs available to stream, people look for the comfort of listening to familiar favourites. But the worrying thing is that only three years ago people listened to twice the amount of newly produced music (Gioia 2022). The overall music market is growing, but *all of the overall growth* appears to come from people listening to old music. The new music market is shrinking at a disturbing rate. Instead of investing in new acts, the major music firms are acquiring the rights to well-established acts. Since 2019 the rights to acts including Taylor Swift, Shakira, Whitney Houston, Dolly Parton, David Bowie, Bob Dylan, and James Brown have been acquired for large sums. Naturally, the major firms will want to recoup their investment, so it is only logical that they will promote these acts. In terms of pure commercial logic, there is less incentive to sign, develop and promote new acts, no matter how talented they are.

Irish musicians are facing a situation where fewer artists globally are being signed and developed by major firms. Other factors have recently impeded the development of local music acts. Maybe the Irish situation could have been better if COVID-19 had not struck, but the pandemic, inevitably, had a major impact on the local scene. Perhaps one of the most telling expressions of the impact of the COVID-19 pandemic materializes in the contrasting fortunes of grassroots musicians and workers compared to major labels since 2020. March of that year saw live music venues close across Ireland, and they remained closed for more than 18 months. Musicians, technical crew and many of those who deliver ancillary services for this sector found themselves largely or entirely out of the work force overnight. By mid-2021 some 5,000 people in Ireland's arts and entertainment sectors were surviving on the Pandemic Unemployment Payment, a social welfare payment for those left without income due to the coronavirus (O'Connor 2021). Much media commentary centred on how the Irish music and entertainment sectors were 'utterly devastated by the impact of Covid-19 … particularly … the live music sector' (Stokes 2021).

In early 2021, the Music and Entertainment Society of Ireland (a body representing workers in Ireland's music and entertainment sectors) declared that 'March 13th [2020] was the day the music died in Ireland' (Conboy 2021). An earlier survey of 1,000 members carried out by the same organization found that more than three-quarters of respondents stated that they experienced mental health problems resulting from the impact of COVID-19 on their livelihoods (Cox 2020). In light of the unfolding pandemic, the Irish Music Rights Organisation (IMRO) set up and administered the Irish Music Industry COVID-19 Relief Fund to support Irish music creators by providing recipients with a one-off payment of €750. This was co-funded by IMRO, the Irish Recorded Music Association (IRMA), and Spotify (as part of its worldwide contribution of €10m to COVID-19 music relief).

Such a picture of music industry gloom and despair contrasts somewhat starkly with the results achieved by the world's largest labels across the same period. For example, during the third quarter of 2020, in the midst of the global pandemic, Universal announced strong growth, with global revenues up by 23 per cent on the previous year's equivalent quarter, and proceeds from streaming alone surpassing $1.1bn (Ingham 2020c). The company's overall recorded music revenues for the first half of 2021 grew by 20 per cent, with streaming revenues up 25 per cent compared with the first six months of 2020. Its music publishing and merchandising operations were also on an upward trajectory, by 4 per cent and 22 per cent, respectively across the same period (Paine 2021).

December 2021 saw Warner report an overall intake of more than $5.3bn for the fiscal year. This marked an increase of 18 per cent on 2020, making 2021 the company's most successful year to date in terms of revenues (Warner Music Group 2022). The company achieved $1bn+ revenues from recorded music sales for four straight quarters (Stassen 2021). Similarly, Warner's global music publishing revenues grew by 16 per cent year-on-year (ibid.). Likewise, 2021 saw revenues surge for Sony, who posted a 54 per cent increase in revenues for recorded music in quarter one, with the company taking nearly $2bn worldwide in combined digital and physical sales (King 2021). Such a trend, which continued across quarter two, helped offset the Sony Corporation's COVID-related declines in its motion pictures division (Haithman 2021). The year 2021 also saw Sony demonstrate strong growth in music publishing revenues, with quarter two signalling a 48 per cent increase on the same period in 2020 (Aswad 2021). In this context, *Music Business Worldwide*, a music industry analysis site operated by former *Music Week* editor, Tim Ingham, estimated that the three major labels were enjoying a combined 'hourly' turnover of $2.5m by August 2021 (Ingham 2021b).

Taking the global record industry as a whole, the IFPI report that 2020 trade revenues show year-on-year growth of 7 per cent to a total of approximately $22bn (IFPI 2021). It is highly likely that the global recording industry will continue to expand for a seventh straight year. In terms of the music publishing sector, global revenues edged towards $6bn in 2020 (*Statista* 2021b). Again, in light of the quarterly postings of the three major labels to date, steady growth was predicted for 2021.

Overall, such developments bring into sharp focus issues of inequity and inequality between local artists and global labels in economic terms. However, the COVID situation has simply accentuated a trend that has long been evolving. Since the turn of the millennium, the majors have gradually adapted to a changing technological environment by modifying and remodelling their structure and organization. Following the emergence and widespread diffusion of digital platforms for the distribution of music, and in particular, the proliferation of peer-to-peer file-sharing sites (which were widely blamed for generating a severe crisis for the music industry in industry, media and policy circles alike), the world's biggest record companies sought to expand the range of revenue streams available to them in order to offset the concomitant decline in physical sales. An increasing body of scholarly literature has documented and critiqued how these changes have taken form (e.g., Arditi 2019; Hughes et al. 2016; Marshall 2012; Rogers 2013). In essence, the nature of contractual arrangements between labels and artists has evolved to grant the labels control over a much broader array of rights. Multi-rights recording contracts are now the conventional model. This effectively means that major record companies have developed a range of interests across the music industry's core sub-sectors and beyond, with the breadth and depth of revenue streams leading back to UMG, WMG and SME reflecting this expansion. As UMG Ireland's marketing manager, David Harris explains:

> [W]e give you an advance to record the album ... but you are fully signed to us, so we will look for rights within merchandising, touring, branding, everything, which is pretty standard ... This doesn't include publishing, but within the deal, Universal get first option on publishing ... so yes, it's in there ... We get an aspect of live as well. It would be commercially naïve of us not to do that ... [Y]ou mightn't be able to sell that many records, but you could have many brand associations through being a desirable, marketable act, and that can keep you signed as a recording artist. So, it's not just about record sales, that's what I'm trying to say. It's about revenue. (Harris 2014)

Labels now receive returns from stand-alone music products and services (physical recording, streamed music, digital downloads etc.); from the use of music as a 'secondary' media form, i.e., through television, film, digital games, advertising and other new media platforms; from artists' live revenues; and from any other space or place in which the brand of an artist can be exploited. Music lawyer Ailish McKenna describes these developments as a fundamental shift in investment strategies on the part of the majors, who are now 'funding the artist to create a brand, and feel they need to be compensated from both core and ancillary areas' in return (McKenna 2014).

Some scholars argue that the digital 'piracy' narrative that dominated music industry discourse over many years represents a deliberate strategy to smooth the way for the normalization of multi-rights recording contracts. For example, David Arditi asserts that the panic generated around online music piracy should be viewed as:

> an ideological attempt to reframe what people think about the recording industry ... In this case, by arguing that digital music harmed musicians, record labels successfully convinced musicians, music listeners, journalists, legislators, and the general public that the recording industry needed to develop new sources of revenue in order for musicians to be able to eat ... [T]his laid the groundwork for the recording industry to expand the means of consumption. (2019: 619)

Earlier work by David Hesmondhalgh highlighted the ambivalent nature of scholarly research carried out on the implications of file-sharing, and points to specific benefits for major labels in emphasizing a contracting music marketplace in terms of 'strengthening arguments that domestic industries need government support in shaping legislation, in carrying out successful litigation, and in gaining the go-ahead for mergers' (2007: 8).

While multi-rights deals have become much more common in the industry, the benefits accruing to the Irish arms of a major label are minimal. As UMG's David Harris again attests:

> Unfortunately, we don't see that [share of revenue from a multi-rights deal] too much on a local level because we haven't signed anybody who has been big enough ... [T]he deals that I mentioned that have had success internationally, like Justin Bieber and Lady Gaga – Interscope and Island-Def Jam in the US would see that [revenue], we don't see that. That all happens at parent company level, we don't get anything locally from that, we don't get a cut. (Harris 2014)

Whether local or international, an additional implication arises for recording artists in the context of multi-rights deals. When different sets of rights emanating from various aspects of an artist's career (recording, publishing, live, merchandising, other) are assigned to just one company (or different arms of the same company), not only is a lot of power concentrated at one source, but cross-collateralization of revenue streams is also likely to apply. This means that the label can use profits generated through one activity to offset any losses deriving from another. As such, it is potentially more difficult for an artist to start earning money, as investments must be recouped across all sub-sectoral activities before the artist can receive any payment. Moreover, the restructuring strategies of labels also carry implications for other aspects of local music production which resonate strongly in an Irish context. For example, individuals or companies operating in the domain of post-production, providing music for film, television, advertising and games, now find themselves in direct competition with major music labels who, in efforts to increase revenues through synchronization, are entering into blanket licensing agreements with television and film production companies and advertising agencies. This fresh and energetic interest in the local audio-visual domain is outlined by Sarah Glennane, CEO of the Irish Screen Composers Guild:

> I was at the Galway Film Festival recently. There were three reps from Sony present. Another from EMI Publishing [a Sony-ATV company]. Companies like these are very active in this area now. [They are] very interested in soaking up this work. They are visiting production companies on a regular basis, essentially taking a music supervision role, where they will help find the track that you are looking for, and help cut and splice it according to your needs. For production companies, availing of the blanket licenses they offer in terms of songs and also music production libraries, can make it seem a lot more economical ... This proliferation of production music is really affecting composers. (Glennane 2019)

What is more, Glennane highlights how major labels now regularly approach Irish film and television production companies with a view to securing rights to bespoke composition for forthcoming productions in return for capital investment in these projects. Such arrangements, which can see the label acquire rights to the music even before a composer is hired, can prove lucrative to a production company as they offer an additional funding mechanism for film and television productions. Overall, such developments can be seen to reduce opportunities for local composers and companies, but also to have the effect of lowering fees for composers as well as diminishing or removing 'bank end' royalties associated with the compositions.

It once appeared that the popular music industry could generate a constant stream of innovative acts who could challenge the established acts and grab the attention of music fans. Now, it is becoming more difficult for new acts to find a large and sustained audience. Some Irish acts like Enya and U2 will logically be expected to be part of the 'repertoire of the future' which will hopefully be enjoyed for centuries. But it would be tragic to think that the opportunities for newer Irish acts to join the pantheon of 'greats' are being lost every day. The drive to 'bring the international record industry to Ireland' may have had an unintended consequence. Once invited, it took over and dominated the local music market.

In the past, the ingenuity of Ireland's music entrepreneurs guided Irish acts on pathways to the global market. Only time will tell if current or future entrepreneurs will manage that feat. But at least they can look back to the examples of Ellen O'Byrne, Horslips, U2, Enya, *Riverdance*, The Corrs and even to the ingenuity of the early members of our boybands.

This book illustrates the positive effects that supportive individuals have on local acts. It also highlights what happens when leisure and play are regulated by people like District Justice Goff. When, in the 1930s, he sentenced a young woman to a month in prison for a public kiss he was using the law in a way that would feel restrictive to many young people. The same authoritarianism was evident twenty years later. Then, one of Ireland's most visible pop exports was a group of chaperoned youngsters from an orphanage who sang religious songs.

Countering this, young innovators like Elvera Butler, Edwina Forkin, Billy McGrath, Kieran Owens and Michael McCaughan turned the country's universities into places where music culture was stimulated and developed. They proved that young people, in alliances with London-based booking agents like Paul Charles, could competently, creatively and passionately redefine Ireland's live music industry and music culture. Later, individuals including Niall McGuirk and Miriam Laird, and their Hope Collective allies, asked and answered the question: If the music scene isn't the way it should be – then why aren't you involved?

Perhaps that is the question that should be constantly asked. If the increasing centralization of the global music industry is harming the chances of certain talented acts from making a living – what good is it? If that industry excludes certain individuals and groups from having a platform – who does it serve? Answers to those questions are particularly important when the message 'anyone can make music and have a hit' is loudly proclaimed. Yet fewer acts seem to break through and have sustained careers.

The honest answer is that the global media firms serve their owners and shareholders. No one should be surprised by that. In many ways their drive for profits is admirable. But the message from Ireland's pop music history is that we shouldn't depend solely on the global music firms for our cultural landscape. Our history proves that challenging the centralized decision-making of the major music firms can be profitable, inspiring and fun!

None of this should underestimate the challenges facing Ireland's current music makers who want to make a living. They are facing huge obstacles. But there are some positive signs of practical encouragement. In March 2023 the Minister for Culture, Catherine Martin, received global media attention for her continuing Government initiative to support artists in a meaningful way with a basic income. The idea was not completely original, but the Irish approach was hailed as setting new standards. To the *New York Times*:

> Ireland's [approach] stands out because it is government-run and involves rigorous analysis of the recipients' finances, work patterns and well-being... (Marshall 2023)

It is too soon to say what the lasting impact of the initiative will be. But it highlights a very important lesson from our examination of the Irish music industry. It's a lesson that might provide hope, and ideas for alliances, to musicians anywhere. Individuals make a difference; supportive communities really matter; artists benefit from local assistance before they engage with major global firms. If *do-it-yourself* is a guiding principle when the music industry seems difficult and hostile, adding a few words to that equation may be helpful. That's certainly the case from Ireland's remarkable success stories.

Do-it-yourself, *you're not alone.*

Bibliography

AEG (2019) About us. *AEG Worldwide*, https://www.aegworldwide.com/about.
Alexander, I. (2007) Criminalising copyright: A story of publishers, pirates and pieces of eight. *The Cambridge Law Journal* 66, no. 3: 625–56. https://doi.org/10.1017/S0008197307000694
Allen, B. (2017) U2's Joshua Tree 2017 tour wraps with $316 million earned. *Billboard* (1 November), https://www.billboard.com/articles/columns/chart-beat/8022273/u2-the-joshua-tree-2017-tour-earnings.
Allen, B. (2018) Coldplay & Guns N' Roses join Top 10 of Billboard's highest-grossing tours of all time. *Billboard* (17 January), https://www.billboard.com/articles/columns/chart-beat/8094876/coldplay-guns-n-roses-top-10-billboard-highest-grossing-tours.
Andrews, S. (1998) As DVD's full U.K. launch draws near... *Billboard* (12 September): 107.
Arar, Y. (1981) Irish rock band U2 performs for teen-age fans. *The Burlington Free Press* (10 June): 48.
Arditi, D. (2019) Music everywhere: Setting a digital music trap. *Critical Sociology* 45, nos 4–5: 617–30. https://doi.org/10.1177/0896920517729192
Aswad, J. (2020) Warner Music revenues flat for fiscal 2020, streaming up in Q4. *Variety* (23 November), https://variety.com/2020/music/news/warner-music-revenues-flat-annual-earnings-report-1234838052/.
Aswad, J. (2021) Sony Music posts strong quarter as streaming rises 56%. *Variety* (4 August), https://variety.com/2021/music/news/sony-music-earnings-streaming-1235034308/.
Atlanta Constitution (1937) Scottish lass and Irish lad can't kiss, b'gad. *Atlanta Constitution* (23 October): 22.
Averill, S. (1977) Editorial. *Raw Power* 1, no. 1: 2. https://doi.org/10.1016/0378-7796(77)90001-3
Averill, S. (2012) Recorded interview with Michael Murphy (8 March).
Averill, S. (2018) Interview with Michael Murphy (27 November).
Baker, G. (1996) Australia declares its commitment to Ireland's Corrs. *Billboard* (7 September): 66.
Bambarger, B. (1996) Ivers, 'Riverdance': Luck 'o labels Irish. *Billboard* (6 April): 116.
Barkham, E. (1990) The Producers (transcription). *New Hi Fi Sound*. London: Haymarket.
Barrett, C. (2010) The visual arts and society. In *A New History of Ireland Volume VII: Ireland, 1921–84*, edited by J. R. Hill, 587–620. Oxford: Oxford University Press.
Barry, A. (2014) Do Irish radio stations play enough homegrown music? *The Journal* (27 July), https://www.thejournal.ie/irish-bands-irish-radio-play-1584875-Jul2014/.
Barry, F. (1979) Eamon Carr's music vocation with Horslips. *Meath Chronicle* (3 March): 24.

Bart, P. (1993) Exec comes full circle after descent into despair. *Variety* (7 February). https://variety.com/1993/voices/columns/exec-comes-full-circle-after-descent-into-despair-1117859405/.
Batchelder, R. (1924) Radio broadcasting... *Boston Globe* (1 June): 79.
Bauman, J., Biles, R. and Szylvian, K. (2012) *The Ever-Changing American City: 1945–Present.* Lanham, MD: Rowman & Littlefield.
Baym, N., Bergmann, R., Bhargava, R., Diaz, F., Gillespie, T., Hesmondhalgh, D., Maris E. and Persaud, C. (2021) Making sense of metrics in the music industries. *International Journal of Communication* 15: 3418–3441. https://ijoc.org/index.php/ijoc/article/view/17635.
Bellafante, G. and Dam, J. (1997) Mr. Big of the new jig. *Time* (Canada edition), 31 March: 60–63.
Bessman, J. (1995) Atlantic makes commitment to Ireland's Corrs. *Billboard* (22 July): 11.
Betts, G. (2004) *Complete British Hit Albums.* London: Collins.
Billboard (1956) Gaelic Singers concert trek hypes disk. (17 November): 17.
Billboard (1957) From Donegal to Galway Bay. (2 March): 34.
Billboard (2011) U2's '360' is officially most successful tour of all time. *Billboard* (11 April), https://www.billboard.com/articles/photos/live/472125/u2s-360-is-officially-most-successful-tour-of-all-time.
Black, S. (1991) Whelan and dealin'. *Evening Herald* (6 December): 31.
Blackhurst, C. (2015) John Reid: A recorded music maestro who's found a new beat at Live Nation. *Evening Standard* (6 February), https://www.standard.co.uk/business/markets/john-reid-a-recorded-music-maestro-who-s-found-a-new-beat-at-live-nation-10028330.html.
Blake, E. (1996) Rocking the boat. *The Age* (Melbourne), 24 July: 29.
Bolger, D. (2021) The Welding Rod's contribution to world literature. In *The 32: An Anthology of Irish Working-Class Voices*, edited by Paul McVeigh. London: Unbound.
Bono, The Edge, Adam Clayton, Larry Mullen Jr with Neil McCormick (2006) *U2 by U2.* London: HarperCollins.
Boosey, W. (1931) *Fifty Years of Music.* London: Ernest Benn Limited.
Bracefield, H. (1998) Let Erin remember: The Irish-American influence on traditional music in Ireland. *Writing Ulster* 5: 29–44.
Bradby, B. (1989) God's gift to the suburbs? *Popular Music* 8, no. 1: 109–116. https://doi.org/10.1017/S0261143000003226
Bradley, S. (1997) Just Corrs. *The Age* (Melbourne), 2 February: 65.
Brennan, H. (2001) *The Story of Irish Dance.* Lanham, MD: Roberts Rinehart.
Brocklebank, P. and Molony, S. (2013) *Where the Streets Have 2 Names: U2 and the Dublin Music Scene 1978–1981.* Dublin: Liberties Press.
Brooks, T. (1978) Columbia Records in the 1890s: Founding the record industry. *ARSC Journal* 10, no. 1: 5–36.
Brooks, T. (1979) A directory to Columbia recording artists of the 1890s. *ARSC Journal* 11, nos 2–3: 102–138.
Brooks, T. (2002) High drama in the record industry: Columbia Records, 1901–1934. *ARSC Journal* 33, no. 1: 21.

Burke, A. E. (1995) Employment prospects in the Irish popular music industry. *Journal of Statistical and Social Inquiry in Ireland* XXVII, Part II: 93–120.

Buxton, D. (2005) Rock music, the star system, and the rise of consumerism. In *On Record: Rock, Pop and the Written Word*, edited by S. Frith and A. Goodwin, 427–40. London: Taylor & Francis.

Byrne, G. (1988) Enya – the next big thing. *Irish Independent* (22 October): 16.

Byrne, G. (1995) Be proud…Begorrah! *Irish Independent* (5 December): 26.

Byrne, N. (2015) How music works: Why the Irish music industry is failing. *The Irish Times* (30 July), http://www.irishtimes.com/culture/how-music-works-why-the-irish-music-industry-is-failing-1.2302033.

Campbell, S. (2011) *Irish Blood, English Heart: Second Generation Irish Musicians in England*. Cork: Cork University Press.

Campbell, S. and Smyth, G. (2005) *Beautiful Day: Forty Years of Irish Rock*. Cork: Atrium.

Carr, E. (1994a) The rap. *Evening Herald* (4 March): 5.

Carr, E. (1994b) The men in the moneyzone. *Evening Herald* (11 June): 15.

Carr, E. (1995) Boyz in the hall. *Evening Herald* (5 October): 21.

Carr, E. (1996) It's a toss up for the Corrs. *Evening Herald* (16 January): 21.

Carr, E. (1998) The Boyz are tops. *Evening Herald* (10 August): 3.

Carroll, J. (2016) Radio silence: stations which play the least Irish music revealed. *Irish Times* (27 December), https://www.irishtimes.com/culture/tv-radio-web/radio-silence-stations-which-play-the-least-irish-music-revealed-1.2902810.

Carter, B. (1937a) 'But…', *The Palm Beach Post* (26 October): 1.

Carter, B. (1937b) 'But…', *Ogden Standard-Examiner* (26 October): 4.

Cartwright, G. (1998) 'The Corrs', *The Guardian* (19 March): 39.

Casey, M. (2017) 'Was Victor Herbert Irish?' *History Ireland* (January), https://www.historyireland.com/volume-25/victor-herbert-irish/.

Cash, J. with Carr, P. (1997) *Cash: The Autobiography*. San Francisco: HarperSanFrancisco.

Charles, P. (2016) Recorded interviews with Michael Murphy (October).

Christman, E. (2015) Sony Music acquires German hard rock label Century Media Records. *Billboard* (24 August), https://www.billboard.com/articles/news/6671448/sony-music-acquires-german-hard-rock-label-century-media-records.

Christman, E. (2018) Publishers quarterly: Big lead for Sony/ATV at No. 1. *Billboard* (4 May), https://www.billboard.com/articles/business/8454566/publishers-quarterly-top-ten-sony-atv-warner-chappell-universal.

Christman, E. (2020) After Hipgnosis' purchase of 33,000 songs, what's next for Kobalt Music Group?' *Billboard* (10 November), https://www.billboard.com/pro/kobalt-music-group-deals-analysis-hipgnosis-copyright-fund/.

Clarion Ledger (1957) 'Ten Commandments' for our teen-agers. (27 October): 36.

Clarke, S. (2009) Smells Like Green Spirit. *Hot Press* (18 November): 35.

Clayton-Lea, T. (2012) *101 Irish Records (You Must Hear Before You Die)*. Dublin: Liberties Press.

Clayton-Lea, T. (2014) Steve Averill's life in Irish rock, from the sleeve to the stage. *Irish Times* (8 October), https://www.irishtimes.com/culture/art-and-design/steve-averill-s-life-in-irish-rock-from-the-sleeve-to-the-stage-1.1955142.

Clayton-Lea, T. and Taylor, R. (1992) *Irish Rock: Where It's Come from; Where It's at; Where It's Going*. Dublin: Gill and Macmillan.

Clifford, G. (2014) *Those Good Gertrudes: A Social History of Women Teachers in America*. Baltimore, MD: Johns Hopkins University Press.

Cloonan, M. (1999) Pop and the nation-state: Towards a theorisation. *Popular Music* 18, no. 2: 193–207. https://doi.org/10.1017/S0261143000009041

CNN (2000) Clear Channel buys SFX. *CNN Money* (29 February), https://money.cnn.com/2000/02/29/bizbuzz/sfx/.

Collins, L. (2011) What put The Corrs manager in Mandela's cell? *Sunday Independent* (4 December): np.

Conboy, J. (2021) Interview with Jackie Conboy, the Music and Entertainment Association of Ireland. *Breakfast Briefing* (5 January), https://www.newstalk.com/podcasts/breakfast-briefing/breakfast-briefing-5th-january-2021-jackie-conboy-the-music-entertainment-association-of-ireland.

Connacht Tribune (1934) 'Whither Ireland?' (17 February): 8.

Connaught Telegraph (1969) Town stages a hippy boycott. (4 December): 1.

Connolly, E. (2003) It's the wedding that style forgot. *Evening Echo* (16 August): 24.

Coogan Byrne, L. (2020) Gender disparity data report on Irish radio (23 June), https://lindacooganbyrne.com/2020/06/23/gender-disparity-data-report-on-irish-radio/

Cooper, J. (1997) Irish sighs. *The San Francisco Examiner* [Datebook], 6 July: 31.

Coopers & Lybrand (1994) *The Employment and Economic Significant of the Cultural Industries in Ireland*. Dublin: Temple Bar Properties.

Cork Examiner (1907) Pirated music: Prosecution in Youghal. (2 September): 8.

Cork Examiner (1922) New justices (28 October): 6.

Cork Examiner (1935) Justice's comments (24 June): 4.

Cowell, S. (2004) *I Don't Mean to be Rude, But...: The Truth about Fame, Fortune and My Life in Music*. London: Ebury Press.

Cox, A. (2020) Musicians fret over Covid-19 impact on industry. *RTE News* (29 July), https://www.rte.ie/news/2020/0729/1156214-musicians-covid19/.

Criminal Law Amendment Act, 1935. http://www.irishstatutebook.ie/eli/1935/act/6/section/18/enacted/en/.

Cunningham, M. (2013) *Horslips: Tall Tales – The Official Biography*. Dublin: O'Brien Press.

Deegan, G. (2012) O2 Dublin fifth best attended venue in world. *Irish Independent* (18 January), https://www.independent.ie/entertainment/music/o2-dublin-fifth-best-attended-venue-in-world-26812330.html.

Deloitte/IMRO (2015) *The Socio-economic Contribution of Music to the Irish Economy*. Dublin: Irish Music Rights Organization.

Deloitte/IMRO (2017) *The Socio-economic Value of Music to Ireland*. https://www.imro.ie/wp-content/uploads/2017/11/Imro-Report-2017_12.10-final.pdf.

den Drijver, R. and Hitters, E. (2017) The business of DIY: Characteristics, motives and ideologies of micro-independent record labels. *Journal of Art & Anthropology* 6, no. 1: 17–35. https://doi.org/10.4000/cadernosaa.1192

Denieffe, M. (1971) Skinhead gangs battle at new community hall. *Evening Herald* (24 April): 1.

Des Moines Tribune (1957) 'Moral insanity and Elvis Presleyism. (1 December): 3.
Devane, F. (1933) Commercialised country dance halls. *Irish Independent* (25 February): 10.
Devlin, P. (1979) *The Vogue Book of Fashion Photography*. London: Thames & Hudson.
Devlin, P. (2003 [1983]) *All Of Us There*. London: Virago.
Digital Music News (2018) Sony has officially acquired EMI Music Publishing. Officially', *Digital Music News* (15 November), https://www.digitalmusicnews.com/2018/11/15/sony-completes-emi-music-publishing-acquisition/.
Dillane, A. (2002) *The Ivory Bridge: Piano Accompaniment on 78 rpm Recorded Sources of Irish Traditional Music, America c. 1910–1945* (unpublished dissertation).
Dillane, A. (2021) Raging Mother Ireland: Faith, Fury and Feminism in the Body, Voice and Songs of Sinéad O'Connor. In *Made in Ireland: Studies in Popular Music*, edited by Á. Mangaoang, J. O'Flynn and L. Ó Briain, 54–66. New York: Routledge.
Dillon, A. (2003) Early Irish fanzines. *Loserdom* (13 October), http://www.loserdomzine.com/earlyirishfanzines.htm.
Dillon, A. (2012) Recorded interview with Michael Murphy (18 January).
Dillon, C. (1994) Boyzone are no mere Chippendales. *Irish Press* (27 May): 9.
Diner, H. (1983) *Erin's Daughters in America: Irish Immigrant Women in the Nineteenth Century*. Baltimore, MD: Johns Hopkins University Press.
Ditto Music (2018) How are the music charts calculated? *Ditto Music*, https://dittomusic.com/en/blog/how-are-the-music-charts-calculated/.
Donegal Democrat (1979) An original and beautiful sound – that's Clannad. (24 August): 14.
Donegal News (1931) "ADDICTS" OF JAZZ. (14 February): 6.
Donohoe, M. (2013) Lunch with… *Irish Independent* (28 September): 86.
Dowling Almeida, L. (2013) Irish immigration to the United States in the 20th century. In *The Irish-American Experience in New Jersey and Metropolitan New York: Cultural Identity, Hybridity, and Commemoration*, edited by M. Deyrup and M. Harrington, 77–92. Lanham, MD: Lexington Books.
Dredge, S. (2020) Sony Music revenues grew to $4bn in 2019, fuelled by streaming. *Musically* (5 February), https://musically.com/2020/02/05/sony-music-revenues-grew-to-4bn-in-2019-fuelled-by-streaming/.
Drogheda Independent (1926) Drunks. (21 August): 6.
Duffy, T. (1994) Enya strikes a universal chord. *Billboard* (23 July): 119.
Dundalk Democrat (1993) Corrs. (25 December): 5.
Dunning, J. (1997) Moral duel with light and smoke. *New York Times* (7 March): C3.
Durling, E. (1937) On the side. *Los Angeles Times* (29 October): 28.
Dwane, D. (1995) The Corrs – Making it big. *Western People* (22 November): 16.
Editor (1935) 'Corpus Christi celebrations', 'The dance craze', *Drogheda Independent* (29 June): 6.
Editor (1941) Native and foreign dancing. *Drogheda Independent* (27 September): 2.
Elder, B. (1997) Things are looking up… *Sydney Morning Herald* (21 January): 3.
Ernberg, L. (1984) *Steppin' Out: New York Nightlife and the Transformation of American Culture, 1890–1930*. Chicago: University of Chicago Press.
Evening Echo (1977) City Hall concert cancelled. (11 May): 1.
Evening Herald (1940) Jazz at Dundalk District Court. (2 October): 1
Evening Herald (1971) Cardinal raps sex obsession. (24 April): 1.

Evening Herald (1993) Name that band and score a winner! (18 November): 19.
Fallon, B. (1997) *Boyzone Go East!* London: Chameleon.
Filan, S. with Gittins, I. (2014) *My Side of Life: The Autobiography*. London: Penguin.
Fisher, J. (2021) Interview with Michael Murphy (3 July).
Fitzgerald, H. (2014) Email correspondence with Michael Murphy (28 September).
Fitzgerald, M. and O'Flynn, J., eds (2016) *Music and Identity in Ireland and Beyond*. London: Routledge.
Fitzpatrick, E. (1996) Columbia reshods 'Riverdance' vid for U.S. *Billboard* (31 August): 110.
Flaherty, A. (1987) Music of a race. *Irish Press* (15 May): 8.
Flatley, M. with Thompson, D. (2006) *Lord of the Dance*. London: Pan Macmillan.
Flick, L. (2000) After 5 years without Enya album, Warner offers 'Day Without Rain'. *Billboard* (28 October): 96.
Flynn, C. (1987) 7,000 revellers at Trinity Ball. *Irish Press* (16 May): 4.
Foley, K. (2002) Man and boyz. *Sunday Times* (13 October), https://www.thetimes.co.uk/article/ireland-cover-story-man-and-boyz-wnpf0b380bb.
Foley, S. (1994) Royal goings on. *Limerick Leader* (30 April): 34.
Forkin, E. (2011) Recorded interview with Michael Murphy (27 March).
FORTE (1997) *Access All Areas: Irish Music – An International Industry*. Report for the Minister for Arts, Culture and the Gaeltacht. Dublin: Government Publications Office.
Foster, R. (2018) We cannot resemble our fathers. *Translations* programme, National Theatre.
Freeman, M. (1999) Top 20 singles and albums of the nineties. *Music Week* (18 December): 28.
Galavan, B. (2014) Recorded interview with Jim Rogers (21 February).
Gaster, P. (1999) *The Corrs: Corner to Corner: The Authorized Behind-the-Scenes Book*. London: Andre Deutsch.
Gedutis, S. (2005) *See You at the Hall: Boston's Golden Era of Irish Music and Dance*. Boston, MA: Northeastern University Press.
Gee, T. (1970a) The local scene. *Drogheda Independent* (30 October): 20.
Gee, T. (1970b) The local scene. *Drogheda Independent* (6 November): 22.
Gibson, C. and Jung, K. (2006) Historical census statistics on the foreign-born population of the United States: 1850 to 2000. *U.S. Census Bureau*, https://www.census.gov/library/working-papers/2006/demo/POP-twps0081.html.
Gillett, C. (1970) *The Sound of the City*. New York: Pantheon.
Gillon, S. (2006) *10 Days That Unexpectedly Changed America*. New York: Random House.
Gioia, T. (2022) Is old music killing new music? *The Atlantic* (23 January), https://www.theatlantic.com/ideas/archive/2022/01/old-music-killing-new-music/621339/.
Glatt, J. (1997) *The Chieftains: The Authorised Biography*. New York: Da Capo Press.
Glennane, S. (2019) Recorded interview with Jim Rogers (July 2019).
Gould, N. (2008) *Victor Herbert: A Theatrical Life*. New York: Fordham University Press.
Graham, B. (1979) U-2 could be a headline. *Hot Press* (8 March): 9.
Graham, B. (1989) *U2, the Early Days: Another Time, Another Place*. London: Mandarin.
Griffiths, G. (2022) Ireland's official biggest singles of 2021 revealed. *Official Charts* (9 January), https://www.officialcharts.com/chart-news/irelands-official-biggest-singles-of-2021-revealed__34917/.

Gritten, D. (1997) Ethereal girl. *Daily Telegraph* (6 December): M52.

Gronow, P. and Saunio, I. (1999) *International History of the Recording Industry*. New York: Bloomsbury.

Gubbins, H. and Ó Briain, L. (2020) Broadcasting rock: The Fanning Sessions as a gateway to new music. In *Made in Ireland: Studies in Popular Music*, edited by Á. Mangaoang, J. O' Flynn and L. Ó Briain, 31–41. New York: Routledge.

Gunderson, E. (2005) U2 tour has the concert business getting dizzy. *USA Today* (23 January), https://usatoday30.usatoday.com/life/music/news/2005-01-23-u2-tour-dates_x.htm.

Haithman, D. (2021) Sony music and games Q2 growth helped offset declines in movies and TV. *The Wrap* (27 October), https://www.thewrap.com/sony-music-and-games-q2-growth-helped-offset-losses-in-movies-and-tv/.

Hanlon, A. (2021) "Missing from the Record": Zrazy and women's music in Ireland. In *Made in Ireland: Studies in Popular Music*, edited by Á. Mangaoang, J. O' Flynn and L. Ó Briain, 67–78. New York: Routledge.

Hannon, K. (1993a) Search is on for an Irish Take That. *Evening Herald* (1 November): 10.

Hannon, K. (1993b) 'They're all set to get the girls swooning' and 'Take That Irish-style'. *Evening Herald* (16 November): 3.

Hannon, K. (1994) I was there for the birth of a band. *Evening Herald* (8 December): 23.

Harris, D. (2014) Recorded interview with Jim Rogers (February 2014).

Hartigan, P. (1997) Our show thus far: the Riverdance backstage drama. *Boston Globe* (5 January): N6.

Harvey, D. (2005) *A Brief History of Neo-liberalism*. Oxford: Oxford University Press.

Harvey, D. (2011) *The Enigma of Capital and the Crises of Capitalism*. London: Profile Books.

Haskins, D. (2010) Interview with Michael Murphy (22 January).

Haugh, D. (1996) Corrs for sell out Castlebar concert. *Connaught Telegraph* (1 May): 2.

Hayden, J. (2012) Recorded interview with Michael Murphy (29 March).

Hayes, D. (1988) Enya reaches a watermark. *Irish Press* (14 September): 51.

Healy, L. (2004) Brian's lonely debut as top stars snub debut. *Evening Herald* (27 November): 3.

Healy, S. (1994) Ted to the rescue. *Evening Herald* (11 July): 70.

Heaney, M. (2011) Look of the Irish: Why we're now a visual culture. *Irish Times* (17 September), https://www.irishtimes.com/culture/art-and-design/look-of-the-irish-why-we-re-now-a-visual-culture-1.602645.

Heffernan, J. (1932) Death of Tom Shanley recalls Tenderloin days. *Brooklyn Times Union* (14 October): 6.

Hensher, P. (2010) The X-factor: a money-making machine. *Telegraph* (30 October), https://www.telegraph.co.uk/culture/tvandradio/x-factor/8097727/The-X-Factor-a-money-making-machine.html.

Hesmondhalgh, D. (2007) *Digitalisation, Music and Copyright*. CRESC Working Paper Series: Working Paper No. 30. Milton Keynes: Centre for Research on Socio-Cultural Change, Open University.

Hesmondhalgh, D. (2018) *The Cultural Industries* (4th edn). London: Sage.

Hesmondhalgh, D. (2020) Is music streaming bad for musicians? Problems of evidence and argument. *New Media & Society* 23, no. 12: 3593–3615. https://doi.org/10.1177/1461444820953541

Hesmondhalgh, D. (2021) Streaming's effects on music culture: Old anxieties and new simplifications. *Cultural Sociology* 16, no. 1: 3–24. https://doi.org/10.1177/1749975521101997

Hiatt, B. (2014) Trying to throw their arms around the world. *Rolling Stone* (6 November): 54–61.

Hickey, D. (1975) It's a problem being a saint. *Sunday Independent* (16 November): 88.

Himes, G. (1984) Films brought Chieftains fame. *Baltimore Sun* (13 March): 27.

Hogan, E. (2010) 'Earthly, sensual, devilish': Sex, 'race' and jazz in post-independence Ireland. *Jazz Research Journal* 4, no. 1: 57–79. https://doi.org/10.1558/jazz.v4i1.57

Hopkins, J. (1977) Elvis. *St Petersburg Times* (22 August): 4 DX.

Hot Press (2020) *Hot Press Yearbook 2020*. Dublin: Hot Press.

Hughes, D., Evans, M., Morrow, G. and Keith, S. (2016) *The New Music Industries: Disruption and Discovery*. Cham, Switzerland: Springer.

Hulbert, D. (1997) Lord of the Flashdance. *The Atlantic Constitution* (16 September): 11.

Huston, J. (2009) *In Bloom: Irish Bands Now*. Blackrock, County Dublin: Currach.

IBEC Music Industry Group (1995) *Striking the Right Note – A Submission to Government on the Development of the Irish Music Industry*. Dublin: IBEC.

IBEC Music Industry Group (1998) *Raising the Volume: Policies to Expand the Irish Music Industry – A Submission to Government*. Dublin: IBEC.

IFPI (2002) *The Record Industry in Numbers*. London: International Federation of Phonographic Industries.

IFPI (2006) *The Record Industry in Numbers*. London: International Federation of Phonographic Industries.

IFPI (2009) *The Record Industry in Numbers*. London: International Federation of Phonographic Industries.

IFPI (2010) *The Record Industry in Numbers*. London: International Federation of Phonographic Industries.

IFPI (2013) Digital music report 2013: Engine of a digital world. http://www.ifpi.org/downloads/dmr2013-full-report_english.pdf.

IFPI (2014) Global top selling albums of 2014. http://www.ifpi.org/best-sellers.php.

IFPI (2020) *Global Music Report*. London: International Federation of Phonographic Industries.

IFPI (2021) *Global Music Market Overview*. https://gmr2021.ifpi.org/report.

Ingham, T. (2017) Sony bought Ministry of Sound for £67m, Century Media for £12m. *Music Business Worldwide* (11 January), https://www.musicbusinessworldwide.com/sony-bought-ministry-of-sound-for-67m-century-media-for-12m/.

Ingham, T. (2020a) Universal claims 80%-plus share of 2019's Top Ten global artists – led by Taylor Swift. *Music Business Worldwide* (2 March), https://www.musicbusinessworldwide.com/universal-claims-80-plus-share-of-2019s-top-10-biggest-global-artists-led-by-taylor-swift/.

Ingham, T. (2020b) The three major publishers generated more than $3.2 billion in 2019 – that's $369,000 per hour. *Music Business Worldwide* (2 March), https://www.rollingstone.com/pro/features/the-three-major-publishers-generated-more-than-3-2-billion-in-2019-thats-369000-per-hour-959699/.

Ingham, T. (2020c) Universal Music Group just generated over a billion dollars from streaming in a single quarter, in a global pandemic. *Music Business Worldwide* (20 October), https://www.musicbusinessworldwide.com/universal-music-group-just-generated-over-a-billion-dollars-from-streaming-in-a-single-quarter-during-a-global-pandemic/.

Ingham, T. (2021a) Sony Music Publishing returns with a modern vision – via a re-brand of Sony/ATV. *Music Business Worldwide* (10 February), https://www.musicbusinessworldwide.com/sony-music-publishing-returns-as-a-modern-vision-and-a-global-re-brand-of-sony-atv/.

Ingham, T. (2021b) The three major companies now turn over $2.5m every hour – and will generate more than $20bn between them this year. *Music Business Worldwide* (10 August), https://www.musicbusinessworldwide.com/major-music-companies-now-turn-over-2-5mevery-hour-and-will-generate-more-than-20bn-between-them-this-year/.

Inglis, T. (2008) *Global Ireland: Same Difference*. London: Routledge.

Irish Examiner (1907) Pirated music: Prosecution in Youghal. (2 September): 8.

Irish Independent (1928) Drink at dances. (6 January): 8.

Irish Independent (1935a) The dancing craze may die. (24 June): 10.

Irish Independent (1935b) "Motor-hawks" at dances. (11 September): 12.

Irish Independent (1935c) Improper conduct in public places. (11 September): 12.

Irish Independent (1940a) D.J.'s stand for Irish dancing. (19 February): 4.

Irish Independent (1940b) People demoralised. (19 September): 7.

Irish Independent (1957) Mr Bartholomew Goff. (24 October): 10.

Irish Independent (1970) Bishops greet Dana in Derry. (24 March): 22.

Irish Independent (1992) Art changes... (27 March): 11.

Irish Press (1934) Dr Collier deals with dance hall evils. (19 February): 7.

Irish Press (1937a) Temperance movement. (26 June): 2.

Irish Press (1937b) Scandalous scenes. (12 July): 4.

Irish Press (1937c) Embraced in public. (16 October): 13.

Irish Press (1937d) D.J. and press, Louth "embracing" case recalled. (6 November): 9.

Irish Press (1937e) Girl who embraced in public. (22 October): 2.

Irish Press (1939a) 70 boys and girls at barn dance in court. (4 March): 14.

Irish Press (1939b) Dance halls. (2 December): 11.

Irish Press (1941) D.J. wants dance laws amended. (20 January): 8.

Irish Press (1943) Boys may still be birched, D.J. warns. (10 November): 3.

Irish Press (1966) Art cleavage a design tragedy. (5 October): 7.

Irish Press (1969) I.C.A. warning to hippies. (18 November): 3.

Irish Standard (1916) Irish weep for their slain patriots. (20 May): 1. Minneapolis.

Irish Times (1937) London letter: the next objective. (23 October): 8.

IRMA/PPI (2014) *Submission in Reply to the Copyright and Innovation Consultation Paper*. https://enterprise.gov.ie/en/consultations/consultations-files/irma-and-ppi.pdf.
Jackson, J. (2001) Louis Walsh. *Hot Press* (20 March), https://www.hotpress.com/music/louis-walsh-416908
JNLR (Joint National Listenership Research) (2020) *Ipsos MRBI/JNLR 2020/3 Summary Results*. https://www.ipsos.com/en-ie/ipsos-mrbijnlr-20203-summary-results.
Johansson, O. (2020) *Songs from Sweden: Shaping Pop Culture in a Globalized Music Industry*. Palgrave Singapore.
Jones, M. (2012) *The Music Industries: From Conception to Consumption*. London: Palgrave.
Kavanagh, D. (2014) I was so tired I literally fell asleep at the wheel… In *North Side Story: U2 in Dublin 1978–1983*, edited by N. Stokes, pp. 186–87. Dublin: Hot Press.
Kelly, K., ed. (2000) Cool Hibernia: The story of the Corrs. *World of Hibernia* (Spring): 36–40.
Kenny, K. (2000) *The American Irish: A History*. New York: Routledge.
Keogh, P. (1993) Getting in tune with the Irish music industry. *Irish Press* (13 September): 23.
Kerr, C. (1999) From Budweiser to Boyzone: the man behind the brands. *Irish Independent* (16 September): 48.
Kibler, A. (2015) *Censoring Racial Ridicule: Irish, Jewish, and African American Struggles over Race and Representation, 1890–1930*. Chapel Hill, NC: University of North Carolina Press.
King, A. (2021) Sony Music is up: company reports $1.8 billion increase in quarterly revenue. *Dancing Astronaut* (5 August), https://dancingastronaut.com/2021/08/sony-music-is-up-company-reports-1-8-billion-increase-in-quarterly-revenue/.
Kipnis, J. and Legrand, E. (2005) Enya expands lyrical language. *Billboard* (26 November): 56.
Klamath News, The (1937) Lass exiled from Irish Free State for public kiss. (23 October): 1.
Klein, H. (2022) Music biz has deteriorated not because of musicians, but because of… extreme capitalism. *Down with Tyranny* (23 January),
https://www.downwithtyranny.com/post/music-biz-has-deteriorated-not-because-of-the-artists-but-because-of-extreme-capitalism?fbclid=IwAR3KrN4Mnn47ME3kA92aELR_LYCX3pH_xmImC9Sn69tf7r2m-zp4sentPeA.
Kolodin, I. (1976) *The Opera Omnibus: Four Centuries of Critical Give and Take*. New York: Dutton.
Kosta, B. (2009) *Willing Seduction: The Blue Angel, Marlene Dietrich, and Mass Culture*. New York; Oxford: Berghahn.
Krueger, A. (2020) *Rockonomics: What the Music Industry Can Explain the Modern Economy*. London: John Murray Press.
Laing, D. (2013) The recording industry in the twentieth century. In *The International Recording Industries*, edited by L. Marshall, 31–52. Oxon: Routledge.
Laird, M. (2011) Recorded interview with Michael Murphy (2 July).
Leonard, M. (2016) *Gender in the Music Industry: Rock, Discourse and Girl Power*. Oxon: Routledge.
Liberator, The (1937) Irish dancing is doomed. (11 September): 5.
Liberator, The (1938) War on jazz. (3 September): 13.

Limerick Leader (1963) All-star concert. (16 October): 21.
Limerick Leader (1970) Grand all-star concert. (7 November): 32.
Lincoln Star Journal (1937) To prison for a kiss. (22 October): 29.
Live Nation (2019) Festivals. *Live Nation*. https://www.livenation.co.uk/festival.
Longhurst, B. (1995) *Popular Music and Society*. Cambridge: Polity Press.
Lucey, B. et al., eds (2019) *Recalling the Celtic Tiger*. Oxford: Peter Lang.
Lynch-Brennan, M. and O'Rourke Murphy, M. (2014) *Irish Bridget: Irish Immigrant Women in Domestic Service in America, 1840–1930*. New York: Syracuse University Press.
Mac Anna, Ferdia (2006) *The Rocky Years: Story of a (Almost) Legend*. London: Hodder.
Mac Anna, Ferdia (2018) Interview with Michael Murphy (6 June).
MacCafferty, J. (n.d.) Interview. Available online at: www.jamesmaccafferty.com (accessed 3 March 2014).
MacRuairi, T. (1978) Folklore. *Irish Press* (18 August): 13.
MacRuairi, T. (1979) Invaders "take over" stadium. *Irish Press* (4 January): 4.
Maguire, M. J. (2002) Foreign adoptions and the evolution of Irish adoption policy, 1945–52. *Journal of Social History* 36, no. 2: 387–404. https://doi.org/10.1353/jsh.2003.0025
Mall, A. (2018) Concentration, diversity, and consequences: Privileging independent over major record labels. *Popular Music* 7, no. 3: 444–65. https://doi.org/10.1017/S0261143018000375
Malm, K. and Wallis, R. (1992) *Media Policy and Music Activity*. London; New York: Routledge.
Mangaoang, Á., O'Flynn, J. and Ó Briain, L. (2021) *Made in Ireland: Studies in Popular Music*. New York: Routledge.
Marshall, A. (2023) Ireland asks: What if artists could ditch their day jobs? *New York Times* (23 March). https://www.nytimes.com/2023/03/23/arts/ireland-basic-income-artists.html (accessed 28 March 2023).
Marshall, L., ed. (2012) *The International Recording Industries*. New York: Routledge.
Marshall, L. (2013) The 360 degree deal and the 'new' music industry. *European Journal of Cultural Studies* 16, no. 1: 77–99. https://doi.org/10.1177/1367549412457478
Masson, G. (2003) There is either a very good future or there is no future. *Billboard* (18 October): 64.
Masson, G. and Sexton, P. (2000) Web issues seen as key... *Billboard* (15 July): 10. https://doi.org/10.1080/10528008.2000.11488703
Matthews, B. (2021) Protecting the value of your music. In *Music Unites Us, ASCAP Annual Report 2019*. New York: ASCAP.
May, V. (2011) *Unprotected Labor: Household Workers, Politics and Middle-Class Reform in New York, 1870–1940*. Chapel Hill, NC: University of North Carolina Press.
Maybury, P. and McNulty, D. (2008) *Underground*. Dublin: Image Text Sound.
Mayo News (1969) Hippies decide on island community. (29 November): 1.
McAnailly Burke, M. (1989) The importance of being Enya. *Sunday Independent* (26 November): 15–16.
McAvoy, M. (2016) *Cork Rock: From Rory Gallagher to The Sultans of Ping*. Cork: South Bank Press.
McCarthy, E. (2016) Irish casting agent Ros Hubbard... *Irish Examiner* (19 November): 76.

McCaughan, M. (2009) Recorded interview with Michael Murphy (27 December). https://doi.org/10.1068/d3809b

McDermott, D. (2003) Snap! Georgina and Nicky net €850,000 for wedding pictures. *Irish Independent* (30 July).

McDonagh, M. (2004) X marks the spot for Sligo's Tabby on the brink of stardom. *Irish Times* (4 December). https://www.irishtimes.com/news/x-marks-the-spot-for-sligo-s-tabby-on-the-brink-of-stardom-1.1168766.

McDonald, R. (2011) "Anything about Ireland?": Reading in Ireland 1969–2000. In *The Oxford History of the Irish Book, Volume V: The Irish Book in English*, edited by C. Hutton and P. Walsh, 180–208. Oxford: Oxford University Press.

McEntee, J. (1987) Composer criticises Eurovision 'parody'. *Irish Press* (30 April): 5.

McGarrigle, J. (1988) Enya Ni Bhraonain. *Donegal Democrat* (12 February): 18.

McGrath, B. (2013) Recorded interview with Michael Murphy (13 February).

McGuirk, N. (2002) *Document: A Story of Hope*. Dublin: Hope Publications.

McGuirk, N. (2010) Recorded interview with Michael Murphy (18 January).

McGuirk, N. (2011) Interview with Michael Murphy (21 March).

McKenna, A. (2014) Recorded interview with Jim Rogers (April 2014).

McLaughlin, N. and Braniff, J. (2020) *How Belfast Got the Blues: A Cultural History of Popular Music in the 1960s*. Bristol: Intellect.

McLaughlin, N. and McLoone, M. (2012) *Rock and Popular Music in Ireland: Before and After U2*. Dublin: Irish Academic Press.

McRae, C. (2006) Interview with Michael Murphy (1 June). https://doi.org/10.1145/1279682.1279683

Meath Chronicle (1931) Making town jazzless. (13 June): 6.

Meath Chronicle (1937) Protest by justice. (22 May): 13.

Meath Chronicle (1957) Ex-district Justice Goff's death. (2 November): 7.

Meisner, N. (1995) Now it's an emerald globe. *Times* (London), 8 June: 36.

Meriden Journal (1961) Soloists... (5 January): 6.

Moloney, M. (1982) Irish ethnic recordings and the Irish-American imagination. In *Ethnic Recordings in America: A Neglected Heritage*. Washington: American Folklife Center, Library of Congress.

Mooney, P. (1972) Horslips first album. *Longford Leader* (15 December): 11.

Moore, J. N. (1977) *A Matter of Records: Fred Gaisberg and the Golden Era of the Gramophone*. New York: Taplinger.

Morash, C. (2010) *A History of Media in Ireland*. Cambridge: Cambridge University Press.

Morris, J. (2014) Recorded interview with Jim Rogers (February 2014).

Mulligan, M. (2014) *The Superstar Artist Economy: Artist Income and the Top 1%*. London: Midia Research.

Mulligan, M. (2021) Recorded music revenues hit $23.1 billion in 2020, with artists direct the winners – again. *Midia – Music Industry Blog* (15 March), https://midiaresearch.com/blog/recorded-music-revenues-hit-231-billion-in-2020-with-artists-direct-the-winners-again.

Murphy, G. (2015) The truth about Ireland's music business. *Journal of Music*. http://journalofmusic.com/focus/truth-about-irelands-music-business.

Murphy, L. (2015) Enya breaks her silence on fame, privacy and music. *Irish Times* (13 November), https://www.irishtimes.com/life-and-style/people/enya-breaks-her-silence-on-fame-privacy-and-music-1.2428630.

Murphy, M. (2014) Punk and post-punk in the Republic of Ireland: Networks, migration and the social history of the Irish music industry. *Journal of Punk and Post-Punk* 3, no. 1: 49–66. https://doi.org/10.1386/punk.3.1.49_1

Murphy, M. (2016) Anarcho-punk in the Republic of Ireland: The Hope Collective. In *The Aesthetic of Our Anger: Anarcho-Punk, Politics and Music*, edited by Mike Dines and Matthew Worley, 199–226. Colchester: Minor Compositions.

Murphy, M. (2017) Punk's secret agent: How Paul Charles brought punk to Ireland, Britain and the international market. *Journal of Punk and Post-Punk* 6, no. 3: 431–41. https://doi.org/10.1386/punk.6.3.431_7

Murphy, M. (2018) Elvera Butler: Ireland's ground-breaking New Wave female entrepreneur. *Punk & Post Punk* 7, no. 3: 409–419. https://doi.org/10.1386/punk.7.3.409_7

Murphy, M. (2021) A history of Irish record labels from the 1920s to 2019. In *Made in Ireland: Studies in Popular Music*, edited by Á. Mangaoang, J. O'Flynn and L. Ó Briain, 19–30. New York: Routledge.

Music Board of Ireland (2003) *The Economic Significance of the Irish Music Industry*. Dublin: Music Board of Ireland.

Music and Copyright (2021) UMG and SME put the market share squeeze on WMG and the independent sector. *Music and Copyright* (21 April), https://musicandcopyright.wordpress.com/tag/market-share/.

Music Week (2017) Sony Music accounts reveal Syco stake. *Music Week* (12 January), https://www.musicweek.com/labels/read/sony-music-accounts-reveal-syco.../067119.

Nachman, G. (2009) *Right Here on Our Stage Tonight!: Ed Sullivan's America*. Berkeley: University of California Press.

Napa Journal (1937) Kiss bars girl from Irish Free State forever. (23 October): 1.

Negus, K. (1996) *Popular Music in Theory: An Introduction*. Cambridge: Polity Press.

Ness, J. (2016) A conversation with Enya about sampling, the nature of fame, and how to control your career. *Forbes* (20 June), https://www.forbes.com/sites/passionoftheweiss/2016/06/20/a-conversation-with-enya-about-sampling-the-nature-of-fame-and-how-to-control-your-career/.

New York Times (1905) Receiver for restaurant. (7 November): 11.

New York Times (1906) "Covers for two": a gastronomic study. (2 September): 24.

New York Times (1907) Old rule withdrawn. (12 January): 8.

New York Times (1918) Shanley's. (1 March): 8.

New York Times (1920) Shanley's. (20 July): 10.

New York Times (1921) Join in the dancing. (14 January): 9.

New York Times (1922) Shanley revue. (21 September): 18.

Newman, M. and Flick, L. (2000) How the U.K. lost its grip on the U.S. *Billboard* (9 September): 1.

Ní Fhuartháin, M. (1993) *O'Byrne De Witt and Copley Records: A Window on Irish Music Recording in the U.S.A., 1900 to 1965*. Cork: University College.

Niles Weekly Register (1843) Abolition and the repealers. (1 July): 286.

Nolan, J. (2004) *Servants of the Poor: Teachers and Mobility in Ireland and Irish-America.* Notre Dame, IN: University of Notre Dame Press.
Nolan, J. (2009) Women's place in the history of the Irish diaspora: A snapshot. *Journal of American Ethnic History* 28, no. 4: 76–78. https://doi.org/10.2307/40543472
NZ Top 40 (2022) Official Top 40 albums. https://nztop40.co.nz/chart/albums.
O'Brien, T. (1989) Music tax no hit with industry. *Evening Herald* (10 June): 8.
O'Connell, R. (2013) Critical essay—Your granny's gramophone: the cultural impact of 78 rpm recordings on Ireland and Irish America. *technoculture*, https://tcjournal.org/vol3/oconnell.
O'Connor, B. (2003) Privacy is on sale to highest bidder. *Sunday Independent* (17 August): 21.
O'Connor, N. (2021) Entertainment industry group 'disappointed' after meeting with Minister. *The Journal* (18 August), https://www.thejournal.ie/music-entertainment-industry-live-events-return-reopen-date-5525640-Aug2021/.
O'Dwyer, C. (2011) Recorded interview with Michael Murphy (29 June).
O'Flynn, J. (2004) *Perceptions of Irishness in Irish Music: A Sociological Study of the National Identity and Music.* PhD Thesis, Mary Immaculate College, University of Limerick.
O'Flynn, J. (2009) *The Irishness of Irish Music.* London: Routledge.
Ó Gráda, C. (2008) The Irish economy half a century ago. *Working Paper Series*, UCD School of Economics, August.
O'Halloran, D. (2006) *Green Beat: The Forgotten Era of Irish Rock.* Belfast: Brehon Press.
O'Hanlon, P. (1996) The Corrs. *Anglo Celt* (7 November): 36.
O'Hara, M. (2012) *Travels with my Harp: The Complete Autobiography.* London: Shepheard-Walwyn.
O'Kelly, F. (2020) Recorded interview with Michael Murphy (4 February).
O'Neill, G., ed. (2019 reissue) *Vox 80.–83.* Hi Tone Books.
O'Neill, S. and Trelford, G. (2003) *It Makes You Want To Spit!: The Definitive Guide to Punk in Northern Ireland, 1977–1982.* Dublin: Reekus.
O'Sullivan, M. (1998) Corr blimey. *Sunday Independent* (8 March): 12.
O'Toole, F. (2004) *After the Ball: Ireland After the Boom.* Dublin: New Island Books.
O'Toole, F. (2009) *Ship of Fools: How Stupidity and Corruption Sank the Celtic Tiger.* London: Faber.
Official Charts (2022a) The Official Top 40 biggest albums of 2021. https://www.officialcharts.com/chart-news/the-official-top-40-biggest-albums-of-2021__34858/
Official Charts (2022b) Ireland's official biggest albums of 2021 revealed. https://www.officialcharts.com/chart-news/irelands-official-biggest-albums-of-2021-revealed__34901/
Official Charts (2022c) Official Irish singles chart Top 50. https://www.officialcharts.com/charts/irish-singles-chart/
Official Charts (2022d) Official Irish albums chart Top 50. https://www.officialcharts.com/charts/irish-albums-chart/20220128/ie7502/
Official Charts Company (n.d.) How the Official Charts are Compiled. https://www.officialcharts.com/getting-into-the-charts/how-the-charts-are-compiled/

Owens, K. (2012) Recorded interview with Michael Murphy (8 March).

Paine, A. (2021) UMG streaming revenues up 25% in first half of 2021 ahead of IPO. *Music Week* (28 July), https://www.musicweek.com/labels/read/umg-streaming-revenues-up-25-in-first-half-of-2021-ahead-of-ipo/083815.

Peterson, R. A. and Berger, D. G. (1990) Cycles in symbol production: The case of popular music. In *On Record: Rock, Pop and the Written Word*, edited by S. Frith and A. Goodwin, 140–57. London: Routledge.

Phelan, A. (1994) Boyz show their stuff at the POD. *Irish Independent* (28 May): 38.

Plunkett, J. (2010) The X Factor phone votes bring in £5m. *The Guardian* (13 December), https://www.theguardian.com/media/2010/dec/13/x-factor-phone-votes.

Pollstar (2018) Top 100 promoters. *Pollstar.com*, https://www.pollstar.com/Chart/2018/07/2018MidYearWorldwideTicketSalesTop100Promoters_661.pdf.

Post Standard, The (Syracuse) (1957) Elvis' TV appearances scored by Fr. Shannon. (27 October): 16.

Prendergast, M. (1987) *Irish Rock: Roots, Personalities, Directions*. Dublin: O'Brien Press.

Pride, D. (1999) Global music pulse. *Billboard* (19 June): 53.

Quinlan, R. (2017) From Boyzone to Ballymore and beyond. *Irish Independent* (16 April), https://www.independent.ie/business/irish/from-boyzone-to-ballymore-and-beyond-35626262.html.

Read, O. and Welch, W. L. (1959) *From Tin Foil to Stereo: Evolution of the Phonograph*. Indianapolis: Howard W. Sams.

Reddington, H. (2012) *The Lost Women of Rock Music: Female Musicians of the Punk Era*. Sheffield: Equinox.

Rennie, S. (2013) Interview with Pat Magnarella, published 26 January, at https://www.youtube.com/watch?v=J_tQWjhb1TQ.

Rogers, J. (2013) *The Death and Life of the Music Industry in the Digital Age*. New York: Bloomsbury.

Rogers, W. and Anderson, N. (2013) Keeping the tradition alive. In *The Irish-American Experience in New Jersey and Metropolitan New York: Cultural Identity, Hybridity, and Commemoration*, edited by M. Deyrup and M. G. Harrington, 25–46. Lanham, MD: Lexington Books.

Rogers, J. and Cawley, A. (2016) A song for Ireland? Policy discourse and wealth generation in the music industry in the context of digital upheavals and economic crisis. In *Networked Music Cultures*, edited by R. Nowak and A. Whelan, 189–208. London: Palgrave.

Rosenwaike, I. (1972) *Population History in New York City*. New York: Syracuse University Press.

Ryan, C. (2020) Made in Ireland: Fit for consumption? Fanzines and fan communication in Irish DIY music scenes. In *Made in Ireland: Studies in Popular Music*, edited by Á. Mangaoang, J. O'Flynn and L. Ó Briain, 207–223. New York: Routledge.

Santa Ana Register (1937) Coleen is sent to jail for kiss. (22 October): 1.

Scandinavian Design Group (1962) *Design in Ireland*. Irish Export Board.

Scott Cain, M. (2004) Mary Black: For the joy of music. *Rambles*, http://www.rambles.net/black_ijoy14.html.

Seales, B. (2012) Recorded interview with Michael Murphy (1 February).

Sexton, P. (1998) Ireland's Corrs looking to put U.S. in their "corners"... *Billboard* (4 April): 10.
Shanley, L. (1990–1991) The Shanleys of Broadway. *New York Irish History* 5: 16–20. https://doi.org/10.1080/03612759.1991.9949448
Share, P., Tovey, H. and Corcoran, M. (2007) *A Sociology of Ireland* (3rd edn). Dublin: Gill and Macmillan.
Sheehan, P. (1996) Gael force. *Sydney Morning Herald* (12 July): 49.
Sheridan, M. (1988) We're poor record buyers. *Irish Press* (23 November): 19.
Sheridan, M. (1989) Ireland holds dismal record. *Irish Press* (21 June): 15.
Simpson Xavier Horwath Consulting (1994) *A Strategic Vision for the Irish Music Industry – A Submission to Government*. Dublin: Simpson Xavier Horwath.
Sligo Champion (1997a) Huge demand for Boys band tickets. (27 August): 17.
Sligo Champion (1997b) The boys are back in town. (10 September): 19.
Sligo Champion (1997c) I O You delight large crowd. (5 November): 21.
Sligo Champion (1997d) I O YOU single launch on Friday. (3 December): 23.
Sligo Champion (1997e) Getting in tune... (3 December): 1.
Smith, H. G. (1975) For artists, a tax haven in Ireland. *The New York Times* (26 January): 172.
Smith, S., et al. (2023) *Inclusion in the recording studio?: Gender and race/ethnicity of artists, songwriters & producers across 700 popular songs from 2012–2022*. Los Angeles, CA: USC Annenberg.
Smyth, G. (2005) *Noisy Island: A Short History of Irish Popular Music*. Cork: Cork University Press.
Smyth, J. (1993) Dancing, depravity and all that jazz: The Public Dance Halls Act 1935. *History Ireland* 1, no. 2: 51–54.
Smyth, P. (1996) European challenge to IRTC would be contested. *Irish Times* (18 January), https://www.irishtimes.com/news/european-challenge-to-irtc-would-be-contested-1.22726.
Smyth, S. (1996a) *Riverdance: The Story*. London: Andre Deutsch.
Smyth, S. (1996b) Watching the money flow. *Irish Independent* (10 February): 31.
Sony Music Publishing (n.d.) *Company Overview*. https://www.sonymusicpub.com/en/about
Spain, J. (1979) Horslips...the men who can beat America. *Irish Press* (5 January): 7.
Spottswood, R. (1990) *Ethnic Music on Records: A Discography of Ethnic Recordings Produced in the United States 1893 to 1942*. Urbana, IL: University of Illinois Press.
Stahl, M. (2013) *Unfree Masters: Recording Artists and the Politics of Work*. London: Duke University Press.
Stano (2011) Interview with Michael Murphy (29 June).
Star Press, The (Indiana) (1937) She got thirty days for this. Miss Clarke shows a reporter just what a 30-day kiss was. (26 November): 19.
Stassen, M. (2021) Warner's music revenues just topped $1bn for the fourth straight quarter. *Music Business Worldwide* (15 November), https://www.musicbusinessworldwide.com/warners-recorded-music-revenues-just-topped-1bn-for-the-fourth-straight-quarter/.

Statista (2018) Leading music promoters worldwide in 2017, by number of tickets sold. *Statista: The Statistics Portal*. https://www.statista.com/statistics/304982/leading-music-promoters-worldwide/.

Statista (2020) Revenue market share of the largest music publishers worldwide from 2007 to 2021. *Statista: The Statistics Portal*. https://www.statista.com/statistics/272520/market-share-of-the-largest-music-publishers-worldwide/.

Statista (2021a) Revenue market share of the largest music publishers worldwide from 2007 to 2021. *Statista: The Statistics Portal*. https://www.statista.com/statistics/272520/market-share-of-the-largest-music-publishers-worldwide/.

Statista (2021b) Music publishing revenue of the Universal Music Group from 2007 to 2021. *Statista: The Statistics Portal*, https://www.statista.com/statistics/314363/universal-music-group-music-publishing-revenue/.

Stewart, K. (1989) Ireland: Artistic, creative, professional and very cost effective. *Billboard* (20 May): 16. https://doi.org/10.1071/EG989229

Stokes Kennedy Crowley (1994) *A Report on the Irish Popular Music Industry*. Dublin: Stokes Kennedy Crowley.

Stokes, N. (2021) Can the live music industry recover from the devastation of lockdown? *The Institute of Directors in Ireland*.
https://www.iodireland.ie/resource-media/media-hub/blog/can-the-live-music-industry-recover-from-the-devastation-of-lockdown.

Strachan, R. and Leonard, M. (2004) A musical nation: Protection, investment and branding in the Irish music industry. *Irish Studies Review* 12, no. 1: 39–49. https://doi.org/10.1080/0967088042000192103

Strong, C. and Raine, S. (2021) *Towards Gender Equality in the Music Industry*. London: Bloomsbury.

Sullivan, C. (1998) Eire of their ways. *The Guardian* (11 December), Arts: 12–13.

Sunday Independent (1970a) Bishop wishes Dana luck. (15 March): 3.

Sunday Independent (1970b) Group is angry with Curate. (8 November): 3.

Taylor, C. (2000) Corrs prepare strategy to win U.S. *Billboard* (9 September): 101.

Telling, G. (2015) Enya's heavenly comeback. *Entertainment Weekly* (20 November): 109.

Temin, C. (1997) "Lord of the Dance": Fancy footwork going nowhere. *Boston Globe* (28 April): C9.

Tennessean, The (1959) Nashville's Top 10. (16 August): 31.

Times-Picayune, The (New Orleans) (1843) Mr O'Connell and abolition. (6 July): 2.

Tovey, H. and Share, P. (2003) *A Sociology of Ireland* (2nd edn). Dublin: Gill and Macmillan.

Trousers, T. (2011) Interview with Michael Murphy (20 June).

Tschmuck, P. (2006) *Creativity and Innovation in the Music Industry*. Dordrecht: Springer.

Turner, T. (2015) Space Celts and a voyage into the avant-garde. *The Quietus* (24 November), https://thequietus.com/
articles/19296-enya-interview-roma-nicky-ryan?curator=MusicREDEF.

Ulster Herald (1956) Little Gaelic singers. (25 August): 3.

Vallely, F. (2008) *Tuned Out: Traditional Music and Identity in Northern Ireland*. Cork: Cork University Press.

Van Der Grift, J. (1923) Woman who made $200,000 out of $100, tells how she did it. *The Newcastle Herald* (17 January): 9.

Van Nguyen, D. (2017) Where the streets have no statues: why do the Irish hate U2? *The Guardian* (12 July), https://www.theguardian.com/music/2017/jul/12/where-the-streets-have-no-statues-why-do-the-irish-hate-u2.
Variety (2018) Live Nation reports a record 2017 in year-end results. *Variety* (27 February), https://variety.com/2018/biz/news/live-nation-reports-a-record-2017-in-year-end-results-1202712461/.
Villette, M. and Vuillermot, C. (2009) *From Predators to Icons: Exposing the Myth of the Business Hero*. Ithaca, NY: Cornell University Press.
Waco News Tribune (1937) Public kiss bars pretty girl from Ireland visit. (23 October): 1.
Wainright, J. P. (2006) England 1603–1642. In *European Music, 1520–1640*, edited by J. Haar, 509–21. Woodbridge: Boydell.
Walker, F. (1872) *Population of the United States*. Washington: Government Printing Office.
Walsh, C. (2010) Interview with Michael Murphy (4 July).
Warner-Chappell (n.d.) *What We Do*. https://warnerchappell.com/what-we-do/.
Warner Music Group (2022) *Annual Report 2022*. https://investors.wmg.com/financial-information/annual-reports.
Welch, N. (1994) The Boys hit town. *Irish Examiner* (25 June): 41.
Western Journal (1979) Horslips special. (12 January): 18.
Westlife (2009) *Our Story*. London: HarperCollins.
White, C. (2001) *Reading Roddy Doyle*. New York: Syracuse University Press.
Wikström, P. (2020) *The Music Industry: Music in the Cloud* (3rd edn). Medford: Polity Press.
Williamson, J. and Cloonan, M. (2007) Rethinking the music industry. *Popular Music* 26, no. 2: 305–322. https://doi.org/10.1017/S0261143007001262
Wilmington Morning News (1937) Kiss in Ireland brings life exile. (23 October): 1.
Wilson, Z. (1957) Voice of the people. *Arizona Daily Star* (23 October): 30.
Witkin, R. W. (2003) *Adorno on Popular Culture*. London: Routledge.

Films

The Commitments. Directed by Alan Parker, 1991.
The Frog Prince. Directed by Brian Gilbert, 1985.
Roll Up Your Sleeves. Directed by Dylan Haskins, 2008. Hideaway Films, DVD.
The Year of the French. 1982. Directed by Michael Garvey.

Albums

Boyzone. 1999. *By Request*. Polydor 547 404-2, album.
The Cake Sale. 2006. Self-titled. Oxfam CD-1, compact disc.
Cleary, Father Michael. 1970. *The Singing Priest*. Release Records, BRL 4008, album.
The Corrs. 1995. *Forgiven, Not Forgotten*. Atlantic 7567-92612-2, album.
The Corrs. 1997. *Talk on Corners*. Atlantic 7567-83051-2, album.
The Corrs. 2000. *In Blue*. Atlantic 7567-83352-2, album.
Enya. 1986. *Enya*. BBC Enterprises, REB 605, album.
Enya. 1988. *Watermark*. WEA 243875, album.

Enya. 1991. *Shepherd Moons*. WEA 9031-75572, album.
Enya. 1995. *The Memory of Trees*. WEA 0630-12879, album.
Enya. 1998. *Paint the Sky with Stars*. WEA 3984 20895, album.
Enya. 2000. *A Day Without Rain*. WEA 8573-85986, album.
Girl Band. 2012. *France 98*. Any Other City, 12" EP.
Hannigan, Lisa. 2009. *See Saw*. Self-released, compact disc.
Horslips. 1972. *Happy to Meet – Sorry to Part*. Oats, MOO3, album.
Horslips. 1978. *The Man Who Built America*. Horslips Records, MOO 17, album.
IOYOU. 1997. *Together Girl Forever*. Sound Records, SUN CD16, compact disc single.
Little Gaelic Singers. 1957. *From Donegal to Galway Bay*. Decca Records, DL 8435, album.
Logan, Johnny. 1980. *What's Another Year*. Release Records, RL 1005, single.
Logan, Johnny. 1987. *Hold Me Now*. Epic, EPC 650893 7, single.
McFadden, Brian. 2004. *Irish Son*. RCA, XPCD2988, promotional compact disc single.
The Priests. 2008. Self-titled. Epic, 88697 33969 2, compact disc.
U2. 1983. *War*. Island, ILPS 9733, album.
U2. 1987. *The Joshua Tree*. Island Records, U26, compact disc.
U2. 1997. *Pop*. Island Records, CIDU210, 524 334-2, compact disc.
Various Artists. 1984. *Touch Travel*, T4, tape cassette.
The Virgin Prunes. 1982. *Pagan Love Song*. Rough Trade, RT 106, single.
Westlife. 1999. *Swear It Again*. RCA, 663572, compact disc single.
Zig and Zag. 1994. *Them Girls Them Girls*. RCA 74321 25103-7, single.

TV

An Eye On The Music (1991). RTE.

Index

3Arena (Point Theatre) 49
4FM 55
78 records 14
143, label 123

'A Day In The Life' 112
A Day Without Rain (album) 108
'A Musical Nation: Protection, Investment and Branding in the Irish Music Industry' (article) 179
A&M 43, 105
A&R (artist and repertoire) 49, 84, 106, 117, 159, 162
ABBA 67, 122
Abbey Theatre 72
'Abide with Me' 9
AC/DC 47
Act of Parliament (Britain) 10
Act Up AIDs campaign 104
Adams, Bryan 54
Adoption Act (1952) 65
Advent 32
Ahern, Bertie 165
Aiken Concerts 51, 97
Alexander, Isabella 10–11
All of Us There (book) 69
Allied Irish Bank 138
All-Priests Show, The 68
Alternative Distribution Alliance 44
Alternative Radio Dublin (ARD) 55
America (U.S.) 39, 76, 83, 102, 104, 107, 113, 121, 126
America's Got Talent 162
American Idol 162
An Eye on the Music 122, 134
Ancient Order of Hibernians 64
Annie Get Your Gun 160
Anschutz Entertainment Group (AEG) 42, 47–8
ANÚNA 136–7
Any Other City, label 175
Apple 6
Apprentice Boys Hall 63
Arditi, David 186
Arista 46

Arkansas 27
Arks, advertising agency 171
Armstrong, Billie Joe 102
Armstrong, Roger 79
Arnheim 105
Arts Council of Ireland 57–8, 160
ASCAP (American Society of Composers, Authors and Publishers) 12
Asia 48
Aslan 95–6
Associated Television (ATV) 45
Astley, Virginia 108
Astor, John Jacob 22
Astor, New York 25
Athy 155
Atlanta Constitution 38
Atlantic, label 44, 120, 123–5, 127–8, 131
Atrix, The 88, 93
Australia 47, 107, 127–9
Austria 180
Austrians 34
Averill, Steve 8, 87,
    assisting local music scene 79, 80–2
    graphic design 168, 170–6
    Horslips 74–5
Avis, Meiert 92
Azzoli, Val 124

B*witched 3
Babes in Toyland 97, 105
Bachelors, The 2
Backstreet Boys 160–1
Bailey pub 87
Baker, Don 134
Ballagh, Robert 138
Ballisodare 111
Ballyfermot College of Further Education 57
Bambi 141
Barrett, Cyril 169
Barrett, Paul 155
Bauman, John 64
Bawnboy 69
Baxter, Carrie 181
Baym, Nancy 177
BBC 114, 129, 149
BBC *Radio 1* 55

Beatles, The 45, 71, 112
Bee Gees, The 46
Been There, Seen That, Done That (album) 174
Beethoven 46
Belfast 74, 122
Bell, Brian 86
Berkeley, Sara 90
Berlin, cabaret 24
Berlin, Irving 46
Bernstein, Elmer 134
Bertelsmann 43
Bertelsmann Music Publishing 46
Beverley Hills 132
Beverley Hills, 90210 127
Bieber, Justin 186
Big D 55
Big Self 95
Billboard Top 200 125
Billboard, magazine 63, 117, 126, 141, 156
BIMM Dublin 57
Bis 97
Bishop of Ossory 30
Björk 2
Black Belt Jones 105
Black, Mary 5
Blackpool 101
Blackrock Vigilance Committee 36
Blades, The 95
Blarney Stone 37
Bloody Jellies 105
Bloom, Luka 98–9, 134
BMG 43
BMG Rights Management 46
Bolger, Dermot 90
Bolger, Smiley 105
Bolton, Michael 125
Bond, James 120
Bono 76–8, 85, 88, 146
Boomtown Rats, The 2, 51, 84, 90, 155
    counterculture 68
    Falling Asunder tour 93–4
    management of, 79, 91, 108, 112, 121
Bord Fáilte 169
Bord Gáis Energy Theatre 50
Boston 119, 123
Boston Globe 139
Bothy Band, The 142
Bow Lane 49, 54
Bowie, David 44, 49, 54, 183
Boy Scoutz, The 81
Boyzone 3, 8, 163
    management and skills 146, 148–52, 155–9
    signing record deal 15

Bracefield, Hillary 3–14
Bradby, Barbara 77
Brady, Paul 134
Braniff, Joanna 3
Bray, County Wicklow 104
'Breathless' 127, 130
Breen, Joe 86
Brennan, Helen 39
Britain 121, 126, 130, 137, 145–6, 155–7, 170, 179
British 162
Broadcasting Authority of Ireland (BAI) 56
Brocklebank, Patrick 3, 85
Brooks, Tim 13
Brosnan, Pierce 120
Brown, James 183
Budweiser 152
Burke, Alexandra 162
Bush, Kate 54, 182
Butch Cassidy and the Sundance Kid (film) 144
Butler, Elvera 88, 92, 94–5, 188
Butler, Jean 134, 136, 139
Buxton, David 168
Buzzcocks 93
By Request (album) 156
Byrne, Gay (Gaybo) 87, 138
Byrne, Georgina 165
Byrne, Nicky 164–5
Byrne, Seamus 78

cabaret 68, 125, 146, 148
    New York 24
Cabaret Voltaire 108
Cactus World News 96, 105, 172
Cake Sale, The 175
Callaghan, Tabby 147
Campbell, Sean 3
Canada 47, 102, 107
Cannon, Seán 111
'Canvas of Life' 120
Capel Street 120
Capitol 43
Carlow 142
Carlsberg 152
Carpenter, Karen 124
Carpenters, The 122
Carr, Eamon 82, 151–2, 155–6, 171
Carr, Jude 80
Carraroe 163
Carrickmacross 35
Carrick-on-Shannon 18
Carroll, Jim 55–6, 178
Carroll, Ted 73, 79–80, 172

Casey, Marion 11
Cash, Johnny 27
Cassidy, Maurice 138
Castlebar 17
Castlerea 161
Catholic Church 28–9, 35, 62, 102
    influence in Ireland 29–31, 35, 39, 63–5, 68–9, 71–2, 103, 135
    Irish Catholics in the US 19, 26, 62–3
Catholic Interracial Centre 63
Catholic Sun 62
CBS, label 82–84
CD (compact disc) 49, 153–4
Celtic Heartbeat, label 91, 136
Celtic Records 14
Celtic Tiger 51, 163, 166
Celts, The (TV series) 114
Century Media Records 44
Chaila, Denise 3
champagne 22
Channel 4 149
Chappell & Co. 46
Charles, Paul 92, 188
Charles, Ray 46
Chateau d'Esclimont 164
Cheiron Studios 162
Cherry Lane Music Publishing 46
Chevron, Phil 77–8
Chicago, city 14, 27, 141–2
Chicago, group 119, 123
Chieftains, The 114, 134, 142, 145
China 43
Chippendales 151
Chiswick records 73, 79, 82, 172
Chomsky, Noam 101
Christian Brothers 142
Chrysalis Music Group 46
Chumbawamba 97, 100, 103
Church & General 136
Church of Ireland 68, 102
cinema 33, 38
Ciunas 105
Clancy Brothers, The 2, 66, 142
Clannad 91, 110–13, 136, 155, 172
Clapton, Eric 46, 130
Clare 17
Clarke, Julia 37–8
Clash, The 94, 170
Clayton, Adam 79–80, 82
Clayton-Lea, Tony 3
Clear Channel Communications 47
Cleary, Father Michael 68
Clipper Carlton showband 63

Cloonan, Martin 8
Cobain, Kurt 47
Cohen, Leonard 45
Cole, Lloyd 134
Collective Soul 125
Columbia records 13, 43
Columbia Tri-Star 141, 144
Comhaltas Ceoltóirí Éireann 142
Commitments, The (film) 119–20, 122, 134
Communist Party 101
Condon, Richard 53
Connacht Telegraph 71
Connacht Tribune 30
Connecticut 64
Connolly, Emma 165
Conservative party (Britain) 10
copyright law (US, Britain) 10
Córas Tráchtála 169
Cork 88, 92–5
    City Hall 95
    county 9
    Institute of Technology 57
    University College Cork (UCC) 95
Coronas, The 181
Corpus Christi 31
Corr, Andrea 121–2, 124, 128
Corr, Gerry 122
Corr, Jim 121, 124
Corr, Sharon 124, 130
Corrs, The 3, 7, 119–31, 134, 179, 188
Costello, Elvis 54, 172
Costello, Tom 54
Coughlan, Mary 172
Coulter, Phil 114
country and western 70
COVID-19 178, 183–4
Cowell, Simon 44, 158–9, 161–3, 166
Cranberries, The 3, 5, 122, 126, 179
Craven, Beverley 134
Creagh, Séamus 111
Criminal Law Amendment Act (1935) 36–8
Croatian immigration to US 19
Crosby, Brian 175–6
Crosstown Songs 46
Cry Before Dawn 98–9
Cure, The 54

D Mob 116
Dallas (TV series) 108
Daly, Jackie 111
Dana 3, 67–8
dance halls 29
Dance Halls Act (1935) 39

dancing 29, 32–5
Dandelion Market, The 85
'Danny Boy' 66–7
Davey and Morris (album) 53
Davey, Shaun 54
DC Nien 85–7, 172
de Burgh, Chris 84
De Danann 111
de Valera, Éamon 36, 38–9
Decca Records 13, 64–5
Deeny, Michael 73
Deep Blue Something 125
Def Jam 43
Def Leppard 54
Deko 102
Delmonico's, New York 24
Department of the Taoiseach 135
Depeche Mode 172
Design in Ireland (report) 169
Detroit 142
Deutsche Grammophon 45
Devane, Father 30
Devlin, Barry 69, 171
Devlin, Polly 69
DeWitt, Justus 14
Dickins, Rob 114–6, 129
Dillane, Aileen 13, 68
Dillon, Anto 80, 101
Diner, Hasia 19, 26
Dion, Celine 56, 119, 125, 127
Disney 133, 141
DIY (do-it-yourself) music scene 5, 7, 70, 75, 85–6, 88–90, 102, 104–6, 119, 131, 154, 168, 175, 188
    fanzines 80–2
    Hope Collective 96–7, 99–105
    students 90–9
Doherty, Moya 121, 132–4, 136–40, 143, 145
Donegal 107–8, 111, 114
Donleavy, J.P. 53
Donnelly, Philip 113
Donoghue, Emma 69
Dookie (album) 104
Doonican, Val 2
Dowling Almeida, Linda 18
Down, county 17
Doyle, Roddy 119
Dr Feelgood 86
Dr. Dre 46
'Dreams' 129–30
Drogheda Independent 31, 34, 72
Dromod, county Leitrim 18

Dublin 8, 49, 72, 74, 76–7, 79, 81–6, 88, 93–5, 100–2, 105, 107, 109, 112, 117, 119, 121–3, 126–7, 132, 136–8, 145–6, 148, 156, 158, 166, 170
Dublin Institute of Technology 57
Dubliners, The 66, 134, 172
Dún Laoghaire 102
Dún Laoghaire Technical School 171
Dundalk 33, 35, 122, 125
Dundalk Institute of Technology 57
DVD 130
Dylan, Bob 54, 183
Dynasty (TV series) 108

Eagles, The 122
Eamonn Andrews Studios 53
East 17 151
Easter Rising, 1916 28
Easy Rider (film) 144
Ed Sullivan and *Ed Sullivan Show* 61–6
Eddy, Duane 74
Edge 76, 78
Egan, Kian 159, 160, 162
Egan, Richie 105
Ehrich House of Fashions 22
Einstürzende Neubauten 108
EMI 45, 95, 136, 154
EMI Music Publishing 45, 187
Emilíana Torrini 2
Emotional Fish, An 174
Engine Alley 134
England 42, 102
English, T. J. 21
entertainment (Ents) officer, university 80, 88, 90–100, 103
Enya 3, 5, 7, 91, 107–18, 125, 129, 179, 187–8
Epic, label 43
Epiphone 76
Ernberg, Lewis A. 23
Europe 48
European Commission 44, 56
European Union (EU) 49, 163
Eurovision Song Contest 67, 123, 132–3, 135–7, 148
Evans, Gwenda 76
Evening Herald 35, 55, 71, 149–51, 165
Evening Press 55
Everything But The Girl 125

Fairplay for Airplay 55
Fairport Convention 95
Falling Asunder, tour 93

Famous Music 45
Famous Music UK 46
Fanning Show, Dave 84, 92, 94
fanzines 80–2, 96, 97, 103
'Father and Son' 155
Faughnan, Margaret 18
Faulkner, Jimmy 111
Feehily, Mark 159
Fenians 16
Ferrari 41
Ferrograph tape recorder 112
Fianna Fáil Ard Fheis 39
Filan, Shane 159–60, 163–4, 166
Finance Act, 1969 53
First Music Contact 57
Fisher, John 85
Fitzgerald, Hugo 101
Fitzgerald, Mark 3
Fitzpatrick, Jim 170
Five 158
Five Go Down to the Sea 99
Flannery, Mick 181
Flatley, Michael 134, 136–7, 139, 142–5
Fleetwood Mac 129–30
Flom, Jason 123
Flynn, Bernadette 140
Fonn (TV series) 72
Fontaines DC 3, 181
Forbes magazine 107, 144
Forgiven, Not Forgotten (album) 125–7, 129
Forkin, Edwina 103, 188
Foster, David 119, 120
Foster, David 123–5
Foster, Roy 73
Fountainhead, The 80, 88, 105, 125, 172
Fowley, Kim 81
Foxx, John 108
France 43, 153, 165, 180
France 98 (EP) 175
Freemans' Journal 21
Freep fanzine 170
French Riviera 76
French-Canada (Quebec) 56
Friday, Gavin 168, 173
Friends of Irish Freedom 11
Frog Prince, The (film) 114
From Donegal to Galway (album) 64–5
Frontline 48
Fruupp 93
Fugazi 7, 97, 100, 103
Furstenburg 152

Gaelic Athletic Association (GAA) 33–4

Gaelic culture 28
Gaelic League 28, 34
Gaiety Investments 51
Galavan, Barbara 136–7
Gallagher, Rory 2, 86
Galway 17, 92, 95, 164
Galway Film Festival 187
Gaskell, Carole 140
Gately, Stephen 150
Gedutis, Susan 14
Geffen 45
Geldof, Bob 90, 93
German immigration to US 19
Germany 44, 102, 107, 180
Gershwin, George 46
Gibbons, Luke 169
Giddens, John 129
Gilbert and Sullivan 46
Gilla Band 3
Gioia, Ted 182–3
Girl Band 175
Glenageary 102
Glennane, Sarah 187
God Knows 3
Goff, Bartholomew 28–39, 62, 122, 188
Golden Disc, record shop 75, 81, 170
Golden Horde, The 97, 99
Goo Goo Dolls 125
Google 47
Gould, Neil 11–12
Graham, Bill 79, 82, 84, 87, 92
Gramophone Company 12
Gramophone Company and Victor 12
Great Western Squares, The 175
Greek immigration to US 19
Green Day 7, 100, 104, 108, 160
Guardian, The 146
Guggenheim family 66
Guggi 168, 173
Guinness 53, 152
Gweedore 110

Halliday, Johnny 74
Hamilton, Diane 66
Hammond, Albert 47
Hanlon, Ann-Marie 68
Hannigan, Lisa 175
Hannon, Katie 149–50, 154
Hannon, Neil 175
Hansard, Glen 175
Happy to Meet – Sorry to Part (album) 75, 171
Harp, lager 72, 171
Harris, David 185–6

Harvey, Thelma and the Big Beauty Cast 24
Haskins, Dylan 104
Hawk's Well Theatre 160
Hawkins, Sophie B. 125
Hayden, Jackie 58, 79, 82–4, 172
Hayden, Tommy 148
Healy, Shay 123
Heaney, Mick 169
Hearst 22
Heat, fanzine 80, 170
Heathers 104
Hebdige, Dick 168
Hello magazine 164–5
Henry VIII 42
Herbert v. Shanley Co., legal case 17
Herbert, Victor 11–12, 17–18
Hesmondhalgh, David 177, 186
Hideaway, label 104
Higgins, Tommy 138
Hingerton, Larry 71
Hipgnosis 47
hippies 71
History Channel 61
HMV label 9
Hogan, Eileen 28
'Hold Me Now' 135
Holly, Buddy 74
Hollywood 132, 144–5
Holy Show, The 68
Hope Collective 96–7, 99–105
Horan, Niall 181
Horgan, Conor 173
Horslips 2, 7, 69–75, 79, 84, 86, 151, 170–2, 188
Hot Press 8, 77, 79, 84, 86, 88, 92, 116, 170
Hothouse Flowers 98, 99, 134, 172
Houston 116
Houston, Whitney 125, 183
How to Dismantle an Atomic Bomb (album) 175
Howth 87
Hozier 3, 49, 51, 181
Hubbard, Ros 121
Hudson Taylor 181
Hughes Vision 121
Hughes, Bill 155
Hughes, John 120–3, 126, 131
Hughes, Willie 120
Hurley, Red 125
Huston, Jenny 3
Hype, The 80

I Don't Mean to be Rude, But... (book) 159
'I Useta Love Her' 95

Iceland pop success 2
IFPI (International Federation of the Phonographic Industry) 5, 130, 153, 179–80, 184
'I'll Take You Home Again Kathleen' 27, 66
In Blue (album) 130
In Dublin, magazine 86–8
In Motion 105
In Tua Nua 172
Industrial Revolution 18
Ingham, Tim 184
Inhaler 3, 181
Innisfail 17
International Online Distribution Alliance (IODA) 43
Interscope 43, 186
Intoxicating Rhythm Section (IRS), The 99
IOYOU 160–1
Ireland 84, 145, 147, 159, 168, 169
  demographics 91
  economic development 6
  emigration, poverty, diaspora 6, 9, 17, 19–21, 61, 141–2
  female emigration 18, 21
Irish Americans 62, 123, 142
Irish Association for the Prevention of Intemperance 29
Irish Countrywomen's Association (ICA) 71
Irish culture 29, 61, 136, 142, 144, 169
Irish Derby 152
Irish Free State 28
Irish in America (US) 9, 12–13, 17, 25–6, 41
  females 26–7
  music 13–14, 16–17
Irish orphans in the US 64
Irish Independent 31–2, 116, 154
Irish music in the US 13
Irish Music Rights Organisation (IMRO) 50–1, 183
Irish Nationalist Party 10
Irish Press 29–30, 32, 36–7, 69, 86, 91, 109
Irish Radio and Television Committee (IRTC) 56
Irish Recorded Music Association (IRMA) 183
IRMA/PPI 57
Irish Screen Composers Guild 187
Irish Society for the Prevention of Cruelty to Children 102
'Irish Son' 166
Irish Times 37, 55, 86, 147
Island, record label 43, 77, 83, 94
Island-Def Jam 186
Italian immigration to US 19

ITV 122

Jackson, Janet 108
Jackson, Joe 148
Jackson, Michael 45
Jafaris 3
Jam Jar Jail 105
Jamaica 8
James, Gavin 181
Japan 107, 134
Jape 105
jazz 29, 31, 33, 35, 62
Jennings, Ollie 92, 95
Jesuit order 103, 135
Jewish immigration to US 19
Jews 35
Joan of Arse 105, 175
Jobs in Music, campaign 55
Jobs, Steve 76
Johansson, Ola 2, 4–5, 162
John, Elton 46, 166
Jones, Michael 4
Joshua Tree, The (album) 95, 168
Jubilee Allstars 175
Junior Catholic Women's Club 63
Just for Kicks (album) 94
Just Mustard 181

Kahn, Gus 46
Kaliber beer 152
Kampus venue 94
Kavanagh, Dave 91–2, 94, 136
Keane, Dolores 125
Keating, Ronan 130, 150, 156
Keineg, Katell 105
Kelly 122
Kelly, Anne Louise 106
Keltic Konviction 105
Kennedy Smith, Jean 119, 123
Kennedy, Dermot 51, 178, 181
Kennedy, John Fitzgerald 123
Kennedy, Ted 123
Kenny, Pat 149
Kenya 8
Keogh, Paul 152–7
Keys, Bobby 74
Keystone studio 53
Kick record label 94
Kid Rock 123
Kilcoole 104
Kilkelly, Father 71
Kilkenny 39
Kilkenny, Ossie 92

Kill Devil Hill 101–2
King, Larry 144
kiss (scandal in Ireland) 36, 38–9
Klamath News, The 38
Klein, Howie 108, 182
Knebworth festival 85
Knickerbocker, New York 25
'Knock on Wood' 121
Kobalt Music Publishing 46–7
Kodaline 3, 49, 51, 56
Kojaque 3, 181
Korea 107
Kraftwerk 86
Kynsy 3, 181

L'Andromeda (opera) 41
Labour party (Britain) 10
Lady Gaga 186
Laing, Dave 12
Laird, Miriam 101, 188
Lake Pontchartrain 21
Lankum 3, 181
Las Vegas 164
Late Late Show, The 7, 155
Lava, label 123
Lawnmowers, The 105
Led Zeppelin 46, 74
Leeds 20
Leitrim 14, 18, 24, 41, 166
Lennon, John 47, 71
Lennon, Sonia 151
Leno, Jay 144
Lent 32
Leonard, Marion 113, 179
Let Me Be Frank (album) 166
Levine, Ian 154
Lewis, Leona 162
Liberal party (Britain) 10
Liberator, The (newspaper) 31–2
Licensed Grocers and Vintners Association 30
Lichtenstein, Roy 174
Lightbody, Gary 175
Limerick 82, 135
Lincoln Star Journal 38
Lisdoonvarna 111
Little Gaelic Singers from County Derry, The 62–8
Little Mix 162
Live Aid, concert 90
Live Nation Entertainment (LNE) 42, 47–9, 51, 96
Lockhart, Jim 73
Logan, Johnny 135, 148

216 Index

Loggins, Kenny 123
Lombard studio 53–4
London 54, 71, 74, 77, 78, 82–4, 86, 93, 96, 106, 108, 129, 137–8, 142–3, 145, 156, 171
London Star 37
Longford Leader 74
Lord of the Dance 139–41, 143–4
Los Angeles (LA) 125, 128
Los Angeles Times 38
Loserdom fanzine 101
Louth Hunt Ball 31
Louth 31
Love, Courtney 100
Ludus 108
Lunny, Donal 111, 135
Lynch, Shane 149–50
Lyttle People 148

M.E. Association 102
Mac Anna, Ferdia 86–7
Mac, Steve 161
MacBride, Tiernan 78
MacCafferty, James 63
Madison Square Garden 49
Madonna 125, 130, 154
Magherafelt 92
Maguire, Moira J. 64–5
Makay, Tolü 3, 181
Makem, Tommy 66
Malibu 123–4
Mall, Andrew 44
Malm and Wallis 8
Molony, Sinéad 3, 85
Man Who Built America, The (album) 70, 75
Manchester 20
Manelli 41
Mangaoang, Áine 3
Marley, Bob 47
Marshall, Lee 179
Martin, Catherine, Minister for Culture 188
Martin, Linda 125, 148
Maserati 76
Matchbox Twenty 123
Mavericks, The 172
May, Imelda 3, 49, 181
Maybury, Peter 3
Mayo 148
Mayo 5000 136, 143
McAloon, Paddy 134
McAvoy, Mark 3
McCabe, Patrick 90
McCarthy, Shane 173
McCaughan, Michael 97–100, 188

McColgan, John 133, 136–40
McCormack, John 9, 13
McCormack, Niall 175
MCD Capital 47
MCD concerts 51, 96, 97
McDonagh, Mary 160–1
McFadden, Brian 163–6
McGrath, Billy 88, 92–4, 188
McGrath, Shaughn 172
McGuinness, Paul 54, 78, 82, 91, 99, 106, 121, 136, 138
McGuirk, Niall 96, 100–4, 188
McKaye, Ian 103
McKenna, Ailish 185
McLachlan, Sarah 125
McLaren, Malcolm 134
McLaughlin, Noel 3, 86
McLoone, Martin 3, 86
McNally, Charlie 92, 94
McNulty, Dennis 3
McQuaid, Archbishop John Charles 65
McRae, Catherine 174
Meduza, featuring Dermot Kennedy 178, 181
Meehan, Sean 114
Melba, Dame Nellie 13
Membranes, The 101
Memory of Trees, The (album) 107, 125
Merchant, Natalie 125
Mercury 43
Mestel, Lawrence 46–7
Metallica 46, 160
Mexican Pets 105
Microdisney 95
Midday TV show 127
Middle Earth club 170
Midnite label 82, 172
'Mikey' (Graham, Michael) 150
Ministry of Sound label 44
Minor Detail 120–2
Mississippi river 21
Mohill 18
Molloy, Brian 54
Molloy, Matt 142
Moloney, Mick 14
Moloney, Paddy 145
Monaghan 31, 39
Moore, Christy 111, 113
Morash, Christopher 88–90
Morini, Albert 63
Morris, James 53, 54, 92
Morrison, Bryan 78
Morrison, Van 2, 5, 74
Morristown, New Jersey 18

Mother label 176
Motown 45
Moving Hearts 95, 172
MTV 54, 177
Mugabe, Boz 175
Mullen, Larry 87, 106
Mullingar 17
Murder Capital 3, 181
Murphy (Cork police constable) 9, 10
Murphy, Gareth 59–60
Murray, Frank 98
Murray, Ruby 2
Murs, Olly 162
Music and Entertainment Society of Ireland 183
Music Board of Ireland 51, 58
Music Business Worldwide 184
Music Corporation of America (MCA) 46
music publishing industry 10
Music Week 184
Musical Copyright Act, 1906 (Britain) 10–11
Musicbase 57

Nachman, Gerald 62
Napa Journal 38
Nashville Top 10 66
National College of Art and Design (NCAD) 169–70
National Stadium 93–4
Navan 72–3
Nazareth House, Derry 65
Nenagh 69
Netherlands, the 102, 107
Nevermind (album) 104
New Basin canal 21
New Hi-Fi magazine 112
New Order 108
New Orleans 21
New York 14, 17, 19, 27, 49, 123, 131, 141
   cabaret 23
   dining 22
   Irish emigration to 8, 25
New York Times 23–4, 65, 140, 188
New Zealand 153, 182
Newman, Randy 46
Ní Fhuartháin, Méabh 13–14
Nicaragua Solidarity campaign 100
Nirvana 104, 108
No Doubt 125
No Means No 97
NOFX 97
Nolan, Janet 20, 26
Norris, Gillian 140

North America 48
Northern Ireland 30, 63, 83, 102
Norway 102
Not Our World 103
Nutter, Alice 103

O2 Arena *see* 3Arena
O 175
Ó Braonáin, Fiachna 98
Ó Maoinlaí, Liam 98
Ó Riada Suite 135
Ó Riada, Seán 135
O'Byrne, Ellen 14–17, 27–8, 188
   record company 16
   shop 14, 16, 28
O'Connell Street 100
O'Connell, Roxanne 14
O'Connell, Daniel 21
O'Connor, Aine 72
O'Connor, Charles 75, 170, 171
O'Connor, Sinéad 3, 68, 91, 98–9, 179
O'Connor, T.P. 10–12, 17
O'Duffy, Alan 74
O'Dwyer, Colm 103
O'Flynn, John 3, 178
O'Halloran, Daragh 3
O'Hara, Mary 65
O'Kelly, Fachtna 79, 91, 108, 111, 121
Ó Briain, Lonan 3
O'Neill, Sean 3
O'Neill, Eoghan 95
O'Neill, Lisa 181
O'Shea, Eoin 85
O'Sullivan, Gilbert 2, 155
O'Toole, Fintan 90, 163–4
OATS label 75
Oberstein, Maurice 152–3, 157
Obskur 181
OK! magazine 164
Oliver Twist (musical) 160
One Direction 3, 162
Ono, Yoko 71
Opportunity Knocks (TV series) 146
Orchard, The 44
'Orinoco Flow' 116, 129
Osborne, Joan 125
Oscar, awards 144
Our Story (book) 159
Outcasts, The 85
Owens, Kieran 80, 88, 92, 105–6, 188
Oxfam 175

'Pagan Love Song' 168

Index

Page, Jimmy 74
Paint the Sky with Stars (album) 108
Palm Beach Post 38
Palm, Luka 181
Pandemic Unemployment Payment 183
'Paradise' 178
Paranoid Visions 102, 175
Paris 164
Parlophone label 44
Parov, Nikola 137
Parton, Dolly 183
Pat Kenny Show 122
Pathé News 38
PBS 141
Penal Laws 31
Performing Rights Society 50
Pet Lamb 105, 175
PIAS Group 44
Picture This 3, 181
Pilger, John 101
Pillow Queens 3, 181
Pink Floyd 44
pirate radio 88
Pirates (group) 86
Planxty 111, 113, 135–6
Pleasure Cell, The 97, 99
POD, nightclub 149, 151
Pogues, The 98–9
Point Theatre (O2 Arena) 138, 155
Police, The 120
Polydor label 43, 58, 105, 120
PolyGram 152–7
Pop (album) 174
Power Rangers, The 159
Prefab Sprout 134
Prendergast, Mark J. 3
Presley, Elvis 7, 61–4, 66
Price, Pete 80
Priests, The (album) 68
Primary Wave 46
Prince 47, 108
Principle Management 106
Prine, John 113
Protestant (religion in Ireland) 30
Public Enemy 96
punk music 90
Puttnam, David 114

Queen 45
Quicksand 97

Radiators from Space, The 77, 79, 81–2, 170, 172

Radio Dublin 88
Radio Éireann 55
Radiohead 46
Raine, Sarah 113
Rape Crisis Centre 102
Rat Pack 164
Raven Arts Press 90
Raw Power fanzine 80, 170
RCA 43, 136
Reading festival 85
Reading, Pennsylvania 63–4
Record Mirror 77
Rector's, New York 25
Red Hot Chili Peppers 108
RED distribution network 43
Reddington, Helen 113
Redmond, John 10
Redneck Manifesto 105
Reed, Lou 45
Reekus record label 95
Reeves, Jim 148
Reid, John 96
Reid, John (Michael Flatley manager) 143
Remick Music Corporation 46
Reprise label 108, 182
Reynolds, John 148, 151–2, 154
Reznor, Trent 47
Rhino label 44
Rhys Myers, Jonathon 121
RIAA (Record Industry Association of America) 5
Rice, Damien 3, 175
Riverdance 7–8, 91, 121, 132–41, 143–5, 169, 188
Riverstown 111
Robson and Jerome 159
Rocky de Valera and The Gravediggers 86–7
Rogers, Kenny 123
Roll Up Your Sleeves (documentary) 104
Rolling Stone magazine 76, 86
Rolling Stones 45, 49, 74, 125
Ronan, Saoirse 121
Rondor 46
Roscommon 28
Rosemary's Baby (film) 144
Royal Albert Hall 129, 142, 152
Royal Blues, The 148
RTÉ 72, 89, 113, 122, 132–4, 137–8
   Choice Music Prize 56
   Concert Orchestra 134
   RTÉ Radio 2 (2FM) 55–6, 84, 88
'Runaway' 125, 127–8
Runaways, The 81

'Running Up That Hill' 182
Rush 108
Russian language 114
Rwanda 137
Ryan, Ciarán 80
Ryan, Nicky 91, 109–14, 116, 121
Ryan, Roma 91, 109–10, 114, 116
Rykodisc label 44

Salem, Massachusetts 37
San Francisco 27
Santa Ana Register 38
Saturdays, The 3
Saw Doctors 95
Scandinavia 169
Scarlet Letter, The (book) 37
Science Gallery, The 169
Scotland 37, 102
Scots-Irish 18
Script, The 3, 49, 56, 181
Scullion 112
Seagram 43
See Sew (album) 175
Selló 181
Seville Suite, The (composition) 135
Sex Pistols 134
sexism 24
Shakira 183
Shanley family
  Andrew 22
  Annie 22
  Barney 22
  in Ireland 17–18
  in New York 17, 22–6
  James 22
  Michael (father), death 18
  Michael (son) 22
  Patrick 22
  'Pear Shanley' 24
  Peter 22
  restaurants 23–4, 28
  Rose, wife of Bernard 25
  Shanley Revue 24
  Tom, attitude to women customers 25
  Tom, attitude to self-improvement 25
  Tom, emigrates to US 18, 21
  Tom, success in New York 22
Shannon, Rev. William 62
Shapiro, Ron 126
Share, Perry 132
Shaw, George Bernard 53
Sheeran, Ed 49
sheet music 9

Shepherd Moons (album) 107
Sherry's, New York 25
Showband 146
Sigur Rós 2
Silent Running 96
Silent Scream, The (documentary) 133
Sillerman, Robert 47
Simon and Garfunkel 122
Simple Minds 54
Sinatra, Frank 74, 164, 166
Sinitta 148
Sinn Féin 28
Sinn Féin Music House 16
Sisters of Mercy 26
Six As One 160
slavery 21
Sligo 28, 142, 147, 159–61, 163
Sligo County Council 147
Sligo Rovers 161
Sloth 105
Slowest Clock, The 103
SM Corporation, The 170
Smash Hits 149, 156, 162, 164
Smyth, Gerry 3
Smyth, Jim 39
Sniffin' Glue fanzine 80
Soak 56
Soda Blonde 181
Solomon firm 74
Something Happens! 174
Son Records 137
SONGS Music Publishing 47
Sony 68, 105, 133, 136
Sony Music Entertainment (SME) 42–4, 148, 154, 184, 185
Sony/ATV, publishing 45–6, 187
Sonya 148
Soulé 3
Sound Affair 122
Sound Records 161
South America 48
Spain 102, 107, 137
Spandau Ballet 120
Spice Girls 158
Spillane, Davy 137
Spotify 177
Square Meal 85
St Francis Xavier Hall 103
St Patrick's Day 129
St Vincent De Paul charity 37
Stagalee 93
Stahl, Matt 4, 5
Stano 86–7

Stansfield, Lisa 54
Star Press, The 38
Stars of Heaven, The 99
Stefani, Gwen 125
Steiger 152
Stein, Amelia 173
Stewart, Alison 77
Stewart, Ken 73
Sticky Fingers 85
Stiff Little Fingers 2
Stiff Records 99
Stokes, Dermot 92
Stokes, Niall 84, 86, 92
Stop Animal Experiments fund 102
Strachan, Rob 179
Stranger Things 182
Stranglers, The 95
Streisand, Barbara 46
Strong, Andrew 134
Strong, Catherine 113
Strougers, The 85
STS studios 155
Sub Pop, label 44
Subculture: The Meaning of Style (book) 168
Sugarcubes, The 2
Sunday Independent 72
Sutton, John 119
'Swear It Again' 161
Sweden (pop success) 2, 4, 5, 8, 162
Swift, Taylor 183
Swiss immigration to US 20
Switzerland 180
Syco 44, 148, 159, 162

Táin, The 72
Taiwan 107
Take That 47, 146, 149, 155
Talk on Corners (album) 129
TalkTalk 147, 154
Tansey, Séamus 142
Taoiseach 71, 151, 165
Taste Travel cassette 108
Teatro San Cassiano 41
Teenage Express magazine 73
Telefís 181
Telegraph, The Daily 146
Tell Tale Heart 170
Ten Columbians, The 63
Tencent 43
Tennant, Bill 143–4
Tension 105
Terry, Todd 125, 129

'The Promise of Life' 10
'The Stack of Barley' 16
'The Star of Bethlehem' 10
'Them Girls Them Girls' 159
Therapy? 3, 105
Thin Lizzy 2, 51, 54, 73–4, 79, 86, 170
Thorn, Tracey 125
Those Handsome Devils 97, 99
Three Ring Psychosis 102
Thuillier Jr., Harry 174
Ticketmaster 47–8, 51
Tikaram, Tanita 134
Time Machine 148
Time Out magazine 86
Times, London 144–5
Times-Picayune New Orleans 21
Time-Warner 44
Tipperary 74
Tipping, Paul 92
Titanic (film) 56
Today FM 55, 113
'Together Girl Forever' 160
Tóibín, Colm 90
Toohey, Ailish 155
Top of the Pops 116, 164
Tops of the Town (talent show) 147
Tovey, Hilary 132
Trad Rave 181
Trempeleau, Wisconsin 26
Trend Studios 53
Trinity College, Dublin 80, 82, 92, 94, 97–8, 103, 152
 Ball 96, 152
Trouble Pilgrims, The 170
'Troubles, The' 83
Trousers, Tommy 102–3
TTFM radio station 127
Tubes, The 119
Turner, Luke 112
Tuxedomoon 108
TV-AM 133
Tyrone 69

U2 2, 5, 7, 41, 49, 53–4, 90, 93–5, 115–16, 122, 135–7, 148, 153, 155, 168, 172, 174, 176, 179, 187–8
 and Dublin music scene 77–85
 and early local supporters 86–9
 management 91, 99, 106, 121, 136
U2 by U2 (book) 79
U2, the Early Days (book) 82
UK charts 180–1

UK music industry 44, 46, 50, 51, 54, 83, 114, 117, 122, 128, 129, 130–1, 141, 148, 152–3, 156–7
Ultra Montaines 175
Ultravox 120, 134
Umbrellas, The 105
Under A Blood Red Sky (album) 77
Undertones 2
Unforgettable Fire, The (album) 77
Union Square Hotel 22
Universal Music Group (UMG) 42–4, 105, 143, 184–5
Universal Music Publishing Group 45–6
University College Dublin (UCD) 28, 97
  student's union 92–3
Ure, Midge 134
US music industry 44, 56, 128, 131, 141

V2, label 105
Vallely, Fintan 13
Vanderbilt, Mrs Cornelius 24
Vangelis 114
VCI 140
Vegetarian Society of Ireland 102
Venice 41
Vertigo (film) 43
Verve 45
VHS video tape 130
Victor 12, 13
Villette, Michel 5
Virgin Music, publishing 46
Virgin Prunes 80, 86–7, 99, 105, 168, 170, 172–3
Virgin, label 46, 174
Virgin-EMI 43
Vivendi 43
Vogue Book of Fashion Photography, The 69
Vox fanzine 86
Vuillermot, Catherine 5
Vulpynes 3
VVL 143–4
VW *Beetle* 76

Waco News Tribune 38
Waits, Tom 46
Wales 8, 102
Walsh, Colm 99, 106
Walsh, Louis 146–52, 154, 156, 158–9, 161, 163
Walsh, Phil 171

Waltham, Massachusetts 26
Walton, Mark 149
War (album) 77, 135
Warner Chappell, publishing 45–6
Warner Music Group (WMG) 42, 44, 105, 110, 114, 116, 136, 184–5
Warner Music Nashville 44
Washington, DC 103
Washington, George 18
Watermark (album) 107, 112
'We are Family' 128
Webb, Jimmy 134
'We Call it Acieed' 116
Westland studio 49, 54
Westlife 3, 8, 41, 130, 148, 158–66, 181
Westport 71
Westwood, Chris 77
'What's Another Year' 135
Whelan, Bill 122–3, 134–7, 139
Whelan's club 123
Whipping Boy 105
White Anglo-Saxon Protestant (WASP) 18
White Stripes, The 46
Who, The 108
will.i.am 47
Williams, Robbie 166
Wilmington Morning News 38
Wilson Phillips 124, 128
Wilson, Ian 92, 94
Windmill Lane studios 49, 53, 92
Winslet, Kate 121
Witkin, Robert W. 13
women in the music industry 120
World War I (anti-British sentiment in the US) 11
Wrangler 149

X-Factor, The (TV show) 146–9, 162

Year of the French, The (TV series) 145
Yes 124
Yeu, Guo 134
York label 54
Youghal 10

Zebra 85
Zig and Zag 159
Zomba 46
Zrazy 68

www.ingramcontent.com/pod-product-compliance
Lightning Source LLC
Chambersburg PA
CBHW061244230426
43662CB00020B/2426